Dear Reader:

The book _____ latest bestseller from th_____ry, the imprint *The Nev*_____e crime!" The True Cr_____g accounts of the lates_____that have captured the natio_____St. Martin's is the publisher of John Glatt's riveting and horrifying SECRETS IN THE CEL-LAR, which shines a light on the man who shocked the world when it was revealed that he had kept his daughter locked in his hidden basement for 24 years. In the Edgar-nominated WRITTEN IN BLOOD, Diane Fanning looks at Michael Petersen, a Marine-turned-novelist found guilty of beating his wife to death and pushing her down the stairs of their home—only to reveal another similar death from his past. In the book you now hold, FATAL JEAL-OUSY, Colin McEvoy and Lynn Olanoff document a hor-rific account of obsession and multiple murder.

St. Martin's True Crime Library gives you the stories behind the headlines. Our authors take you right to the scene of the crime and into the minds of the most no-torious murderers to show you what really makes them tick. St. Martin's True Crime Library paperbacks are bet-ter than the most terrifying thriller, because it's all true! The next time you want a crackling good read, make sure it's got the St. Martin's True Crime Library logo on the spine—you'll be up all night!

Charles E. Spicer, Jr.
Executive Editor, St. Martin's True Crime Library

FATAL JEALOUSY

Colin McEvoy and Lynn Olanoff

St. Martin's Paperbacks

FATAL JEALOUSY

Copyright © 2014 by Colin McEvoy and Lynn Olanoff.

All rights reserved.

For information address St. Martin's Press, 175 Fifth Avenue, New York, NY 10010.

EAN: 978-1-250-00971-5

Printed in the United States of America

St. Martin's Paperbacks edition / February 2014

St. Martin's Paperbacks are published by St. Martin's Press, 175 Fifth Avenue, New York, NY 10010.

10 9 8 7 6 5 4 3 2 1

ACKNOWLEDGMENTS

We would like to extend our thanks to our agent, Jake Elwell; to Charles Spicer and April Osborn at St. Martin's Paperbacks; to copy-editor Laura Jorstad; and to attorney Michael Cantwell for his legal review. You are all wonderful to work with and we deeply appreciate your wisdom and guidance.

We would also like to extend our gratitude to Rick Olanoff, John Gebhardt and Art McEvoy for reading through the various stages of our manuscripts, just as they did for our first book, *Love Me or Else*. A special thank you to reporter Sarah Cassi, for her willingness to share her knowledge and observations about the Michael Ballard trial. We'd also like to thank Brad Rinehart, news director for WFMZ, for graciously providing us access to photos from Michael Ballard news reports.

Lastly, we would like to thank everybody who took the time to be interviewed for this book, as well as everyone in our families for all their support and enthusiasm along the way.

CHAPTER 1

JUNE 26, 2010

The four-door gold sedan was speeding and swerving all over the road, and Mark Rowlands could see that it was about to crash.

The Pennsylvania State Police corporal was off-duty that Saturday afternoon. Wearing a T-shirt, shorts, and flip-flops, he was heading home in his unmarked police car, driving west on Route 329 in rural East Allen Township. An eight-year veteran with the state police, Rowlands had just taken the vehicle to a car wash and was driving toward Northampton, a small working-class borough on the western edge of Northampton County, Pennsylvania.

Although a major roadway in the township, Route 329, also known as Nor-Bath Boulevard, is a fairly quiet country road, with trees and foliage on Rowlands's right and grassy clearings and a few small businesses on his left. He was approaching a traffic light at the intersection of Route 329 and Savage Road, near the Miller Supply Ace Hardware store, when he saw the Pontiac Grand Prix GT speeding toward him from the opposite direction.

Observing the erratic driving, Rowlands immediately suspected a drunken driver. Just as it approached the intersection, the car cut across the opposite lane of travel, not quite close enough to strike Rowlands.

He pulled his own car over to the side of Route 329 as the Pontiac careened off the roadway, where it became airborne for a few moments before crashing into a patch of trees in a grassy shoulder area just past the intersection.

Rowlands switched on the emergency lights of his car and radioed in to the state police barracks in the nearby city of Bethlehem, which covers this area of Northampton County. He notified the station about the crash and asked them to send the trooper assigned to that zone before exiting his car to head back to the crashed Pontiac. A few people were already milling around as Rowlands approached. Despite his casual attire, he identified himself as a police officer and ordered them to stand back as he approached the driver's-side window.

The front driver's side of the car had struck the trees, causing extensive damage and forcing both the driver and passenger air bags to deploy. As Rowlands glanced inside, he found a man slumped over with his lower torso on the driver's side but his upper body lying across the passenger seat, his head nearly resting on the front passenger door. There were no other passengers in the car. The man—a Caucasian who appeared to be in his mid- to late thirties—seemed to be unconscious, and Rowlands could hear his slow, shallow breaths.

Rowlands called out to the man, but got no response. As he looked closer, he saw that the man was covered in blood, particularly around his lower torso and crotch area. Both the driver's and the front passenger seats were drenched in the man's blood.

"Keep an eye on him," Rowlands said as he turned to-

ward a woman standing near the scene. "Let me know if
the breathing stops or anything like that."

Rowlands returned to his car and called the dispatch
center to update them on the seriousness of the incident.

"Step up the responding unit, it looks like a pretty
serious crash," Rowlands said before rushing back to the
wrecked car, where the woman still stood watching the
driver. After about two minutes, the injured man started
to stir and appeared to regain consciousness.

"My name is Corporal Mark Rowlands with the Pennsylvania State Police," Rowlands told the man. "You've just
been in a motor vehicle accident. Do not move."

Rowlands started asking the driver questions to test
his memory and cognitive abilities, hoping to keep him
focused and conscious.

"What is your name?" Rowlands asked.

"Michael," the man said slowly, still obviously dazed
and in a great amount of pain. He had blue eyes, short
strawberry-blond hair, and a goatee.

"Where are you coming from, Michael?"

"I just killed everyone."

Rowlands was taken aback by the response, but maintained his composure and professionalism.

"What do you mean by that?" Rowlands asked.

"It's obvious," Michael replied. "I just killed everyone."

Officer Joseph York from the Northampton Police Department was the first to arrive at the scene of 1917 Lincoln Avenue. It was 4:50 p.m., just three minutes after a
call had gone out over the radio about a disturbance involving a stabbing at that address. York was one of twelve
full-time officers and six part-time officers in the department covering a borough of just over two and a half

square miles, where reported stabbings were hardly a common occurrence.

York pulled onto Lincoln Avenue with his white patrol car, the siren blaring, the word NORTHAMPTON printed in red letters along the side of the vehicle. Just a block away from a series of blue-collar row homes, the 1900 block of Lincoln consisted of nicer middle-class town houses. Number 1917 was one half of a relatively large double atop a small grassy hill with a brick front porch and tan siding on the upper half of the house beneath a peaked roof.

The windows had white trimming, and boxes containing an assortment of colorful flowers sat along the edges of the porch. Rows of neatly trimmed bushes ran alongside the front of the home, which was accessible on either side by concrete walkways leading up to a set of steps on both sides of the porch. Several people were staggering around the front yard as York stepped out of his police cruiser.

Most of them were screaming.

Among the crowd was Janet Zernhelt, a fifty-four-year-old woman who said she lived in 1915 Lincoln Avenue, the other half of the twin home. She was nearly hysterical with panic and difficult to understand, but she indicated to York that her husband was inside 1917 and had been hurt badly.

"Help him! Help them!" she kept shouting. "Help them!"

York ordered the people to stay put and wait for him to assess the scene. They would have to be interviewed later, but for now York had to find out exactly what he was dealing with. He rushed up the steps on the 1917 side of the porch, where a small brick wall separated the two halves of the twin home. A bicycle that looked small enough for a young teen lay in a heap in the corner next to a black metal table and set of patio chairs.

York's eyes were immediately drawn to the blood.

A trail of red droplets stained the porch floor in a tiny path leading from the front door toward the steps. It was a light drizzled pattern—almost like someone had flicked a line of red paint with a brush onto the floor—and it stopped before it reached the stairs, as if somebody had started to leave that way from the front door but doubled back inside. A screen door was closed but the front door was wide open and York, who had probable cause to enter the house due to the blood, opened the screen door and stepped inside.

The front door opened into a living room area with a television sitting on a brown wooden stand in the corner, and a red-and-black-plaid couch across from it behind a wooden coffee table. The carpet, like the porch, was stained by a trail of blood, and a pair of legs was just visible, sticking out between the couch and the coffee table, which had been knocked askew.

York rushed over and found the body of a man curled on his left side almost in a fetal position, his arms folded atop each other in front of him, the fingers from his right hand outstretched as if he were trying to shake someone's hand. His bloodied face, which bore a brown mustache and light stubbly beard, lay in a grape-colored puddle of blood on the carpet.

Wearing a white T-shirt and pair of black athletic shorts, the man had been stabbed repeatedly and was covered in blood, with deep stains especially around his face and down the back of his shirt below the neck. The tip of his left thumb was completely severed from the hand. Some plastic children's toys lay on the floor next to him.

Aside from the screaming of the people standing outside, York could hear very little within the home except what sounded like a television set in a room deeper inside.

York stood and walked toward the next room, a dining area accessible from a large open doorway.

Painted on the wall above that doorway was an inscription in black letters that read: LEARN FROM YESTERDAY, LIVE FOR TODAY, HOPE FOR TOMORROW.

The dining room was empty except for a large oak hutch with a few framed photographs along the edges and a dining table with piles of papers and junk on top. There was nothing unusual except for a familiar trail of blood drops leading into the next room. York followed that trail into the kitchen, where he found a scene even grislier than that in the living room.

The blood-soaked body of a woman lay flat on her back in the middle of the floor, with a huge crimson puddle splayed out alongside her, staining the brown Formica tiles. Her arms and legs were spread out, as if she were about to hug someone. Like the man in the living room, she wore black shorts and a white T-shirt, although her body was so covered in blood that it was difficult to see what color the shirt was at all.

She looked as if she had been stabbed dozens of times, even more times than the dead man in the living room. A tattoo of a multicolored rose was just visible on her ankle amid all the blood, as was a tattoo of a stylized dragonfly on her right foot.

York tore his eyes away from the woman and quickly surveyed the rest of the kitchen. The cluttered table contained an array of regular household items: plastic cereal containers, piles of mail, a loaf of bread, a plastic tub of pretzels, a few prescription bottles of pills, and a red-and-black plastic children's lunch box.

The dead body lay in front of a black refrigerator, a white dishwasher, and a row of white cupboards. A few of the cupboards were stained with blood, particularly those just above the dead woman's head, where a large crimson smear was visible. A few drops of blood were still running down from it, dripping onto the floor.

York noticed what appeared to be a couple of bloody footprints around the corpse. Even at a glance, it was obvious that whoever had done this had worn boots. The noise from the television set was even louder now, and he could tell it was coming from a room through a doorway on the other side of the kitchen. The dead woman's left arm was stretched out directly toward that doorway, as if it were pointing, or perhaps reaching for the room.

York stepped from the tiled kitchen onto a pepper-colored Berber carpet. It was a tiny room, much of which was taken up by a hospital bed in the corner. In the middle of the room sat an elderly man in a wheelchair, his head leaning back, sitting just a few feet away from a small television atop a folding table. A baseball game was playing on the TV, and at first glance you might believe the man had simply fallen asleep while watching the game—if not for the gruesome gash in his neck.

It was a ghastly sight, even after the two horribly maimed corpses elsewhere in the house. The man couldn't have been much younger than ninety. His head lay back against the headrest of his wheelchair, his eyes shut, his toothless mouth wide open, his neck cut open in a bloody slash about three or four inches wide. A purplish stream of blood ran like a waterfall from his neck all the way down his gray T-shirt into the seat of his chair, where blood dripped through onto the carpet underneath. A Lifeline alarm was still wrapped around his neck, drenched in blood. The middle finger on his left hand looked shredded, with a bloody chunk of skin peeled away from the knuckle up, as if he'd tried to block the attacker with his hand before he died.

After a few more moments of investigation, York cleared the remaining rooms on the first floor and found nobody else, alive or dead. He reported what he had found into the radio, and let the dispatcher know they were dealing with multiple homicide victims.

CHAPTER 2

An ambulance from Northampton Regional Emergency Medical Services pulled up to the scene of the Route 329 crash. Emergency responders Ronald Bauer and Rob Fallstich rushed toward the wreck, where they met a visibly stunned Corporal Mark Rowlands speaking to a dazed, bloody man in the driver's seat. Rowlands, still confused by the driver's sudden, shocking confession, took a few steps backward to allow the EMTs to do their work.

Like Rowlands, Bauer and Fallstich found that the man had lost dangerous amounts of blood. The driver was conscious, or at least semi-conscious, but was not immediately responsive to them. After a few moments, however, Michael appeared alert and was able to accurately answer when asked what month and what day of the week it was.

Fallstich asked whether the man was experiencing any pain and whether he was aware of what had just happened. Upon hearing the question, Michael slowly turned his head and looked Fallstich directly in the eye.

"It doesn't matter," he told the EMT, "because I killed them all."

It was a chilling statement, but Bauer and Fallstich were professionals and they had to stay focused on helping the man. As they continued their treatment, Michael suddenly stuck two of his fingers into his mouth and down his throat to gag himself until he vomited. Afterward, he looked up at the two EMTs.

"Way too drunk. Needed to get the alcohol out," he said before passing out.

Bauer and Fallstich quickly placed the unconscious man onto a long spine board stretcher and removed him from the crashed car. The man kept slipping in and out of consciousness as they took him back toward the ambulance. Once he was extricated from the vehicle, the emergency responders could see he was wearing jeans and a pair of work boots, both of which were soaked in blood. He was also wearing an empty knife sheath on his belt.

It seemed that the man's injuries were not caused solely by the crash. He appeared to have a large gash on his right thigh, which was the source of much of the blood in his lower torso area.

Bauer and Fallstich also noticed that the tip of his left ring finger was missing, and had seemingly been sliced off.

Michael continued to bleed profusely, and it was clear to the two emergency responders that he was very near death. They attempted to obtain his blood pressure, but it was difficult to do so because of his heavy perspiration. After a few minutes, a helicopter arrived and a medevac unit came out to assist the emergency responders and prepare for an airlift transfer to St. Luke's Hospital in Fountain Hill, just outside Bethlehem. The medevac crew sedated Michael and inserted a plastic air tube into his trachea to secure his airway and assist with breathing.

Meanwhile, the police ran the license plate number of

the 2004 Pontiac Grand Prix that Michael had been driving, and found that it was registered to a woman named
Denise Merhi. She lived on 1917 Lincoln Avenue in the
borough of Northampton.

It didn't take long for the authorities to identify the three
stabbing victims inside 1917 Lincoln Avenue. The woman
found dead in the kitchen was Denise Merhi, the owner of
the house and a thirty-nine-year-old divorced mother of
two. The police were still trying to locate her children, a
thirteen-year-old boy named Trystan and a ten-year-old
girl named Annikah.

The deceased elderly man was Alvin Marsh Jr., Denise's eighty-seven-year-old grandfather, who had been
living with Denise along with her father, the sixty-two-
year-old Dennis Marsh. Dennis's current whereabouts
were unknown.

The dead man in the living room just inside the front
door was Steven Zernhelt, Denise's fifty-three-year-old
neighbor from 1915 Lincoln Avenue, the other half of the
twin home. He was the husband of Janet Zernhelt, the
woman who had hysterically confronted Joseph York
when he arrived on the scene.

After York reported what he had found at 1917 Lincoln
Avenue and more police officers and emergency officials
arrived to help secure the scene, the next step was to talk
to the witnesses. One of the first people the police spoke
with was Debbie Hawkey, the wife of Denise's cousin and
one of her very closest friends.

She was also the first person to find Denise's body and,
after listening to her story, it became clear to the police
that she could have very easily been one of the murder
victims herself.

Debbie and her two sons, ages three and five, had just

spent the last three days with Denise and her daughter Annikah at the beach in Seaside Heights, New Jersey. They had gone there to celebrate Annikah's birthday; she had turned ten on Wednesday, June 23. The five of them arrived back home on Friday and planned to later make arrangements for Debbie to pick up her keys from Denise, who was borrowing Debbie's van while her own car was in the shop.

Debbie and Denise had exchanged text messages earlier in the day, she told the police. Debbie said she'd received a text that her van was back, and she'd arranged for Denise to leave the keys in the mailbox so Debbie could pick the van up later. Somewhere around four forty-five that afternoon, Debbie's husband dropped her off in front of Denise's house. She opened the mailbox, only to find that the keys were not inside.

Debbie went up to Denise's front door, and when nobody answered her knock she turned the doorknob and stepped inside. The door was unlocked, but it wasn't unusual for Denise to leave her door unlocked during the day, and Debbie often came in and out freely.

"Hello?" Debbie had called as she entered. "Hello? Is anybody here?"

Debbie walked through the living room into the dining room and saw her keys sitting on the table. As she picked them up, she believed she heard noises in the kitchen, as if someone was cooking something. Placing her purse on the dining room table, Debbie stepped into the kitchen where, to her horror, she found Denise sprawled out on the floor in a pool of blood, dead.

Debbie didn't see anybody else at the time, but believed she heard some rustling coming from somewhere deeper inside the house. Terrified, she ran back through the dining and living rooms out the front door, hoping to find her husband waiting for her out front.

He has to call 911, she was thinking. *We need to call 911.*

But her husband had moved his car farther down the block and he couldn't see Debbie. Still shaken from what she had just seen, she thought to call 911 herself, but realized she had left her cell phone in her purse, which was still in the house. She raced back up the porch and entered the house again, rushed to the dining room, and swept up her purse.

As she did so, she heard noises from the kitchen again. Glancing into the room, she saw a large shadow on the wall. It appeared to be a man.

Absolutely terrified, Debbie ran out of the house again, desperate to find somebody to call 911. In a panic, she ran to the porch on the other half of the twin home and started pounding on the neighbors' door.

Steve Zernhelt answered, and after Debbie told him somebody was hurt, he ran to Denise's house to help. That Good Samaritan act had cost him his life.

After speaking with Debbie, the police spoke to Emily Germani, a fourteen-year-old girl who lived just north of Denise's home. She provided the police with what would prove to be an invaluable piece of information: She had seen the man who likely murdered the three victims.

Emily had heard Debbie Hawkey and Janet Zernhelt screaming; it had sounded like Janet was shouting that her husband was killed. When Emily came out to investigate, she saw a shirtless man come out through Denise's front door onto the porch. He was covered in blood, and was trying to get blood off one of his hands by flicking it toward the ground.

Almost immediately after she spotted him, the man looked directly at Emily and made a surprised expression. Then, she told the police, he immediately doubled back into the house. A little later, Emily saw Denise's car, a gold Pontiac Grand Prix GT, speeding away. The police issued a radio report for other surrounding departments to keep an eye out for that vehicle.

Emily recognized the man as Denise's boyfriend, or at least a man she had dated in the past. His name, she told the police, was Michael Ballard.

CHAPTER 3

Raymond Judge was about halfway through his noon to 8 p.m. shift, catching up on some paperwork in his office, when the call came in about the multiple murders in Northampton borough.

Judge had been with the Pennsylvania State Police for more than fifteen years, during which time he had been involved with at least fifty homicide investigations. He was forty-one years old and, with a strong, square-shaped jaw, he had a youthful look about him, particularly in his big, round brown eyes. He also had a sterling reputation and was well known for his strong work ethic and dedication to the job, as well as his impressive investigative abilities.

Just over three weeks earlier, Judge had played a pivotal role in solving a murder case within hours of it occurring: He'd handled the police interrogation of Darius K. Maurer, a twenty-year-old man from Emmaus, a borough about fifteen miles southwest of Bethlehem. Judge was a member of the criminal investigation unit at the state police's Troop M, which had barracks in the nearby regions of Dublin, Belfast, Fogelsville, and Trevose in addition to Bethlehem. Many of the towns in those areas had no police departments, or had small departments that weren't equipped to handle homicides and other major cases, so the state police were often called in to take over those investigations.

Maurer was the boyfriend of twenty-year-old Donya Sinan Abdulrazzak, also from Emmaus, who had been reported missing the evening of June 4, 2010. According to her parents, she'd left the house that morning for what she claimed would be a ten-minute walk and never came back. When the state police looked into Maurer, they learned that he had called out sick from work that day. His mother told the police he had left the house around 10 a.m., just half an hour after Donya was last seen, and that he'd returned two hours later to change his clothes. He was dirty and sweaty.

That night, Maurer was found after crashing his sport-utility vehicle at Route 309 and Interstate 78 in South Whitehall Township. He had a stab wound on his chest. After he was taken to Lehigh Valley Hospital–Cedar Crest to be treated, Judge interviewed Maurer and he quickly admitted to having killed Donya.

They were in love, he claimed, but her family wouldn't approve of their relationship—he was black, and she was from Iraq—so they decided the only way they could be together was in death, according to Maurer. After having sex in a wooded area of Emmaus—Maurer claimed it was consensual, but authorities disputed that—he punched her, strangled her to death, and left her body alongside a walking trail. Maurer later tried to commit suicide, first by stabbing himself, then by crashing his car.

It was a slam-dunk case for Judge; Maurer would eventually plead guilty to second-degree murder and no contest to rape, and was sentenced to life in prison. Now Judge had a new case on his hands.

According to the police call, they were looking at a stabbing in Northampton borough, possibly involving multiple fatalities. The Northampton Police Department was already at the scene, but they were a small force and it looked as though the state police would be taking over the investigation. Judge was the on-duty criminal investigator that day. His paperwork was going to have to wait.

As Judge started to leave the barracks and head for his car, he was informed that there had also been a motor vehicle accident near the intersection of Route 329 and Savage Road in East Allen Township that could possibly be related to the killings. That was only about a mile and a half away from where the murders took place—a five-minute drive at best.

Judge decided to check out the crash scene first. When he arrived, he found several uniformed police officers still milling around, as well as the off-duty Corporal Mark Rowlands. A damaged gold sedan was still entangled in a patch of trees off the side of the road, but the man who had been driving it—a man named Michael, according to Rowlands—had already been airlifted to St. Luke's Hospital. Apparently, it wasn't looking very good for him.

Judge spoke to Rowlands and others at the scene and got a rundown of what had happened, including the fact that the car belonged to one of the murder victims, and that Ballard had made several remarks about having just "killed everyone." Judge instructed the ranking officer on the scene—Corporal Steven Zellner—that the accident was to be treated as a secondary crime scene. All evidence would have to be preserved, and the scene would have to be cordoned off. He ordered the vehicle to be removed, photographed, and relocated to the Bethlehem barracks for processing.

With little else to do at the crash scene—and a suspect

seeking medical care with no chance of later escaping police custody—Judge headed over to 1917 Lincoln Avenue to see where the killings had taken place.

Janet Zernhelt still appeared to be in a mild state of shock. Although hysterical when Officer Joseph York had first arrived earlier, she was a bit calmer now; several of her neighbors had come and taken her back into her house, trying their best to comfort her. Once she had regained her composure—or at least some semblance of it—she was ready to recall for police the memories that would haunt her for the rest of her life.

The memories of her husband's murder.

Janet told the police she and Steve had been married for thirty-four years. In fact, they had been just one month shy of their thirty-fifth anniversary. They met in high school, when they both worked at a fast-food chicken restaurant on 7th Street in Northampton, and they quickly became high school sweethearts.

Janet was a native of the Lehigh Valley, having lived in the nearby borough of North Catasauqua, which was just a few miles south of where she lived now. Steve's father had been in the US Navy, so the family had moved around a lot during his childhood, but he ultimately settled in Allentown, the largest city in the region. He had most recently been working as a technical service adviser for US Supply, a construction and repair supply company in West Conshohocken, a northern suburb of Philadelphia.

Janet and Steve had lived at 1915 Lincoln Avenue for just under thirty years, having moved there one year before their oldest child was born. All three of their kids had been raised there. It was a nice neighborhood, Janet said. The kind of place where she could let her children play with the other kids across the street without worrying about their safety. The kind of place where you never even thought about locking your door.

On this particular Saturday, Janet and Steve had been alone at home, watching a movie. They had originally been planning to take their boat up to Beltzville Lake, which was just under twenty miles north of Northampton in nearby Carbon County. Boating had always been one of Steve's passions, Janet said. But instead, they decided to stay in and relax together.

They were doing just that when they heard a scream from next door, according to Janet. It was a loud scream, and an unusual one. Janet had trouble describing it except to say that it didn't sound like a normal noise someone would make.

"That didn't sound right," Steve had said to her after hearing it. "Maybe someone got hurt."

Janet knew her neighbors Denise and Dennis, of course. She didn't speak with them very often, but Janet had known the family even before she moved into the house because she had gone to high school with Denise's aunt, who had also grown up in North Catasauqua. In the past, Janet had heard Denise scream after her grandfather Alvin had fallen in the yard, and they thought perhaps something like that had happened again.

Steve went to the next-door porch and knocked on the front door to see if everything was all right. When nobody answered, he walked to the other side of the house to see if Denise or Dennis was in the porch out back, but nobody was there, even though both Denise's and Dennis's cars were parked nearby.

Steve finally returned to his wife and they resumed their movie. But a short while later they heard screaming again, and soon a woman was pounding on their front door. When they opened it, they found Debbie Hawkey—although they didn't know her by name—standing in the doorway shaking, terrified, clutching a cell phone in her hand.

"Call 911!" she screamed. "Call 911!"

"Who are you?" Steve asked.

"I'm the cousin," she said hysterically. "Don't make me go in there! There's blood all over!"

Without hesitation, Steve rushed past Debbie and jumped over the small brick wall that separated the two porches, then rushed through Denise's front door. He went so quickly that he didn't bother putting on his shoes.

"Steve, you don't have your shoes on!" Janet called to him.

It was the last thing she would ever say to her husband.

Janet grabbed a phone from a receiver near the door and called 911. Debbie, still in a panic, ran past her into Janet's kitchen, but Janet was too distracted and frightened to notice. She told the 911 dispatcher there was some sort of disturbance and repeatedly asked them to send someone to their address.

Janet could hear noises next door. She couldn't make out any words, but she heard some sort of commotion, a fight of some sort. At one point she looked out her front door at Denise's porch and saw a figure emerge, but with the screen door blocking her view she couldn't make out who it was.

Janet waited a few more minutes—it felt like a few hours—but the police had still not arrived. She knew something was wrong, and she couldn't stand to leave Steve alone there any longer. She quickly went to her pantry to see if she could find something—a hammer, maybe—anything she could use to protect herself or her husband if she had to. When she couldn't find anything right away, she abandoned the idea and rushed out of her house and over to Denise's door.

"I went in there. I saw my husband in a pool of blood,"

she later said. "I just . . . I was standing there over the body."

Janet knew immediately that Steve was dead. She didn't see how he could possibly be alive. There was just so much blood. At first, she couldn't react. She was in a state of shock; her body had gone completely numb. She couldn't do anything but stand there and stare at the body of her husband.

"I saw him," she later said. "I didn't know how he could have been alive. He bled all over. I saw his face and pools of blood."

CHAPTER 4

John Morganelli's plans for the evening were about to change.

Having returned from a golf outing earlier that day, the Northampton County district attorney had just gotten dressed to go out to dinner with his wife, Diana, and a couple of friends when he received a call from a 911 dispatcher. There was a police officer on the phone, the dispatcher explained, who wanted to speak to him about an incident in Northampton borough.

"What's up?" Morganelli asked once the officer was patched through.

"Well, we've got this murder up here," the officer replied. "It's in a house, and it's looking pretty bad. We wanted to let you know. The coroner's coming."

Morganelli told his wife to go on ahead to the restaurant, adding that he would join her as soon as he could. It was his custom to head out to crime scenes himself whenever a murder occurred. His office had handled around two hundred homicides in the eighteen years he had been in the office, and he made it a practice to personally step foot in as many of those crime scenes as he possibly could.

Morganelli, fifty-four, was first elected district attorney in 1991, when he was thirty-five years old, and he had been reelected four times since. He was a short man with a slight build, a mop of curly brown hair, and a big smile, but the appearance hid a tough prosecutor who believed in taking a hard line against criminals, especially those who had committed violent crimes.

Morganelli had run for Pennsylvania attorney general in 2000, 2004, and 2008. Although unsuccessful in those bids, he nevertheless had garnered statewide attention more than once over the years. In 1995, then-Governor Tom Ridge appointed him to the Pennsylvania Commission on Crime and Delinquency. He was president of the Pennsylvania District Attorneys' Association from 1999 to 2000. In 2003, he was appointed by the state supreme court to a committee focused on capital litigation.

But if you asked him to name his proudest accomplishments during his time as district attorney, the list would probably include some of the murder cases he had personally prosecuted. He had obtained twenty first-degree murder convictions at trial, including some of the most notorious cases in Northampton County history.

Among them was Aragon Pautienus, who strangled his wife inside their suburban Forks Township home in 2008 and stuffed her body inside a plastic storage container, where it stayed for four days until his arrest. It took a jury only half an hour to render a guilty verdict.

Morganelli had also successfully prosecuted the case of Kathy MacClellan, seventy-three, who in 2005 beat her eighty-four-year-old neighbor to death with a hammer in Moore Township after MacClellan claimed the woman had stolen from her. That case was particularly unsettling due to both the age of the killer and her cold demeanor: When the police came to investigate, MacClellan was sitting in her neighbor's porch and said to them, "It's too late. She's dead already."

One of Morganelli's most impressive prosecutions was that of James McBride, who in 1985 killed his wife in his Northampton home and was said to have dismembered her body and disposed of it along the Appalachian Trail. McBride was arrested in 2000 after a grand jury was convened to investigate cold cases, but many believed he would never be convicted because his wife's body was never discovered. Nevertheless, Morganelli handled the prosecution himself and successfully secured a first-degree murder conviction.

At times, Morganelli felt like he had seen almost everything during his years as district attorney. Even so, he wasn't fully prepared for what he was about to see inside 1917 Lincoln Avenue.

After arriving at the Northampton house, Morganelli entered the front door, where his eyes were immediately drawn to the body of Steven Zernhelt curled up in front of the sofa. He could have been napping if not for the half-dried puddles of blood that stained the carpet around him.

Morganelli was greeted by Raymond Judge, the state trooper handling the investigation. The two had met only briefly in the past, when Judge worked with the district attorney's office on the cold-case grand jury investigation of Lucinda Andrews, a fifty-five-year-old woman accused of shooting a man to death in his Northampton apartment in 1985. They had very little contact during that investigation, but Morganelli knew Judge by reputation, and knew him to be a very careful and competent officer.

Judge and Morganelli stepped into the kitchen to survey the rest of the crime scene. Even for a seasoned prosecutor like Morganelli, the bodies were a disturbing sight: Denise Merhi, her arms and legs splayed out, the kitchen soaked with blood in all directions. Alvin Marsh Jr. dead in his wheelchair, the elderly man's neck shredded, his mouth agape, his face frozen in a permanent mask of horror and surprise.

This, Morgnaelli thought, *is probably the worst crime scene I've ever seen.*

It was clear to the district attorney that the Northampton Police Department was too small to handle a case of this magnitude. He directed the Pennsylvania State Police to take control of the investigation, just as they did for most major homicide cases in the county.

Morganelli was also deeply concerned when Judge reported that Denise Merhi had two young children, ages thirteen and ten, who had not been found. He ordered that the rest of the house be searched more thoroughly. There was a chance that they had been home when the murders took place and had run off to another room or closet somewhere to hide.

Or they could have become victims themselves. It was a horrible thought, but one both Morganelli and Judge knew could not be dismissed.

After ordering that he be contacted as new information became available, Morganelli excused himself from the crime scene and left to rejoin his wife and their friends for dinner, although he was quite sure his appetite had just been ruined.

Michael Ballard was rushed to the Bethlehem campus of St. Luke's Hospital, one of two trauma centers in the Lehigh Valley, and the closest to where he had crashed Denise Merhi's car. The hospital emergency room staff had been alerted to a major trauma on the way. A handful of EMTs pushed Ballard into the hospital on a stretcher, his bloodied clothes partially removed and pushed over to the side.

Dr. Timothy Costello, the chief resident of the hospital's emergency medicine residency program, was on duty in the surgical intensive care unit when Ballard arrived at 5:47 p.m. He knew little about the car crash itself, and nothing at all about the horror that had occurred only a few minutes earlier on Lincoln Avenue.

Ballard was covered in blood, with his right leg especially gruesome. Costello immediately took note of the deep, severe cut on his right thigh. Ballard had fallen in and out of consciousness during the flight, and even now he was suffering decreased levels of consciousness.

Ballard's blood pressure was determined to be 80/50, which was dangerously low compared with a normal 120/80. His heart rate was 126, which exceeded the normal range, and his oxygen saturation was 98 percent. Costello ordered that a breathing tube be inserted to protect Ballard's airway. His extreme level of blood loss was life threatening both in itself and because it lessened his body's ability to provide oxygen to his brain.

Death was a real possibility for this man.

Northampton County Coroner Zachary Lysek arrived at 1917 Lincoln Avenue shortly before John Morganelli departed. He had first stopped over at the crash scene on Route 329 upon hearing it was designated a secondary crime scene. Lysek had been coroner since 1992. Before that he spent two years as deputy coroner and about seven years as a police officer in several nearby departments, including Lower Saucon Township, Fountain Hill, and Salisbury Township.

In those nearly thirty years of experience, Lysek had seen more than his fair share of grisly crime scenes. As coroner, he saw an average of between eight and fifteen homicides each year in Northampton County, and had long developed a required level of professional detachment when it came to the violence. Even so, like Morganelli, Lysek felt this particular crime scene was in its own category of atrocity.

This is horrific, Lysek thought as he surveyed the house.

Lysek's job was to document the scene, identify any evidence, assist in the collection of that evidence, and document any injuries on the bodies. Lysek was particularly concerned for the safety of Denise Merhi's children. He was directed by Morganelli to search the house and ensure they were not inside somewhere. Judging by the brutally violent way these three victims had died, the coroner felt certain that whoever committed the murders would not have hesitated in killing the children as well.

Somebody had a lot of anger, Lysek thought. *Obviously this was a crime that took an extended period of time to do, based on the extent of the injuries to the victims.*

Lysek began the search along with Trooper Raymond Judge, members of the state police's records and identification unit, and one other member of Lysek's own office. Gradually, they made their way to the home's basement, which was accessible via a doorway in the kitchen, just across from where Denise Merhi's bloodied corpse lay spread across the floor.

Unlike the floors upstairs, Lysek noticed that none of the basement steps had any bloodstains. The brown stairs, each of which was covered by a black-and-yellow-striped pad, led down to an open door with a multicolored bag dangling from the doorknob, the words HAPPY BIRTHDAY written in bright block letters.

The downstairs opened up into a partially finished basement apartment with multiple smaller rooms, each with a drop ceiling and recessed lighting. Lysek stepped past a tall white rotating fan and a wall-mounted rack with four coats hanging on the hooks. He walked into a small living area with a beige couch, a blue-and-white plaid armchair, a wide-screen television, and a small brown floor table with magazines and empty soda bottles scattered atop.

A pair of legs was visible on the brown-carpeted floor, just in front of the couch.

Lysek rushed over and quickly realized that the legs belonged to an adult, not a child. A white quilt with a pattern of fuchsia stars had been draped over the person. His legs stuck out of one end of the quilt, the feet fitted with a pair of red, white, and blue sneakers and white socks.

On the other side of the quilt, the man's right arm reached outward from beneath the quilt, as if he were a student raising his hand in a classroom. His left hand also poked out from under the quilt, sitting completely still next to the side of the body, resting in a large red bloodstain that was slowly drying on the carpet.

They had discovered a fourth murder victim.

The authorities would later identify him as Dennis Marsh, Denise's sixty-two-year-old father, a parts clerk and truck manufacturer who lived in that basement apartment of Denise's home. Like the other bodies, Dennis appeared to have been stabbed multiple times. The pattern from the extensive bloodstains was consistent with arterial spurting, and all the signs indicated to Lysek that there had been a struggle before he died.

Dennis's white T-shirt was completely soaked in blood. Around the gray-haired man's neck, Lysek found a silver necklace with a MedicAlert tag indicating he had a past medical history of diabetes. A gold wristwatch was intact on Dennis's left wrist. Through the blood, Lysek noticed several tattoos on the man, including one of Mickey Mouse on his left arm, one of singer Jim Morrison on his left calf, one of a semi-clothed woman and a jail cell window on his right calf, and one of a multicolored butterfly on his right upper back.

Looking up from the body, Lysek saw a message written in blood on the white wall: DENISE IS A WHORE.

The coroner stood up and walked closer to the eerie message, which he noticed seemed to have been traced on the wall using a sharp object—possibly the knife used to kill these victims. The letters were only a few inches tall, written in all capital letters next to a framed painting of a beachside ocean scene.

Lysek made another surprising discovery: a light blue T-shirt with a Superman logo resting on the arm of the plaid armchair. The shirt did not appear to be strewn randomly on the furniture, but was instead folded neatly and seemed to have been deliberately placed there. Lysek noticed bloodstains underneath the familiar red S and shield logo.

Lysek wondered if the killer had deliberately placed the T-shirt there after committing the murder.

After conducting a thorough search of the rest of the residence, Lysek and Judge concluded there was nobody else inside the house, living or dead. Lysek called John Morganelli to inform him about the fourth victim, news that both shocked and angered the district attorney. He could hardly believe that the authorities hadn't found the body for more than half an hour after receiving the first 911 call about the murders.

Lysek, however, was less concerned. He knew the police wanted to make sure all the evidence was preserved, and the best way to do that was to quickly secure the crime scene and make sure the house was cleared so nobody would trample over the evidence. Since the quilt concealed the fourth body, he believed it was entirely conceivable that it would have been initially overlooked, and ultimately none of the evidence was compromised.

Regardless, it was now clear that the police were dealing with a quadruple homicide, the first that Morganelli or Lysek could recall in their long careers in Northampton County.

The police later learned that Denise's son Trystan and her daughter Annikah were alive and well. In the days before the murders, Denise had taken the kids down to the New Jersey shore to celebrate Annikah's birthday. CNN reported that John Morganelli said Denise's mother, Geraldine Dorwart, was still at the shore with the children when Denise was killed.

The authorities were extremely relieved. They knew that, if Geraldine and the kids had been home, they could just as easily have suffered her fate.

Geraldine had long been divorced from Dennis Marsh at the time of the killings, having only been married to him a total of seven years. The fifty-five-year-old lived with her sister Karen in Whitehall Township—less than three miles away from her daughter and grandchildren— which was where Geraldine was now taking her grandchildren.

But while Geraldine had escaped physical injury, the emotional pain was immeasurable. Denise was her only child, and they had a very close relationship.

"To know that Denise suffered terrible pain and the utmost fear before her life was taken from her is beyond any heartache imaginable," Geraldine would later say in court.

In recent years, Denise had taken on a sort of caretaker

role in the relationship with her mother. Denise helped
Geraldine complete all of her important paperwork, and
Geraldine sometimes referred to her daughter as her personal secretary and medical adviser. Geraldine had been
undertaking training and schooling to start a new career
path as a certified nursing assistant, and Denise was so
helpful that Geraldine would refer to her as "my coach."

I'll no longer have her to be there for me, Geraldine
thought. *She is no longer a phone call away.*

Denise would have turned forty the following May,
and already Geraldine had been planning a major surprise celebration for her daughter. Denise had gone above
and beyond for Geraldine's fortieth and fiftieth birthdays,
and she wanted to return the treasured gesture to her only
child.

Denise, in fact, was born on Mother's Day in 1971, and
Geraldine considered her daughter a true gift from God
that day. Mother's Day was always an extra-special occasion for the two women, and Geraldine couldn't believe
that the one they celebrated last month would be their last
ever.

Geraldine also considered her daughter the family's
memory maker. Denise loved planning family vacations,
and would organize every little detail: where the family
would go, where they would stay, where they would eat,
and even what they would wear, so they would all match
and look like a family.

And Denise would always document those trips and
other special occasions through photographs. She had put
the family photos into scrapbooks for her two children.
Unfortunately, Geraldine thought, those scrapbooks would
end with photographs of Trystan at age thirteen and Annikah's recent tenth birthday.

She won't be able to take dozens of photos the way she

always did when Trystan and Annikah go to proms, grad-
uations, and weddings, and put these treasures into the
already-started scrapbooks, Geraldine thought.

Even though they had been divorced for decades, Dennis Marsh was still a part of his ex-wife's life. With Denise
and their grandchildren in common, Dennis and Geraldine
attended many of the same family dinners and holiday cel-
ebrations. Geraldine even took care of Dennis's mother
before she died.

Perhaps most valuably, her ex-husband was a caring
grandfather to their grandchildren. Their shared housing
allowed him to experience the simple things with them,
including taking Annikah to school every day and regular trips with both grandchildren to the borough library
and pool. Dennis and Trystan shared a love of cars, and
together were restoring a 1967 Chevy. Trystan was me-
morialized through a tattoo on his grandfather's right
thigh.

Alvin Marsh, her ex-father-in-law, also remained part
of Geraldine's life. In fact, she never thought of him as
her father-in-law—he was more of a father to her than her
own father. She, like many other people, called him
Poppy. Geraldine had known Poppy since she was fourteen, and shared more with him than she did with her
own father or any other male figure in her life. He helped
her through problems, as he did for many people in his
life.

Since he'd become confined to a wheelchair in recent
years, Geraldine had been able to spend even more time
with him. Alvin had served in the US Navy during World
War II, and could tell stories for hours about his time as a
gunman on the USS *North Carolina*. Alvin often spoke
about the future and how much he wanted to be a part of
it. It had always been his dream, Geraldine said, to live
long enough to see Trystan drive.

It breaks my heart knowing he survived the war only to die this way, Geraldine thought.

By now, John Morganelli had rejoined his wife and friends in Bethlehem for dinner, but his mind was never far from the crime scene he had left behind in Northampton earlier that night. The district attorney tried hard to engage in pleasant dinner conversation, but his thoughts kept drifting back to those horrible, bloody images he had seen at the house. And it certainly didn't help that he was receiving constant calls from Trooper Judge and others at the scene with updates about the investigation.

Just as Morganelli started to relax a bit and enjoy his dinner, his cell phone rang with another call from one of the investigators. After again apologizing for the interruptions, he stepped away from the dinner table and answered, trying not to sound too irritable. He was still deeply disturbed from the last call, when he learned about the fourth body, and hoped there wouldn't be any more surprises tonight.

But that hope was dashed once he was told the latest news: The police had been conducting a criminal background check on Michael Ballard, the man who had apparently stolen Denise's car and told emergency officials that he "just killed everyone." That background check was finished, and it turned out he had killed before.

He had previously been convicted for killing a man in 1991. When he was only eighteen years old, Ballard had stabbed the man to death in an apartment in Allentown, Pennsylvania.

The largest city in the Lehigh Valley region, and the third largest in the state—behind Philadelphia and Pittsburgh—Allentown was only about twenty minutes south of Northampton, although they were practically two different worlds. Allentown was a much more urban environment and, Morganelli knew, much more prone to violent murders than the normally quiet borough of Northampton.

Details about that previous murder were still scarce at this point in the investigation, but it appeared that Ballard had killed the man, then stolen the victim's car and attempted to flee to Ballard's home state of Arkansas. If that was true, Morganelli thought, there were already obvious parallels between that killing and the murder of Denise Merhi, whose car it appeared Ballard had also stolen.

Morganelli learned that Ballard had pleaded guilty and been sentenced to fifteen to thirty years in prison for the 1991 murder, but was released in 2006 after serving the minimum. Although it would take some time to track down all the details, it seemed he had been arrested again in April 2008 for a parole violation, then released on parole again on April 19, 2010.

Barely two months ago, Morganelli thought, growing furious. How could this man have been out on the streets? Morganelli had long been a proponent of reforming the parole system in Pennsylvania, particularly when it came to violent crimes. He felt liberal policies from "bleeding-heart do-gooders" had allowed far too many murderers and rapists back on the streets. Now they were dealing with a suspect who had not only killed before and been given a second chance, but had apparently been arrested again after his parole and was set free a second time, giving him the opportunity to commit four murders.

Following his recent parole, Ballard had been released to Allentown Community Corrections Center, a halfway house for state prison inmates, the investigator explained to Morganelli. Inmates there are allowed to be released for limited periods of time for purposes related to work,

education, or treatment. Ballard had been released earlier
in the day, but a warrant had since been issued for his arrest. Ballard had been due back at two o'clock, less than
three hours before Denise Merhi and the others were
killed. He never showed up.

CHAPTER 5

More than 170 miles away, Jaime Zernhelt's phone was ringing.

At age twenty-five, Jaime was the youngest of Steve and Janet's three children. She lived in Laurel, Maryland, not too far from where she worked as an elementary school teacher. This morning, she had several friends and family members over at her home to celebrate the birthday of her fiancé, Lenny Mierzwa. Her two brothers were also there: Justin, twenty-eight, who lived right down the street, and the twenty-six-year-old Ryan, who lived in Philadelphia.

Everybody was having such a good time that Jaime had almost missed the phone ringing, even though it had been ringing for quite a long time. Perhaps, Jaime thought, it was her parents. They had considered coming down for the party today, but Steve Zernhelt had decided everybody would have a much better time without Jaime's parents hanging around.

"You kids have fun," her father had told Jaime on the phone that morning. "You don't need us adults there."

When Jaime answered the phone, however, it wasn't her parents at all, but rather a neighbor who lived across the street from them on Lincoln Avenue. Jaime knew the neighbor; after all, she had grown up in Northampton borough and lived there all her life before going off to East Stroudsburg University to study education.

The neighbor sounded panicked and terrified as she spoke the words that Jaime would never forget.

"Your dad's been stabbed," she said. "But they're working on him."

Jaime fell to the ground, shaking. She was horrified, but also couldn't fully comprehend what had happened. *Stabbed?* she thought. *Stabbed? What happened? It doesn't make sense.*

Somebody—she didn't know who—picked her up off the ground and led her outside to the car. Jaime was in shock, but she must have explained to others at the party what she had just been told over the phone, because the next thing she knew she was in a car heading to Northampton. Lenny, Justin, Ryan, even her dog Ziggy were in the vehicle with her, while her cousin Eric drove and Eric's girlfriend rode along.

It proved to be the longest car ride of any of their lives. Jaime's phone wouldn't stop ringing as concerned family members and friends kept calling, some checking on her, others giving her information and trying to keep her calm. They all kept saying the same thing: "Your dad's okay. They're working on him." The whole time, Jaime just kept praying that her father really would be okay.

But after they were about an hour into the drive, not quite out of Delaware yet, Jaime's uncle Jimmy called. He had heard what others were telling them in the previous phone calls, that Steve was all right, but he insisted that the kids had to know the truth. While on speakerphone so the whole car could hear, Jimmy said he didn't want them to have any false hopes, didn't want them to be wishing and hoping for something impossible.

"I've got to let you know," he said. "He's gone."

Jaime couldn't believe it. She wouldn't believe it. She shook her head forcefully, trying to forget what her uncle had told her.

"It's not true," she said. "He couldn't say that. He didn't mean it."

But looking into her brothers' eyes, she could see that they knew it was the truth. They looked like they were going to be sick to their stomachs, but Justin and Ryan nevertheless tried to maintain strong, stoic faces for Jaime's sake. They had always tried to be strong for her, tried to be her protectors, but she could see in their eyes that they knew the truth, and it made her realize it, too. Her father was dead.

They pulled over at a rest stop and Jaime immediately rushed into the bathroom, where she leaned over the sink and looked into the mirror. She stared at her reflection wishing this would all just go away. That she could wake up from this nightmare.

She thought of her father. They had always had a great relationship. A perfect one, she thought. She couldn't have asked for a better father. Growing up, her dad had always wanted to do everything with his family, whether it was swimming at the pool, playing sports, family dinners— anything just as long as they were together. When she was a young girl, Jaime used to wear a little tool belt and help her dad do work around the house. When she got older, he went out of his way to attend not only her brothers' basketball and football games, but also her cheerleading events all through middle and high school. She had always looked up to him and he was always there to guide her, right up to when he and Jaime's mother put her through college.

Jaime realized she and her brothers were supposed to visit her parents just next weekend. Her dad had just bought a family-sized raft, and they were all going to take it out to the lake. He had been waiting to take it out on the water until they could all go together.

After a few minutes, Jaime returned to the car, where the rest of the long drive was relatively silent. When they pulled up to their childhood home in Northampton borough, the scene was chaotic. The house was sealed off with yellow police tape. News vans and reporters milled on the street, and a helicopter flew overhead.

They pulled up to the front of the house, where Coroner Zachary Lysek confirmed what her uncle had told her a few hours earlier. Jaime collapsed into a nearby man's arms and started sobbing on the front lawn.

My daddy was murdered, Jaime thought. *He's gone.*

CHAPTER 6

While Trooper Raymond Judge continued to take the lead on the quadruple slaying investigation, Trooper McLean Peeke, the head of the barracks' forensic services unit, was tasked with gathering the physical evidence.

Peeke was brought onto the investigation around six o'clock the evening of the murders, and his first stop was the scene of Ballard's car crash on Route 329. With a search warrant yet to be obtained, all Peeke could do was place plastic over the crashed car's windows, so he headed over to the scene of the murders themselves around 7:35 p.m.

Without a search warrant, Peeke couldn't yet collect any evidence, but he could survey the inside of the house. Coroner Zachary Lysek led Peeke through the residence, and although he couldn't obtain any physical items, he was permitted to take photographs and videotape in the rooms where the victims were located: the living room, the kitchen, the back bedroom, and the basement.

Meanwhile, at St. Luke's Hospital, Dr. Costello ordered a rapid blood transfusion for Michael Ballard. He ultimately required three liters of blood and five liters of crystalloid fluid. Eventually, Ballard became stabilized enough that he was ready for surgery. He was transported to a hospital operating room at 6:45 p.m., where the deep stab wound to his leg was to be treated.

The blood transfusion and the surgery ultimately saved his life. Afterward, Ballard was placed into the post-anesthesia care unit, where he would wait until the anesthesiologist determined he was ready to be transferred to the hospital's intensive care unit.

By this time, Costello had been approached by Trooper Gregg Dietz, one of the senior investigators in the state police's Bethlehem barracks criminal investigation unit. The doctor was notified that four people had been brutally murdered in Northampton borough, and that Michael Ballard was the prime suspect. But that made no difference to Costello, just as it would make no difference for any doctor in his situation. Ballard was his patient, and he had to be treated. That was that.

Dietz had earlier asked whether he could question Ballard in the trauma bay, but Costello said it would not have been medically appropriate at that time. By now the police were understandably anxious to interview him and Dietz raised his request again, but Costello refused. Ballard was still recovering from the anesthesia, he explained, and anything he said at this point would be considered suspect.

The trooper asked if he could take Ballard into custody once he was released from the post-anesthesia care unit, but again Costello refused. Typically, he explained, patients coming from the trauma bay remain in the ICU at least twelve to twenty-four hours before they are released. Michael Ballard may have been a suspected murderer, but the doctor had to treat him like any other patient.

However, Costello did not wish to obstruct the police

investigation, either. At the request of one of the police officers, he placed brown paper bags over Ballard's hands so that the bloodstains could be preserved as potential evidence. Hospital staff also gathered Ballard's bloodied clothes and placed them in bags for the state police to take, and police collected the discarded gauze used to wrap Ballard's wounds.

Although the police could not take Ballard into custody, the hospital itself had a policy of restraining patients who had been fitted with a breathing tube so they could not pull it out once they regained consciousness. After Ballard's hands were bagged, they were firmly tied down to the bed. The state police assigned a trooper to guard Ballard's door, but it was clear to them that the suspected killer was not going anywhere.

News of four brutal slayings was enough to shake Northampton borough to its core.

A small town of 9,926 people—located just ten miles north of Allentown—Northampton was once a major center of cement manufacturing. Atlas Cement Company had its headquarters there until 1982, and supplied some of the materials that went into the construction of the Empire State Building and the Panama Canal, among other well-known sites. Now, like many surrounding Pennsylvania towns, the borough's manufacturing days were mostly in the past, although a handful of smaller cement producers were still active in the region.

Northampton still honors its cement manufacturing history through the local Atlas Cement Museum, as well as through the Northampton Area School District, whose sports teams were called the Konkrete Kids. It was a relatively high-performing school district, with a 99 percent graduation rate and 83 percent of those graduates going on to college. The community beamed with particular pride on the school's wrestling team, with its two national titles, seven state team titles, and twenty-one individual state titles.

The town's small business district isn't as successful as it once was, when the art-deco-style Roxy Theatre was a bustling movie house and, later, a live music venue where Bruce Springsteen and Billy Joel played early in their careers. Dating back to 1921, the theater remains a centerpiece of the borough's Main Street, but it now only operates as a second-run movie theater featuring three-dollar shows.

The modest Main Street had seen better days, but still, more of the storefronts were open than not, and it still looked so much like a charming slice of Americana that it was used to portray a typical 1950s Main Street setting in the opening of the 1992 film *School Ties*.

The people of the borough also seemed to take pride in their history, with the nearby Canal Street Heritage Walkway trail following the Lehigh River for more than a mile, boasting some of the more picturesque sights of the area.

Northampton officials chose to have their own police department instead of relying on the state police like many of their neighbors, but serious crimes were rare in the quiet town. Police Chief Ronald Morey had been with the department since 1984, and in that time, prior to this new multiple homicide case, there had been only three murders in the borough.

Two had occurred in 1985. First there was James Mc-Bride's murder of his wife, Kelly, which District Attorney John Morganelli had successfully prosecuted himself. Then there was the fatal shooting of fifty-one-year-old borough resident John Joseph Mayerchak by a prostitute he frequented, Lucinda Andrews, who remained free for twenty-five years before a cold-case investigation led to her arrest. After those two killings, the borough went more than a decade without a murder—until 1997, when Donald Reiman Jr. was lured to the Hokendauqua Creek dam by his girlfriend, Barbara Kitchen, and killed there by another one of her lovers, John Mead.

Another decade had passed before Denise Merhi and three others were stabbed to death inside one of the borough's unassuming homes, a crime that was practically unheard of not only in Northampton borough, but anywhere in the Lehigh Valley region.

"People were shook up, especially because it was four victims. It was something very out of the ordinary," Chief Morey later said. "But then again, stuff like that, it's sad to say, it's happening more and more every day."

The Merhi home was about two blocks from Main Street and about half a mile from the Northampton Area Library, High School, and Middle School. Lincoln Avenue was a street of well-kept modest homes; a prominent Gothic-style church—St. Paul's United Church of Christ— sat almost cattycorner to the residence.

It was considered an excellent place to raise a family—a neighborhood unaccustomed to even the most petty crimes, much less multiple murders.

"I've lived here for twenty years," Ruby Stonewall, a neighbor and family friend, told the *Morning Call,* one of the region's two local newspapers. "Things like this don't happen here."

Even newer residents were stunned by the slayings. A couple that had moved to the neighborhood less than six months ago from Lancaster, Pennsylvania, was especially aghast.

"We moved here because we were told it was quiet," the wife told the *Express-Times,* the other local paper. "Now we're ready to move back."

Such expressions of shock appeared regularly in both newspapers for days. It was one of the biggest stories to ever hit the region, and certainly a noteworthy one for the quiet little Northampton borough. No one could recall another quadruple murder in the county's history.

The story was covered heavily by news agencies in Philadelphia, less than seventy miles away, and also gained mention in newspapers across the country including the *Washington Post,* the *Seattle Times,* and Long Island's *Newsday.*

The region had seen multiple murders in the past. In fact, the *Express-Times* compiled a list of such crimes in the past twenty-five years. But in terms of the number of simultaneous victims, the Northampton quadruple homicide topped it.

New Jersey serial killer nurse Charles Cullen—who has admitted to killing at least forty patients—committed at least eight of those murders in the Lehigh Valley and at least another eight in neighboring counties in New Jersey. And Lehigh Valley resident Ali Davis also has been convicted of four murders, the only other four-time killer in the region's history, as far as the authorities know.

But Cullen's killings occurred over a stretch of sixteen years at ten hospitals before he was arrested. Likewise, Davis's murders were committed in two separate incidents, both in the city of Easton. Davis, who was twenty when he committed his first murder, gunned down a man in the street on May 2007, and then six months later worked with three accomplices to break into a house and murder three people in a gang-related shooting. That triple homicide, which occurred directly across from one of the city's middle schools, was one of the most shocking crimes the Lehigh Valley had ever seen.

That is, until the murders alleged to be committed by

Michael Ballard. The notion of four people meeting such brutal ends all at once sent shock waves through the entire region.

By 9:40 p.m., about five hours after Ballard's car crash, he had recovered enough to breathe on his own again and his breathing tube was removed. That meant Ballard could finally speak, but Dr. Costello was not ready to let the police ask him any questions until he questioned Ballard himself and determined his level of consciousness.

Costello conducted a cognitive exam using the Glasgow Coma Scale, a typical neurological scale used to determine a patient's state of consciousness. He also checked Ballard's eye movement, motor skills, and verbalization.

"Can you tell me your name?" the doctor asked him. "Can you tell me where you are? Can you tell me what happened to you? Can you tell me who the president of the United States is?"

Ballard answered all the questions correctly in complete sentences, and Costello gave him a score of fourteen on the coma scale, the highest possible level. At last, he was ready to be interviewed by the police.

Raymond Judge and Gregg Dietz were called into Ballard's room to conduct the interview. The two troopers introduced themselves and Ballard nodded in recognition. But as soon as they started asking questions about Denise Merhi's house in Northampton borough, Ballard closed his eyes and would not respond.

It was clear to Judge that Ballard was faking sleep or unconsciousness. And although he wasn't fooling the troopers, it was obvious they weren't going to get any answers out of him. At least not right away.

Trooper Christopher Maner was selected to watch Ballard as he slept and to alert Trooper Judge if he awoke. Around eleven o'clock that night, Costello returned to

Ballard's room to check on him. The doctor recalled that a vial of purple fluid was found inside the leather knife holster Ballard had when he arrived at the hospital, so he asked Ballard if there was anything he had ingested that the doctors should be informed about.

Ballard responded that he had consumed a Long Island Iced Tea—a drink well known for its high alcohol content—as well as straight vodka and various multivitamins earlier in the day. Costello ordered a blood alcohol content test for Ballard and it eventually came back at 0.113, over the legal limit for drunken driving in Pennsylvania of 0.08. The test was conducted more than six hours after the murders took place, so the blood alcohol content would have been even higher at that time. His testosterone levels also were higher than usual—possibly from having taken steroids or other supplements—which could have increased his aggressiveness.

After the test, Ballard fell back asleep. Around eleven-thirty that night, Trooper Arthur Johnson was sent to relieve Trooper Maner to stand watch at Ballard's bedside. Ballard awoke just after midnight and looked directly at Trooper Johnson.

"What's your story, dickhead?" he asked.

Johnson identified himself as a trooper with the Pennsylvania State Police who was assigned to observe him.

"How's that going for you?" Ballard shot back.

As Johnson started to tell Ballard that he would like to talk to him about the events from earlier that day, Ballard closed his eyes, once again pretending to be asleep. It was looking less and less likely that he would cooperate with the authorities.

While Johnson watched over Ballard, Judge was on the phone with the Pennsylvania State Parole Board seeking a detainer against Ballard. He had violated his parole by leaving the Allentown Community Corrections Center, and getting a detainer would allow them to hold Ballard until homicide charges could be brought against him.

Later that night, Dr. Costello returned to check on Ballard, who was still resting in his hospital bed. Despite everything they had learned about Ballard from the police, the medical staff still knew little about the car crash that had brought Ballard here, and the doctor needed to learn as many details as he could so they knew how to best provide treatment. The police did not ask Costello to question Ballard on their behalf, nor did he feel pressured to obtain information for them, although Trooper Arthur Johnson was still outside the room guarding Ballard.

Ballard had been uncooperative with police so far, but he seemed more willing to talk to Costello. They spoke for a few minutes about his injuries. The doctor asked about how Ballard had obtained certain wounds, and eventually asked how Ballard sustained the deep puncture wound on his leg.

"I was stabbing some dude, and the knife slipped down and cut my knee," Ballard replied in a cold, casual tone of voice.

Costello was taken aback, and their conversation came to a complete halt. Trooper Johnson, who was standing in the doorway, had also heard Ballard's statement and became immediately alert. Costello left the room a few minutes later, and Johnson asked him to make a written statement about Ballard's startling admission.

Around 1 a.m., Trooper Judge returned to the hospital to speak with Ballard, with the hope that the statement he'd made to Costello indicated he was ready to speak. Ballard didn't close his eyes or pretend to sleep this time, and Judge informed Ballard that he wanted to speak with him about a homicide investigation and read him his Miranda rights. But Judge had no more luck than before, as

Ballard quickly exercised his right to remain silent. He said he would not answer any questions without a lawyer.

Ballard slept for a few hours, and Costello returned at 5:30 a.m. to reassess his patient's condition. Once again, the doctor had not been asked to question Ballard on behalf of the authorities, but the police had continued to keep a trooper—this one named Steven Furlong—standing just outside the doorway to take note of anything Ballard might say.

With a nurse present, Costello performed an examination on his patient and started asking basic questions, including whether Ballard knew why he was in the hospital. Ballard's response was just as frank, and shocking, as a few hours earlier.

"Because I murdered my girlfriend and her family and then the neighbor who came over later," he replied, matter-of-factly. "I was in the process of stabbing them when the knife slipped and stabbed my knee."

Costello repeated Ballard's statement back to him, and Ballard nodded in confirmation. Furlong had trouble hearing Ballard, but could clearly hear Costello as he repeated the information. Costello asked a few more questions, and Ballard seemed better able to articulate how he'd sustained his injuries now than he had been before. It was clear to the doctor that Ballard's alertness and levels of consciousness had greatly improved.

Costello, and the nurse who had been present with him, both again made written statements to the police about Ballard's unsettling confessions.

CHAPTER 7

It was December 6, 1991, when the Allentown communications center received a call from a co-worker of a man named Donald Richard. The caller was concerned because Richard, who was fifty-two, had not shown up for his job at the Allentown State Hospital in three days, and attempts to reach him via phone had been unsuccessful.

The communications center dispatched marked Allentown police cars to Richard's apartment on North 12th Street in the city's downtown. Although that block consisted of mainly single-family homes, Richard's house was divided into separate apartments on the first and second floors.

There was no answer when the police officers knocked on Richard's apartment door. After obtaining a warrant, they eventually entered the apartment, where they immediately detected a rancid odor in the air. An odor that could only belong to a decomposing body.

Inside the apartment, lying on a sofa, was the corpse of Donald Richard.

He had been stabbed eight times—with a serrated knife, by the look of it—three times in the neck, twice in the back and once each in the chest, left shoulder, and lower lip. Blood was splattered all over Richard, the sofa, and the wall behind it. Sitting on a short end table next to the sofa were two opened, unfinished bottles of beer.

Once it was clear that they were dealing with a homicide, the responding police officers called evidence technicians to process the scene. Two different sets of fingerprints were discovered on the beer bottles, one of which matched Richard. The other likely belonged to his killer.

Equally significant was what the investigators did not find: Richard's wallet was missing from the apartment, and his car, a blue-and-gray 1991 Mustang, was nowhere to be seen. The Allentown police issued a nationwide alert with the license plate number and a description of the car, asking any police department that spotted it to stop the vehicle and consider the occupant potentially armed and dangerous.

Meanwhile, Detective Sergeant Dean Schwartz was called in as lead investigator. Having served nine years on the Allentown Police Department, he handled many of the major crimes that reached the department's detective bureau, including homicides, robberies, and rapes. Schwartz began his investigation by interviewing neighbors and co-workers who knew Richard, and a picture of the man's life slowly began to develop.

Schwartz learned that Richard was a gay man who had been seeing several men between the ages of twenty and thirty-five prior to his death. One man who'd previously lived with Richard referred to him as a "trick" and suggested he regularly engaged in sex with other men for money. After looking Richard up in the criminal database, Schwartz learned that on at least one occasion, emergency responders had been called to Richard's apartment because a man in his early twenties—apparently Richard's boyfriend—had become dangerously drunk and needed medical attention.

According to some interviewees, Richard made it a practice of distributing keys to various young men to come in and out of his apartment. With no sign of forced entry at the apartment, it seemed entirely possible that one of these men could wind up one of the prime suspects for Richard's murder.

But by December 8, there was no longer any need to pursue this lead. Donald Richard's stolen car had been found.

Schwartz received a call from the Washington County Sheriff's Office in Fayetteville, Arkansas, informing him the department had stopped a Mustang matching Allentown's nationwide alert. Inside the vehicle, they had discovered Richard's wallet, as well as a serrated knife stained with blood.

They had also apprehended the driver: an eighteen-year-old man named Michael Ballard.

Ballard had been placed under arrest on charges of theft and receiving stolen property. The Allentown Police Department immediately began the process to extradite Ballard back to Pennsylvania on those theft charges.

A check on Richard's credit cards revealed that nearly twelve hundred dollars' worth of purchases of food, gasoline, and other items had been made at various stores from Pennsylvania to Arkansas over the last several days. Ballard hadn't covered his tracks very well. He left a trail of illegal credit card purchases from Pennsylvania all the way to Arkansas, even going so far as to take his friends out to fancy, expensive dinners. Some of the purchases seemed completely random: They later learned he had even stopped to buy a stuffed teddy bear as a gift for an ex-girlfriend.

Also among the items recovered from Ballard was literature from the Ku Klux Klan, including writings con-

demning homosexuality and those who would condone
sodomy. One of the pamphlets cited verses from the bibli-
cal book of Leviticus that homosexuals should be put to
death. Whether Ballard was actually a member the KKK
was not immediately clear.

It was also unclear what relationship Ballard had with
Richard, if indeed he had one at all. But Ballard's connection to the crime scene was obvious, and the case against
him was about to grow that much stronger: His fingerprints
matched the second set found on the beer bottles in Richard's apartment, and DNA testing of the blood found on
the knife matched that of Richard himself.

It was more than enough to charge Ballard with criminal homicide. Shortly after Ballard was committed to the
Lehigh County Prison, however, Schwartz learned that
his case was about to grow even stronger. He had received
a phone call that a nurse from the prison wanted to speak
to the police right away.

Ballard had just confessed to her that he had killed
Richard.

Schwartz sat down with Monica Fabian at the Allentown
Police Department headquarters on December 13 at 10:42
p.m., just over an hour after she had met Ballard for the
first time at the Lehigh County Prison. Visibly nervous
and distressed, Fabian described for Schwartz exactly
what Ballard had told her.

An intake nurse, Fabian had been working in the community services wing near the front of the prison when
Ballard had been brought in that night. He had just been
extradited from Arkansas and, when she first saw him, he
was at the booking counter receiving a mental evaluation
to determine whether any special observations or conditions were necessary for his incarceration.

Afterward, around 9:30 p.m., Ballard was brought

before Fabian for a routine medical evaluation. Once they were alone together, Fabian began asking the familiar questions she asked at all evaluations: Do you have any health problems? Is there any history of health problems in your family? Have you been hospitalized in the past year?

Ballard appeared distracted, but quietly answered all of her questions, at least at first. Then, without provocation, he changed the subject altogether.

"I did it," Ballard said.

"Did what?" Fabian asked, genuinely confused.

"I did it," Ballard repeated. "I killed him."

Fabian was completely shocked. It had been the last thing she had ever expected to hear. Unsure of how to respond, Fabian tried to turn their focus back to the medical evaluation and started asking her routine questions again. But Ballard pressed on, seemingly determined to discuss what he had done.

Ballard explained that he had been serving in the US Army in South Carolina but had been recently discharged. He didn't explain why, nor did he explain why he'd moved from Arkansas to Allentown after his discharge, except to say that he was leaving his home state due to "problems" there.

Ballard continued that he had moved in with his dad's cousin Vera—an older woman he had always called an aunt—and had gotten a job working as a telemarketer. It wasn't the most rewarding job, but he worked hard at it, and quickly developed the second-best sales record of the people in the office.

"I thought maybe I would have a better chance of starting a life over here," he said.

But after a short time, Vera asked him to move out, having discovered Ballard reading a newspaper issued by the Ku Klux Klan.

"Are you involved with the Klan?" Fabian asked.

"No, I just get the newspaper every now and then," Ballard insisted. "I just read the stuff."

One of Ballard's co-workers had given him a telephone number to call, and it turned out to be a long, pre-recorded diatribe of racial propaganda from the Klan. Ballard didn't consider himself a prejudiced man, but he listened to the entire audio recording out of curiosity, then reached out to one of the people associated with the Klan and agreed to attend a meeting.

Ballard drove out to Reading, a Pennsylvania city about forty miles southwest of Allentown, for a rally held by Roy Frankhouser, a Grand Dragon and the state's leading KKK member. A crowd of a few dozen attended, and Ballard stood out like a sore thumb because, as the only non-member, he was the only one not wearing the Klan's signature white robes and headgear.

Ballard never joined the group, and later could not explain why he had decided to attend the meeting at all. But he did bring back to Allentown some of the Klan's literature, which was discovered by his aunt. She was deeply disturbed by the literature, especially because her daughter was married to a black man, Ballard told Fabian. Not wishing to deal with any possible family repercussions by having Ballard around, his aunt asked him to move out.

One of Ballard's co-workers agreed to let him stay at his place until Ballard found somewhere else to live. But what with his problems in Arkansas, his discharge from the army, and now having been thrown out of his aunt's home, Ballard was feeling directionless. Like he wasn't living at all, simply existing.

"I was lost as hell," he later said. "I had no goals. No direction."

Ballard explained to Fabian that one night two Sundays ago—which would have been December 1—he had gone drinking at several Allentown bars and was taking a walk outside when a blue-and-gray Mustang passed him by. Then it passed him another two times. Ballard took notice because he admired fast cars and liked the look of the Mustang.

The car then pulled over not far from him and Ballard approached it to take a closer look at the vehicle. The driver rolled down his window, Ballard claimed, and introduced himself as Donald Richard. They exchanged a few friendly words as Ballard admired the car, then Richard offered to have a drink with Ballard.

Ballard later said he found nothing unusual about the exchange; back home in Arkansas, people would often wave or stop and strike up a conversation while they were driving by. The two went to a nearby bar for a beer and started chatting. They made small talk for a while, chatting about football and whether the New York Giants would make it to the Super Bowl that year.

After talking for about ninety minutes, Ballard explained that he needed to find somewhere new to live. Richard told Ballard he owned an apartment complex on 12th Street with a few vacancies he was interested in renting. It sounded perfect to Ballard, so the two made arrangements to meet at Richard's apartment the next night so that Richard could show him the available rooms.

The next day, as he was leaving his co-worker's apartment to meet up with Richard, Ballard noticed a double-edged boot knife with a six-inch blade sitting in a beer stein next to the door. He picked it up and slipped it into the back of his belt. Later, Ballard would insist that he hadn't expected to use it; nor was he bringing it along for self-defense. He simply thought it was "cool looking," Ballard claimed, so he decided to pocket it.

When Ballard met up with Richard later that day, Richard invited him into his own apartment before taking him to see the vacancies, and then offered Ballard a beer. Ballard accepted and took a seat on Richard's sofa. As he started sipping the beer, however, Richard walked across the room and turned the apartment light off.

Richard then took a seat next to Ballard on the sofa and, according to Ballard's later recollections, started rubbing his hands against Ballard's chest and crotch.

"Do you want me to go down on you?" Richard asked, according to Ballard. "I'll go down on you. Relax. Just relax. Take it easy. I'm not going to hurt you."

Ballard told Fabian that he had never had another man approach him in such a way. He panicked, just "freaked out," he told the nurse. He had no idea what to do.

"The next thing I knew, I saw him laying on the sofa with a knife in his throat," he said.

Ballard told Fabain he had blacked out and didn't remember stabbing Richard. The knife—the same one Ballard had stolen from his co-worker's apartment less than an hour earlier—had been jammed into Donald Richard's throat right up to the handle.

"I don't remember pulling the knife," Ballard said. "The next thing I knew, it was just in his throat. I was all covered with blood."

Ballard claimed he was terrified at the sight of Richard's dead body, at the realization of what he had done. In a state of panic, Ballard claimed, he pulled the knife out of Richard's throat, then took Richard's wallet and keys and rushed out of the apartment.

He told Fabian he stole the Mustang and decided to drive straight to Arkansas, figuring his father would somehow know what to do. He really wasn't thinking about escaping, according to Ballard. That's why he didn't bother getting rid of the knife or think twice about using Richard's credit card for fancy dinners.

Ballard later described the feeling as that of a young,

scared child yearning for safety. And, as a child would, he decided that home was the safest place he could go, even if home was twelve hundred miles away. He hadn't slept for three days after the murder.

"I wish now I would've walked instead of driving," Ballard said to Fabian. "Maybe I wouldn't have been caught."

Fabian sat listening to Ballard in total shock. She had no idea what to say, so instinctively she told Ballard not to tell anybody else what he had told her. She knew from experience that talking to people in prison about the details of their crimes was dangerous, because the other inmates would later use the information to try to get their own sentences reduced. Donald Richard's murder had made a big splash in the paper, so she knew there was a strong possibility that this scenario could happen in Ballard's case. She also knew he wouldn't be particularly safe in prison if word got out that he might be associated with the Ku Klux Klan.

"For your own safety and your own protection, keep quiet what you said here," she said. "I'm not going to say anything."

"Fine, I just want to be protected," Ballard replied. "I'm really scared about being in jail. I don't want anyone trying to hurt me."

With that, Fabian asked the officer standing in the nearby hall to escort Ballard off to be housed in the prison. They had been speaking for just under twenty minutes.

"OK, fine, thank you for your time," Ballard said before he was taken away. Fabian went straight to the police that night.

Details that Fabian shared with the police slowly started to become available to the public. The newspapers took particular interest in Ballard's connection, however vague, with the Ku Klux Klan. Prosecutors made clear that Ballard was not a member of the KKK, and that the killing was not sanctioned by the group, but the fact that Donald Richard was gay made speculation about Klan involvement inevitable.

"Mr. Ballard has never been a dues-paying, card-carrying or robe-wearing member," Ralph Hodges, a Imperial Investigator with the Klan, told the *Morning Call*. Hodges said the police were involved in a conspiracy to pin Ballard's crimes on the KKK, and even claimed that an unnamed police officer had secretly filmed officers talking about it.

"They're attempting to make this a gay-bashing hate crime," Hodges told the newspaper. "They're way out in left field right now."

Lehigh County District Attorney Robert Steinberg denied any such conspiracy, of course. Ballard himself insisted that he wasn't homophobic but had never really had any exposure to homosexuality in the past, so he reacted like a scared child when Richard came on to him.

But Ballard didn't think Steinberg had any interest in the truth of the case. It was an election year and, according to Ballard, Steinberg was reveling in the media attention that the Richard murder was affording him. That made it important for Steinberg to get a conviction, Ballard thought, and so the district attorney took great pains to portray him as—in Ballard's own words—"the most vile piece of shit to walk the Earth."

Over the next few weeks, Ballard met with what he called a "revolving door of attorneys." First his father talked about bringing in a lawyer from Arkansas, but they couldn't afford the fifty-thousand-dollar deposit he required. Next his father hired a lawyer from Williamsport, Pennsylvania, but he dropped the case after Ballard's family had already spent three thousand dollars on his services. Ballard finally got a public defender from

Allentown, but had to get a second one after the first quit the case.

Eventually, Ballard was offered a plea bargain: He could plead guilty to third-degree murder, meaning he had not had a specific intent to kill. That would eliminate the possibility of life in prison under a first-degree murder conviction. Prosecutors said they made the offer due in part Ballard's young age, and because Donald Richard's family was willing to accept it.

The prosecutors also knew that given Richard's shady personal history, it was likely that the defense could try to blame the victim. It was a strategy that had worked in the past, and juries could be unpredictable. Besides, it's illegal to provide alcohol to someone underage, and the fact that Richard had done so could also have proved problematic at trial.

Ballard later said he believed the plea deal was offered quickly and haphazardly, and he would later second-guess whether he should have taken it. But at the time, he knew next to nothing about the legal system, and the problems he had retaining an attorney made him wary about the prospect of facing a trial. He accepted the plea deal.

On November 5, 1992, Ballard appeared before Lehigh County Judge Lawrence Brenner. Wearing a prison jumpsuit and shackles on his wrists and ankles, he pleaded guilty to murder in the third degree, along with additional charges of theft by unlawful taking and illegal use of credit cards.

Ballard reappeared before Judge Brenner on December 14 for sentencing. Detective Sergeant Dean Schwartz was present in the courtroom, as were members of Donald Richard's family, who sat in the front row. They wanted to look Ballard in the eyes before he was incarcerated.

After entering the plea, Ballard turned and spoke directly to the family members. He claimed that he had been trying to forgive himself ever since killing Richard, but that he did not expect the family to forgive him, nor would he ask that of them. He only hoped they could "find it in your heart to understand," according to a report in the *Morning Call*.

Ballard was sentenced to a minimum of fifteen years in state prison and a maximum of thirty years: ten to twenty for third-degree murder and another five to ten years for the theft and credit card charges.

CHAPTER 8

By the end of the day of the quadruple slayings, the police had already prepared a request for a warrant to search Denise Merhi's home. Since the crime had occurred on a weekend, only one of Northampton County's fifteen district judges was on call that day, leaving her to handle everything from minor misdemeanors to homicides. The judge that night was Jacqueline Taschner, a former Northampton County assistant district attorney whose courtroom was in Palmer Township, about a thirty-minute drive from the borough of Northampton.

Taschner, who had prosecuted no shortage of grisly crimes during her time as a prosecutor, wasted no time in signing off on a search warrant before the evening was out. It was in the police officer's hands by nine-twenty that night.

Police gathered sixty-three pieces of evidence in a process that would ultimately take two days to complete. Trooper McLean Peeke started the collection process the night of the murder and obtained and documented twenty-seven items. Trooper Louis Gober, another forensic services unit officer out of the Bethlehem barracks, resumed the collection shortly after noon the following day.

Among the items seized were several knives—including two with broken tips—and a small green duffel bag Ballard had been seen carrying on his travels the day of the murders.

The troopers also cataloged a piece of human tissue believed to be part of one of Ballard's fingertips, according to published reports.

The two broken-tipped knives and a third knife were all recovered in the living room, the same place where Steven Zernhelt's body had been discovered, according to reports. Police also obtained several samples of carpet, draperies, and other stained materials, and investigators took a number of greeting cards—including two sympathy cards—and at least three laptop computers from the home, the *Morning Call* reported. Among Ballard's belongings, the police found a parole notice, a knife sheath, two silver rings, and a silver necklace, according to the newspaper.

State police had seized the car Ballard had crashed not long after the accident, but they did not get permission to search it until three days later. On June 29, they cataloged dozens more pieces of evidence recovered from the car, including two more knives.

At least one of the knives recovered was stamped with the brand name CHICAGO CUTLERY. The name jogged Trooper Raymond Judge's memory: Denise had owned an entire block of knives by the same company.

There was another piece of evidence that the state police were looking to connect to the home: Ballard had been found with one of Dennis Marsh's checks in his pockets. The police believed that Ballard likely had found the checkbook in Dennis's room and ripped out the check after killing Dennis. Police later returned to the house to obtain both Denise's knife block and Dennis's checkbook.

Trooper Judge made arrangements to speak with Marilyn Rivera the morning of June 27. It had been just under twenty-four hours since Denise and the others had been killed, and during the course of Judge's investigation, he had learned that Marilyn Rivera was one of Denise's closest friends. He also learned that Marilyn had spoken to Michael Ballard just a few hours before the murders.

Judge met Marilyn at Denise's home in Northampton borough, which was still roped off with yellow police tape. For obvious reasons, they couldn't go inside the house, so they walked around to the patio setup in the backyard, where they would be out of sight from any passing reporters or curious observers.

It was more than ninety degrees that morning, and both felt extremely uncomfortable in the heat. But they both knew that this interview was an important part of helping the authorities understand just what had happened between Denise and Michael Ballard.

Marilyn explained that she had met Denise about six years ago, right around the time she'd first moved to Allentown. All of her family lived in New Jersey, so she knew very few people in the city and had yet to develop any close friends. She had three children named Robert, Julia, and Carlos, who were sixteen, six, and five at the time.

One summer day, she took her children to Dorney Park and Wildwater Kingdom, an amusement park just a few miles outside of Allentown. It was a fun afternoon for the family until Marilyn turned around for just a moment then realized, with horror, that she had completely lost sight of Julia. Panicking, Marilyn started looking everywhere, screaming her daughter's name, but Julia was no-where to be seen.

That was when a stranger came up behind Marilyn and tapped her on the shoulder. Her name was Denise Merhi, and she explained that Julia had wandered onto a ride in the Camp Snoopy attraction along with Annikah, Denise's own daughter.

Marilyn and Denise exchanged numbers and very quickly became good friends. Their kids were about the same ages, and soon they were doing everything together. Carlos and Annikah attended the same preschool, while Annikah and Julia took the same dance lessons at the Sub-urban North YMCA in Catasauqua. Robert and Denise's son, Trystan, played video games for hours on end with each other. They played soccer, attended dances, had sleepovers, and went for visits to places like the beach and the zoo.

Marilyn and Denise themselves were equally insepa-rable.

"We kind of had this connection that nobody could understand," Marilyn said. "I felt like she was closer to me than my sisters. We just understood each other."

Marilyn described Denise as a very friendly, bubbly woman who loved everybody. But she also had a very strong, domineering personality, Marilyn said, and didn't care what others said or thought about her.

Marilyn's own personality differed from Denise's in this way, but that didn't make them any less close. Mari-lyn's sisters found Denise obnoxious, and Marilyn's hus-band hated the woman, but if Marilyn had been asked to make a choice between the two, the truth is she would have chosen Denise.

"She just got me," Marilyn put it succinctly.

But it wasn't always happy times between the two.

Denise was going through a very difficult period when she met Marilyn, having recently separated from her husband, a man who Denise told Marilyn seemed to delight in playing head games with her.

At one point, Denise suspected he had been cheating on her, but he assured her that she was delusional and had imagined the whole thing. Nevertheless, Denise took the kids and left Puerto Rico, where she had lived with her husband, to start anew.

But she was having trouble coping with life away from him, especially as she struggled through long and dramatic mood swings brought on by bipolar disorder. Sometimes Denise would cry to Marilyn for hours on end. Marilyn tried to convince Denise to again start taking her bipolar medication, which she had long since given up on, but Denise refused. Nevertheless, Marilyn was a good listener, and Denise needed someone to talk to.

Marilyn first met Michael Ballard in the summer of 2007. Denise had recently broken off her engagement to a man named Brian Miller specifically so she could date Ballard, although she spoke very little about what he did or how they met.

That summer, Marilyn hosted a birthday party for one of her sons at her Allentown home, and Denise asked if she could bring Ballard as her date. When he arrived, Ballard particularly stood out among the children and their parents: His sleeves were rolled up, revealing tattoos on his arms, and he had a silver stud piercing in his tongue.

Ballard sat quietly at the table during the party and barely spoke a word to anyone. He obviously made the others guests feel very uncomfortable, although once the party was over he helped clean up and politely thanked Marilyn for having him over.

Marilyn wasn't sure what to make of Ballard at first,

but after a few more encounters she began to warm to him. They had hung out together on several occasions before Denise finally revealed the truth about Ballard's past: He had recently finished serving time in prison for murder.

Denise had met Ballard just the previous March, when he was being released on parole after nearly fifteen years in prison. When he was released he had $177 to his name and no possessions but the clothes on his body. He immediately started looking for work and attempted to join an operating engineers' union.

After a few months of temping and other low-paying work, Ballard was offered a job in February at the Monarch Precast concrete plant in Allentown. It was through that job that he met Denise, who was working as a medical assistant at the doctor's office where Ballard went for a physical exam.

Since the doctor performing the exam was a woman, Denise had to be present for the entire physical, and the two kept sneaking glances at each other throughout the appointment. Eventually the doctor left the room for a moment and the two were alone together.

"And your name is?" Ballard asked.

By the time Ballard left that office, he had told Denise practically everything about his life and his past, including the murder he had gone to prison for. Denise was immediately attracted to him; he projected a "bad boy" image—a sense of living on the edge—that she had always been drawn to, Marilyn explained.

Ballard gave Denise his number, and by the time he got back to the halfway house where he was staying, she had already called him. From that day on, they secretly saw each other every day. At the time, Denise was engaged to Brian Miller, a thirty-seven-year-old information technology technician she had met through the dating website Match.com. They had dated exclusively for almost two years before Miller proposed to her on New Year's Eve in 2006. They seemed happy together, and the couple even built an addition onto Denise's home so that Brian and his two boys could stay there more comfortably on the weekends.

Brian, unlike some of Denise's past boyfriends, seemed like a good man; but Marilyn also felt he wasn't the right type for her. Their relationship began to fall apart one spring day when Denise, Brian, his two children, and two people Denise claimed were co-workers got together for dinner at a Red Robin restaurant. One of those co-workers was actually Michael Ballard, and once everybody took their seats around the table, Brian couldn't help noticing that Denise sat next to Ballard, on the complete opposite end of the table from him.

Brian grew more and more suspicious of Denise and Ballard and, according to later court testimony, eventually confronted her about him. At first, she maintained that she didn't know what she wanted, but by April 2007 Brian was moving out of the house and their engagement was finished. She had chosen Michael Ballard.

Marilyn claimed that Denise "sugarcoated" Ballard's crimes. That, or Ballard sugarcoated them himself when he described them to Denise, Marilyn couldn't be sure which. First, Denise claimed that Ballard had killed someone else in self-defense. Later, she admitted, it wasn't in self-defense at all and that he had killed a gay man after he made an advance. Ballard was from the South, Denise had explained. They weren't used to homosexuals and he just didn't know how to respond, so he went a little crazy.

"When she told me what he did, I was like, 'You're going out with him?!'" Marilyn said.

Nevertheless, Marilyn grew to like Ballard. He had a

steady job and a truck and, most important, he treated Denise like a queen.

For Ballard, Denise marked the first real, meaningful relationship in his life, and he loved the idea of having a "doting girlfriend." After fifteen years in prison, Ballard came to love having the constant attention of a woman. It was like a drug to him. A drug he was quickly growing addicted to.

Denise would speak about not only their strong emotional connection, but their physical one as well, according to Marilyn. Whenever Ballard called Denise's cell phone, the ring tone that played was the Kings of Leon rock song "Sex on Fire." Denise even gave Ballard a nickname because of his sexual prowess: Superman.

That small detail made Judge immediately recall the Superman T-shirt that had been recovered at the murder scene, folded neatly on an armchair next to Dennis Marsh's body in the basement.

Marilyn explained that once Ballard was released from the halfway house, he started renting an Allentown house on Hall Street, but he spent almost all of his time and kept most of his things at Denise's house in Northampton. Ballard, Denise, and Marilyn would often have dinner together, play cards, or just hang out at one another's homes. Even Marilyn's husband, who was no fan of Denise, started to become friends with Ballard.

For Marilyn, Ballard's criminal past was always in the back of her mind, but she felt comfortable enough to hug or kiss him as a greeting. Once, Marilyn even felt comfortable enough to let him pick up her kids from a dance class. Ballard seemed to truly love Denise's children. He spoiled them with gifts, helped them with their homework, tucked them into bed at night, and played the dad role at their birthday parties.

"I liked Michael, I'm not going to lie," Marilyn said.

Under the terms of his parole, Ballard had to take regular anger management courses from an organization called Forensic Treatment Services. Ballard hated the FTS counselors and clashed with them from the very beginning. He felt they were out to get him and just looking for an excuse to throw him back in prison.

The counselors, for their part, believed Ballard was anti-social, did not value other people's feelings, and had entitlement issues and no boundaries whatsoever. They particularly disapproved of Ballard's relationship with Denise, especially because she was engaged to another man when they first started seeing each other.

At one point, the FTS staff asked to speak with Denise about Ballard, and she later told him that they had said horrible things about him and tried to turn her away from him. After that, the two started keeping their relationship a secret from FTS. When Ballard eventually moved in with Denise, he kept renting the Hall Street house to serve as his official parole address.

Marilyn insisted she never saw Ballard act violently or aggressively toward Denise, even as their relationship started deteriorating and they began fighting more often. Ballard was already growing used to Denise's mood swings from her bipolar disorder, and in fact he came to actually enjoy them. It was part of Denise's spontaneity that he found so attractive.

But Denise had trust issues due to the way her ex-husband had treated her, Marilyn said, and she took it out on Ballard. One night, while Ballard was hanging out with Marilyn's husband, Denise became convinced that Ballard was cheating on her, sleeping around with "little hood-rats," as she called them. When Ballard returned home that night, Marilyn watched as Denise scratched and punched him in a fit of jealous rage.

After that fight, Marilyn actually encouraged Ballard to leave Denise, believing she was going to drive him to violate his parole if things continued as they were.

"I told him Denise was going to get him thrown back in jail," Marilyn said later. "She would take things out on him because of her first husband. I said to her, 'You're taking it out on this poor man.' Little did I know . . .'"

Ballard and Denise briefly broke up after that fight, but it wasn't long before they were back together. Denise continued to have her jealousy spells and erratic mood swings, but Ballard adored her anyway. That December, Ballard hung icicle Christmas lights outside Denise's house. It was the kind of family tradition that so many people take for granted but that he'd never had growing up, and he loved it.

Also around that time, while Denise and the children were getting their photos taken with Santa Claus at the mall, Ballard snuck away—Denise didn't like letting him out of her sight—and went to Kay Jewelers to buy her a diamond necklace as a gift.

"It felt great," Ballard later said about that period of his life. "The year before, I had walked out of prison with $177 and nothing but sweatpants. Now I was buying my girl diamonds."

Denise and Ballard even had a mock wedding ceremony together. Alone beneath the shade of a tree—a romantic setting that Ballard compared to a similar wedding scene in the film *Braveheart*—they pledged their love to each other and exchanged rings. Although it was not a legally binding ceremony by any means—Forensic Treatment Services certainly would not have allowed one—Denise still called Ballard her husband, and he considered her to be his wife.

"It was, 'Damn the world if they won't let us, because this is how we feel,'" Ballard later said. "Back then, each one of us was just a half of a whole."

But everything about the relationship between Ballard and Denise drastically changed when Ballard was accused of sexually assaulting a minor, Marilyn said.

The Northampton Police Department investigated the allegations and questioned the juvenile girl, who was known to both Denise and Marilyn. Marilyn said they tested the bedsheets where the assault had allegedly taken place. For a time, the trust both Denise and Marilyn felt toward Ballard was shattered, and neither would let him anywhere near their children.

However, according to Northampton Police Chief Ronald Morey, the alleged victim was unable to specifically articulate exactly what had happened to her. The tests on the sheets turned up nothing, according to Marilyn, who began to have her own doubts as to Ballard's guilt.

Ultimately, the police found there wasn't enough evidence to press charges against Ballard, and soon both Denise and Marilyn felt comfortable being around him again.

But by April 2008, Michael Ballard was back in prison on a parole violation. The official reason given was that Ballard had failed to attend Forensic Treatment Services' required anger management classes and was "not amenable to treatment." But according to Ballard, he had only missed two appointments in the past thirteen months.

Ballard, Denise, and Marilyn each vehemently believed the sexual assault allegations were the real reason for his re-imprisonment, as well as the fact that Ballard had continued dating Denise behind the counselors' backs.

It was a very difficult time for Ballard. He felt he had attained everything he wanted—stability, a family, a normal life—only to have it taken away and be back in prison on charges he insisted were false.

In September 2008, just a few months after he was in-

carcerated again, Ballard was discovered in his cell with
a bedsheet tied around his neck. He received medical attention and his life was saved, and Ballard later insisted
he had not been trying to attempt suicide.

As difficult as it was, Ballard and Denise at first remained devoted to each other, despite his return to prison.
The first day Ballard was back in jail, and Denise was left
at home without him, she collapsed to the ground and
cried out so loudly that Trystan heard her from upstairs
and ran down to check on her. The two embraced each
other as Denise cried hysterically. She later told Ballard
that, at that moment, she felt she didn't want to go on living if he wasn't there with her.

Ballard was forbidden to have any contact with Denise, but they snuck around those restrictions every way
they could. Ballard knew that the prison was monitoring
his mail, so he would write letters to Marilyn and other
friends, and they would in turn pass them on to Denise.
Likewise, Ballard would make his allotted phone calls
to Marilyn, who then secretly passed the phone over to
Denise.

Denise and the children would make scrapbooks with
photos of the three of them and send them to Ballard. He
recalled one specific photo Denise sent from a July 4 celebration without him, where the three of them were smiling and holding hands. On the back of that photo, Denise
wrote that "one hand was missing" from the photo.

"You're still my Superman, my husband," Denise wrote
to him.

Nevertheless, as time passed, Ballard got the sense
that the two were starting to drift apart. He once confided
these fears to Marilyn in a letter to her, where he wrote that
he feared the relationship was going to fall apart.

His fears were not without merit. Denise started seeing
other people and, eventually, she again became engaged

to Brian Miller, the man she had left Ballard for in the first place. She had not been in touch with Brian after their split until December 2009, when he visited the Dominican Republic on a business trip. Knowing Denise spoke Spanish from her time living in Puerto Rico, he sent her a text message with a half joke that she should accompany him as his translator. In later court testimony, he admitted to still harboring some romantic feelings for her.

Denise did not go on the trip with Brian, but they met up two days after he returned. They rekindled their relationship, he moved back into her house, and they made plans to marry in August 2010.

Nevertheless, Denise continued writing letters to Ballard for weeks as if nothing had changed, never mentioning Brian and insisting she still only loved Ballard.

Then, in December 2009, after about a year and a half in prison, Ballard was granted parole once again, with a release date scheduled for the subsequent April. With Ballard's release now fast approaching, Denise realized she could no longer keep her engagement to Brian a secret. Over Marilyn's objections, she wrote a letter to Ballard telling him all about it.

The letter came as a complete shock to Ballard, who was livid with feelings of betrayal. In her letter, Ballard felt like she was trying to play off this engagement as if it were something that had just sprung up within the last week, like it surprised her as much as it did him, but he could tell right away that was not the case.

Incarcerated or not, he still considered Denise his wife, considered her house to be his home. Up to this point, serving this latest stretch of prison time hadn't felt difficult to Ballard because he felt his family was waiting for him when he got out. He would spend his time imagining what he'd be doing if he were back home with Denise:

mowing the lawn, taking Trystan out on the four-wheeler, taking the family to the beach.

Every memory I have that is not prison is that family, Ballard thought at the time. *And now? Now I'm just empty.*

Ballard and Denise had previously made arrangements for Denise to pick him up from prison the day of his release. She was going to drive a friend's car, since he was still not supposed to be seeing Denise at all. But Ballard notified the prison that the car no longer had permission to pick him up. He ended all contact with Denise, refusing to respond to her letters or make any more calls to her.

Ballard received letters from his father and a cousin telling him that ending the relationship with Denise was the right thing to do. They both insisted that Ballard was asking for nothing but trouble if he stayed with that woman. Denise continued writing to Ballard, desperately trying to continue the communication. When Ballard still refused, she became angry, trying to shame him into writing her back, but he did not relent.

"If this is how you feel, then your love was just a farce to begin with," she wrote in one letter.

Denise learned that now, with nobody to pick him up, Ballard would be dropped off at an Allentown bus stop the day of his release. She knew Ballard didn't want her there, but she was concerned about him getting off the bus alone and considered going anyway. Marilyn encouraged her to do it, believing that Denise would hate herself if she didn't, and hoping that it would give her closure and allow her to move on from Ballard once and for all.

When the day arrived, Marilyn and Denise's friend Nicole drove Denise to the bus stop. As the bus approached, Denise stepped outside while her friends waited inside the van. Ballard descended from the bus stairs, and as soon as he saw Denise he turned and walked away from her. It was clear from the look on his face, Marilyn said, that he didn't want anything to do with Denise.

Marilyn waited and watched as Denise spoke to a silent and brooding Ballard for a full forty-five minutes before he finally agreed to get in the van so they could take him to the Allentown Community Corrections Center, the halfway house where he would be staying.

Within a day of Ballard's release, Denise had once again broken off her engagement with Brian to return to Ballard.

"I don't think I ever really decided to let her go," Ballard later said.

He was still forbidden from seeing Denise by Forensic Treatment Services, but they continued their relationship in secret. Few knew that they were back together, according to Marilyn, not even Denise's own children.

Ballard wanted to adopt Denise's kids, move with her to Arkansas, have a baby of their own, and live as a family, and Marilyn knew his feelings were sincere. Denise even shared fleeting thoughts with Marilyn of leaving her children behind and running off with Ballard, though Marilyn knew it was something Denise would never really do.

It was all just part of Denise's obsessive personality, Marilyn claimed, which stemmed from her bipolar disorder. When Denise did something, she threw her whole self into it, and she truly believed Ballard was the one true love of her life.

But once again, the relationship would not last. Marilyn wasn't sure exactly what went wrong this time, but she suspected it was a combination of things.

It was difficult for Ballard and Denise to hide their relationship from both their loved ones and the law. Ballard could only sign out of the halfway house for two hours a day, so they had a very limited amount of time together before having to separate again, and they both hated that arrangement.

There were also the sexual assault allegations, which still made Denise a bit uncomfortable. Denise insisted she believed Ballard was innocent, but some of her friends and family members did not, and the accusation loomed like a cloud during all the time they spent together.

And for his part, Ballard never truly got over his jealousy over Denise getting engaged while he was back in prison. His trust in Denise had been permanently shaken, and they were fighting more often. He found himself becoming more suspicious about what she was doing all the time, and the more he questioned her, the more defensive she became.

"Everything I was fighting for, everything I had loved and was falling in love with, it was all a façade," Ballard later said. "It was all bullshit. It was gone."

All these factors kept building up until Denise could no longer take it. She not only left Ballard, Marilyn said, but entered into a phase where she had multiple flings with various men, none of which was particularly meaningful or long lasting.

"She kind of went crazy and she had sex with a lot of people," Marilyn said. "It was a little too much for me. She had this thing where she went very promiscuous and I was like, 'Okay then . . .'"

Ballard later claimed that Denise confessed multiple infidelities to him. He was convinced that Denise was going out to clubs or having sex with strangers every night. Denise barely even drank when they'd first started dating. Now, Ballard believed, she was out drinking and smoking pot on an almost-nightly basis.

They fought all the time now about Denise's alleged cheating. During one of those fights, Ballard spit in Denise's face and walked away from her.

That brought them to June 25, 2010—the day before the murders. As Marilyn explained to Trooper Judge, Ballard had called Marilyn's cell phone that day to talk about Denise. He had considered Marilyn a friend and often confided in her, so the phone call itself didn't strike her as unusual.

Marilyn was home when she received a call from the Allentown Community Corrections Center. She didn't think she was up to speaking to Ballard at that moment, so she ignored the call. But then he called a second time. And a third. By then, Marilyn figured it might be important, so she answered.

Ballard tried to engage Marilyn in small talk at first, asking how she was doing and how the kids were. But it was painfully obvious that he had called to talk about Denise, and he quickly dropped the charade.

She had stopped taking his calls, Ballard explained. He had called her repeatedly but she wouldn't answer. Marilyn and Denise were actually fighting at the time so they weren't speaking much, but Marilyn knew that Denise had taken Annikah down to the New Jersey shore to celebrate her daughter's birthday.

"Why isn't she answering the phone?" Ballard asked.

"Michael, I don't know," Marilyn said "I don't know why she's not answering the phone."

Ballard said he felt betrayed, as if Denise had broken the trust he thought they shared together. He had stopped wearing the ring she gave him.

Marilyn was startled by Ballard's tone. He was very quiet, very solemn, and obviously very distraught. To Marilyn, he sounded nothing like the Michael Ballard she knew.

Ballard started referring to pictures of Denise he'd seen on her Facebook profile, which he'd viewed on the computer at the halfway house, Marilyn said. He was particularly angry about comments other men had made about Denise on those photos. The more he talked about it, the angrier his voice sounded.

"How could she do this to me? I thought we were meant to be together forever," Ballard said. "She broke my heart. I don't know how I can get over this and I can't live without her."

"You need to walk away," Marilyn said. "This is it. You need to go. She's not for you. You need to find somebody else for you."

Ballard mentioned a photo he had seen of Denise at a Philadelphia Phillies game from earlier in June, about three weeks before. Marilyn knew the one he was talking about. Denise had gone to the game with Peter Hoff, a forty-five-year-old man from Pennsburg, Pennsylvania, whom she had previously met on the dating website PlentyOfFish.com. While they had dated in the past, the thirty-mile distance made their relationship difficult so they called it off. Still, they got together for the occasional date now and then.

Marilyn thought Peter was a very nice man who, she observed, looked exactly like Ballard.

"I see she had a good time at the Phillies game with her mom," Ballard said.

"She didn't go with her mom," Marilyn replied instinctively.

She immediately realized her mistake. Ballard demanded to know who Denise had gone to the game with, listing off the names of men that he knew she had known. Marilyn felt terrible, as if she had given away a secret.

But she later realized that Ballard knew exactly what he had been doing. He had tricked her. Ballard knew

Denise had gone to the game with a man, and he was fishing for more information.

Going through his list of names, Ballard finally mentioned Peter Hoff. Marilyn started to say something, then stopped herself, but again it was too late.

"That's him, right?" Ballard asked.

With a sigh, Marilyn decided to be honest.

"Yes, Michael, that's right," she said. "But you need to talk about this with Denise."

"Oh my God," Ballard said, sounding even more distressed than before.

"I'm sorry," Marilyn said. "I didn't know that you didn't know."

"I don't know what I'm going to do, Mar. I don't know what I'm going to do."

She tried to insist that this was something he had to talk over with Denise, not her, but Ballard just kept repeating himself.

"I don't know what to do. I don't know what to do. I don't know what to do."

Then, abruptly, Ballard asked if he and Marilyn could get together the next morning for coffee. They had done that kind of thing before, so she normally wouldn't think anything of it, but this time it felt different and she was hesitant.

"Please, Mar," he said.

"Okay, Michael," she said, deciding that Ballard just needed to vent a little bit more. "I'm not doing anything tomorrow. I can meet you for coffee."

They made plans for Marilyn to pick Ballard up at the halfway house around eleven o'clock the next morning. But when the next day came, Marilyn still didn't feel very comfortable about the meeting, and one of her friends urged her not to go. He insisted she would only get depressed and that they should do something else instead.

Marilyn decided her friend was right and she would not go. Ballard called Marilyn five times that day, but she missed most of the calls because her daughter had her phone. He finally did reach her, briefly, but Marilyn told him she would not be able to meet for coffee after all.

"Would you come see me after I'm done with what I'm doing?" he asked. Marilyn didn't know exactly what Ballard meant by that, but Ballard was very persistent, and she finally said that she would.

She drove down to Atlantic City with a friend that day and spent the entire day there, without giving Ballard and his phone calls another thought. She didn't get home until very late that night, and it was only then that she learned what Ballard had done.

Looking back on their conversation, Marilyn now believed that the moment Ballard learned Denise had been at the Phillies game with another man was the straw that broke the camel's back.

That was the moment, she believed, that he decided he was going to kill Denise.

That wasn't the only realization Marilyn had reached, she told Trooper Judge. Looking back on Ballard's insistence that she meet him for coffee that morning, Marilyn now felt that Ballard had planned to use Marilyn to get to Denise's house and then get Denise.

"I do believe in my heart that he would have used me to get to Denise's house, and he would've just killed us both," she said.

Oh my God, she thought. *I could not be here for my children. I could've just said, "Oh, I'll meet him for coffee." I could be dead right now.*

It was obvious to Judge that Marilyn was feeling a great deal of guilt over what happened.

"Marilyn, if you had gone that day, you wouldn't be

here," he said. "Don't blame yourself for not going. It's a good thing."

"Maybe things could've been different," Marilyn said tearfully. "Maybe I could've talked him out of it. Maybe . . ."

"It's not going to help you to keep going through it in your mind," Judge said. "It's not your fault. You did the best that you could."

Judge stressed to her that Ballard had bought the knife and gone to Denise's house that day with a purpose. He had planned the whole thing out.

"He was going to do it no matter what," he said. "A person like this, you can't talk sense into him."

CHAPTER 9

Some time after Trooper Judge's interview with Marilyn ended, the state police were finally issued an arrest warrant for Michael Eric Ballard on four counts of homicide and four counts of murder in the first degree. By also charging him with the general term of homicide, a future jury could convict Ballard of a lesser murder charge if they did not agree with first degree. At 2:20 p.m. June 27, Judge and one of his supervisors, Corporal Paul Romanic, went to St. Luke's Hospital to serve Ballard with the warrant.

They also brought along two search warrants, one for the bandages and stretcher sheets used in Ballard's transport to the hospital, and the other allowing them to take photographs of Ballard himself.

The two troopers arrived at Ballard's hospital room and found him lying awake, with his wrists handcuffed to the bed. Trooper Judge informed him that he was under arrest, and the news did not appear to come as any great shock to Ballard. But he did express some confusion when Romanic started taking photographs of his injuries.

"Why are you taking pictures?" he asked. "I ain't contesting this."

That was good news to the troopers. Ballard's blunt admissions to Dr. Costello the night before had certainly indicated that he wasn't trying to hide the fact that he had killed the four victims, but this was the first indication he was going to cooperate with the police.

"We're just being thorough," Judge said in response.

Ballard gave the trooper an icy stare and then, in what seemed like an impatient manner, launched into a succession of quick, brief statements.

"Just give me the papers," he said. "I'll sign it. I'll plead guilty. I shouldn't have lived through it. Make the report. Blame the parole board. What do you want to know?"

"Why all this happened," Judge responded. The trooper didn't really need to discern a motive to get a conviction, but any information along those lines could prove invaluable to an inquisitive jury.

"Any explanation as to why is not worth it at this point," Ballard said. "It's all led up to this. Ask the parole board. Ask Dr. Valliere. Ask Mondello. Ask Denise."

The trooper did not recognize the first two names, but based on Ballard's constant repeating of the phrase "Ask the parole board," they assumed Dr. Valliere and Mondello were people Ballard had dealt with during his first sentence in prison, or during his parole.

"What do you want?" Ballard asked again, pointedly.

"I want a confession," Judge responded.

"I already said I'd plead guilty, what's the point? They're dead and I'm here bleeding," Ballard said. His eyes drifted away from the troopers and up to the muted television mounted on the wall, which was tuned to the Philadelphia Phillies baseball game.

"I'd like to speak to you to find out why," Judge said. "Why it all had to happen like this."

Because Ballard had invoked his right to counsel the night before—and the police could not officially question him without an attorney present—Judge explained that, if Ballard was willing, they could get an attorney for him that day so they could discuss what happened.

But by now, Ballard had little regard for the troopers and was engrossed by the Phillies game, or at least pretending to be.

"Let him watch the game," he said, referring to whatever attorney Judge might get for him.

Judge suggested they could instead get an attorney for Ballard the next morning and set up an interview then. But the trooper could see that Ballard seemed uninterested in speaking to the police at all, and Judge recalled their exchanges the previous day when Ballard refused to answer his questions.

"I can have a lawyer here first thing tomorrow morning," Judge said. "But I don't want to waste everyone's time by getting an attorney down here for you to just tell me to stick it."

Ballard looked Judge in the eyes. He was through with talking to the trooper, and decided to throw Judge's own words back at him.

"Stick it," Ballard said to the trooper. "I want to watch this game."

Ballard was still not fit to be released from the hospital, so a judge was brought in to St. Luke's to arraign him at bedside. Wayne Maura, one of the fourteen magisterial district judges representing the various regions of Lehigh County, arraigned him on four counts each of criminal homicide and murder in the first degree.

District Attorney John Morganelli announced that a press conference would be held later in the afternoon, where information about the homicides and the arrest would be released. Details about the crime had been fairly scant so far in the press accounts. Since the murders had taken place on a Saturday, representatives from the police and district attorney's office were less available to speak to reporters, and the newspapers had to contend with earlier deadlines and a smaller-than-usual cadre of journalists working.

The stories that ran Sunday morning in the *Express-Times* and *Morning Call* reported that a suspect had been taken into custody, but did not identify him by name. The stories also had no official police confirmation for the names of the four victims, although they indicated that the home was owned by Denise Merhi and that her father and grandfather lived there with her. And Steve Zernhelt's brother David, who lived in nearby Allentown, confirmed to both papers that his brother was one of the victims.

"He was trying to do everything he could to help," David Zernhelt had told the *Express-Times*. "I always believed in my brother . . . I know he died a hero."

But the press had plenty of unanswered questions about the murders, the motive, the suspect, and much more. Morganelli, who had a reputation for being press-friendly, arranged for a press conference at the Pennsylvania State Police barracks in Bethlehem. Northampton County Coroner Zachary Lysek and State Police Lieutenant Brian Tobin were present along with the district attorney.

A large number of print reporters, photographers, and television camera crews crammed into the modestly sized meeting room, where the three law enforcement officials sat at the head of the table. Lysek began the press conference by revealing the names of the four victims and their causes of death.

"All four victims died from multiple stab wounds," he

said. "The manner of death on these four cases is classi-
fied as homicide."

Morganelli identified the suspect as Michael Eric Ballard, a name that would become infamous in the Lehigh
Valley region from that moment forward. Ballard was in
custody and was facing four counts of criminal homicide
and four counts of first-degree murder, the district attorney explained. Based on what he'd witnessed personally at
the crime scene and the subsequent investigation by police, Morganelli said it was absolutely clear he was dealing
with four cases of premeditated, first-degree murder.

"It's also a capital case," he went on to announce. "The
fact that he has engaged in multiple homicides is an aggravating factor under the Pennsylvania death penalty
act. We will seek the death penalty in this case."

The authorities provided a partial picture of Ballard's
connection to his victims. They revealed there was "some
type of relationship" between Ballard and Denise, but
gave few details beyond that. There were also numerous
questions the reporters asked that the authorities did not
answer. Who had called 911 to report the killings? How
had Ballard gotten into the house? What was his condition at the hospital? What was his possible motive?

Morganelli declined to answer most of the questions,
but he did reveal that Ballard had previously been convicted for the murder of Donald Richard. Both the
Express-Times and the *Morning Call* had archived stories
about the Richard murder dating back to 1991, and both
papers made note that after Ballard's fifteen-year term in
state prison, he had been incarcerated again for a two-
year stint from 2008 up until April 2010 for a parole violation.

Tony Nauroth, the reporter with the *Express-Times,*
made particular note in the lead of his story that Ballard

had been released just barely two months before the four murders in Northampton borough.

Outside of the press conference, the Associated Press spoke with Denise's cousin Desiray Dolly, as well as her friend Nicole Young. Both confirmed that Denise and Ballard had previously dated. Desiray said she had met Ballard at a birthday party two years earlier, and that he made her feel unnerved.

"He just gave you that kind of feeling, that uneasy feeling," Desiray told the AP. "He was offering us, 'If you ever need [alcohol], just let me know.' Constantly touching, putting hands on shoulders."

Both Desiray and Nicole told the Associated Press that they thought Ballard and Denise had dated for only a brief time and that he had left her alone afterward.

"I just don't get it," Desiray told the media outlet. "He didn't give any kind of warning that I know of."

The *Morning Call,* however, interviewed a neighbor of Denise's who reported that there were prior incidents between Ballard and Denise's family, and that she had recently contacted Northampton police. The neighbor, Rebecca Germani, also knew that Ballard had served time in prison for a previous murder.

"I don't know how he got out," she told the newspaper. "He only did fifteen years prior for slashing somebody's throat."

Multiple reporters camped themselves outside the Northampton double home where the four victims had been slain, and they would remain there for the next several days. "Reporters were gawking at our house for days," as Jaime Zernhelt later put it. Janet and her children couldn't bear to speak to them and politely asked that the press respect the family's privacy. The reporters wanted to know what past relationship, if any, Steve Zernhelt and his family had with Michael Ballard, but Janet couldn't even hear the word "Ballard" without feeling sick, much less talk about him.

The truth was that the Zernhelts had barely known Michael Ballard at all. In fact, Janet wasn't sure Steve had ever even met him prior to that horrible day. She knew him only as one of Denise's boyfriends, and assumed they had broken up long ago because she hadn't seen him in a while.

Janet and Ballard would politely say hello when they encountered each other, but they had only spoken at length once, when Janet was trimming the shrubs outside her house one day. Janet honestly couldn't recall what they even talked about, but she remembered that he gave off a vibe that made her feel unsettled. In fact, Janet recalled that she had actually warned her daughter Jaime to avoid talking with him or being around him whenever she visited home from college.

"Steer clear of him," Janet had previously warned. "That guy gives me the creeps. I just have a feeling about him."

"This guy's a rabid dog and he needs to be put down, and I'm going to put him down with a death sentence," John Morganelli had said at the press conference.

The Associated Press picked up the quote, and it ran in several newspaper stories across the country about the grisly quadruple homicide in Pennsylvania. Morganelli's provocative statement spoke not only to his strong feelings about the death penalty, but also to the shock the community was feeling about the heinousness of the crime and the desire for justice to be served.

Despite the passion and confidence of Morganelli's statement, though, the effectiveness of capital punishment in the state of Pennsylvania was spotty at best. Since 1976, when the state's current capital punishment law was enacted, hundreds of inmates had been sentenced to death, and only three had been executed.

The first was Keith Zettlemoyer, who in 1980 kidnapped and killed a friend who was going to testify against him in a robbery trial. Then there was Leon Moser, a former seminary student who killed his ex-wife and their two daughters after Palm Sunday services at their church in 1985. The most recent was Gary Heidnik, who kidnapped half a dozen women, imprisoned them in his Philadelphia basement, then raped and tortured them to death. Reportedly one of the inspirations behind the "Buffalo Bill" serial killer character in *The Silence of the Lambs,* Heidnik was executed in 1999.

However, in all three of those cases, the inmates had waived all appeal rights and actually asked that their executions be carried out. All others sentenced to death either received a lesser sentence on appeal, died of natural causes in prison, extended their legal battles indefinitely, or were eventually exonerated. In more than thirty-five years, no inmate in Pennsylvania had been executed against his or her will, and of the 191 on death row as of October 2013, few if any would see their sentences carried through.

Morganelli had always been a vocal proponent of reform when it came to the state's death penalty process. In 1993, just two years into his tenure as Northampton County's district attorney, Morganelli filed an unprecedented lawsuit against then-Governor Bob Casey Sr. seeking to compel the governor to sign two death warrants for men who had been convicted in capital murder cases in the Lehigh Valley.

One was Martin Appel, a twenty-eight-year-old man who had shot and killed three bank employees while robbing an East Allen Township bank in 1986. The other was Josoph Henry, who in 1987 murdered a nineteen-year-old

Lehigh University freshman in her Bethlehem dorm room. Henry broke into the dorm seeking money for his drug habit; when the victim woke up in the middle of the robbery, he raped her and then strangled her with a Slinky.

Morganelli was successful in his litigation, but Casey appealed it and the matter remained in the courts for a lengthy period of time. Eventually, Casey was succeeded by Republican governor Tom Ridge, who signed the Appel and Henry warrants. Nevertheless, both cases remained in legal limbo for several more years until the death penalty decisions were ultimately thrown out. They both eventually received new sentences of life imprisonment.

Appel had actually requested the death penalty after he was arrested, but years later, following his sentencing, he changed his mind and fought the punishment. Morganelli wrote a book about the case called *The D-Day Bank Massacre,* and in it he raised a question with interesting ramifications about Pennsylvania's capital punishment law: Did Appel request death because he knew, by exploiting the system, that it was the best way he could avoid it?

Both the Appel and Henry convictions came before Morganelli was elected district attorney in 1991. Since that time, he had never secured a death penalty sentence for a defendant himself, although he came close on several occasions.

The closest he had come was with Christopher Bissey, a twenty-five-year-old drug dealer who shot two teenage girls to death near Lehigh University in 1995 because one of them owed him four hundred dollars for a cocaine purchase. It took only two hours for a jury to convict Bissey of first-degree murder, but one of the twelve jurors could not embrace a death penalty verdict, so Bissey received life imprisonment instead.

Since then, Bissey had become a singer with a prison rock band called Dark Mischief, whose concert was filmed and aired on VH1 as part of the cable network's series *Music Behind Bars*. It was a source of outrage across the country from victims' advocates and conservative commentators who felt that men like Bissey should have been put to death, not given national exposure.

Morganelli and the prosecutors working under him had made more recent efforts at death penalty convictions, but they were equally unsuccessful. In 2007, Ali Davis and three other gunmen broke into a house in Easton and shot to death a twenty-one-year-old man and two young women. Prosecutors said they were gang-related killings committed in retaliation for other gang murders in New Jersey, although none of the victims was directly involved in that crime.

Davis, who was twenty-one at the time, and who had already shot another man to death on the streets of Easton in an unrelated 2007 crime, was the first of the four defendants to face trial in 2010. The death penalty was sought for all of them. Davis was found guilty after three hours of jury deliberation, but when it came to the sentencing phase, they deadlocked on whether to impose the death penalty, resulting in a verdict of three consecutive life sentences. The other three defendants eventually took pleas of life imprisonment as well.

Then came Eugenio Torres, twenty-one, who tortured his girlfriend's three-year-old son Elijah Strickland to death while he was supposed to be babysitting him at an apartment in Wilson Borough, right next to Easton. The boy was badly beaten and burned with scalding hot water. Prosecutors had said he had at least ninety-three bruises all over his body as well as a fractured skull, a lacerated liver, and third-degree burns. Torres said the whole thing was an accident, and that the burns and injuries occurred when he slipped and dropped the boy while they were taking a bath.

Torres was convicted of first-degree murder in 2010. Every member of the jury that convicted him was a parent, and many had trouble sleeping during and after the trial because the testimony was so disturbing to them, the *Express-Times* later reported. However, when it came time to sentence Torres, they deadlocked once again on the death penalty. Two of the twelve jurors could not bring themselves to impose it, so Torres received life as well.

After that verdict, the *Express-Times* ran a story about the difficulty prosecutors faced in securing capital punishment verdicts in Northampton County, leading off with the question on the minds of many following the Torres trial: "If a man convicted of killing a three-year-old boy can't get the death penalty, who will?"

In part due to the difficulties in securing a capital punishment ruling, Morganelli would often use the death penalty as a plea bargaining tool, offering to take it off the table for murderers if they accepted life imprisonment without the possibility of parole and agreed to waive their appellate rights, thus ensuring that no lengthy appeals process would drag through the court system for several subsequent years.

Morganelli had previously offered deals like that to several murderers. There was Douglas Crist, the twenty-two-year-old Allentown man who admitted he beat a Bethlehem woman to death with a hammer in 2001, then set fire to her home. And Russell Buskirk, who shot his friend in the head execution-style and robbed him during a botched drug deal. And Robert White, who was arrested in 2008 for the cold-case murder of a twenty-one-year-old woman in her Easton apartment in 1978.

As a rule, Morganelli almost never pursued the death penalty when a murder suspect was willing to accept such a plea deal.

Any DA that would try it would be crazy to do that, really, because you're risking a potential not guilty or something else when you're getting a guaranteed result here and the appeal process ends, Morganelli believed.

But Morganelli broke his own rule with Michael Ballard. The brutality of the crime, the number of the victims, the fact that Ballard had killed once before: All of those factors meant Morganelli couldn't bring himself to consider any other sentence but the death penalty.

Nevertheless, that spotty track record in both Northampton County and Pennsylvania couldn't help but make the district attorney nervous about his chances.

"I think there is a chance if this guy gets life I may well say to my staff, 'You know what, until I'm done, we're not going to be pursuing these cases anymore because I don't see the point of it,' " Morganelli said. "If we have jurors who can't give this guy the death sentence, who are they going to give one to?"

Less than forty-eight hours had passed since her daughter's killing, but Geraldine Dorwart had business to attend to first thing the morning of Monday, June 28. She had to ensure that Trystan and Annikah would stay in her care so she could help her grandchildren through this tragic period of their lives.

Dorwart filed a handwritten petition for emergency custody that morning. Northampton County Judge Paula Roscioli said it was very rare to receive a handwritten petition. Since it was an emergency petition, the process was expedited and a hearing was held that same day, during which Roscioli announced that Trystan and Annikah's father, Jean-Michael Merhi, had also planned to seek custody.

Geraldine's attorney, Kerry Freidl, argued that Jean-Michael had only seen his children once a year for the past six or seven years, which constituted an absence of any meaningful contact. Geraldine also testified to Jean-Michael's infrequent visits with his children, as opposed to her own regular contact with them, including a period of four years that they had lived with her. Roscioli also noted that a bench warrant had been issued against Jean-Michael due to non-payment of child support, but that it might be vacated in light of the circumstances.

The division had attempted to get in touch with Jean-Michael, but efforts to serve him with paperwork at his home in Puerto Rico were unsuccessful, according to Valerie Camerini, an employee with the Northampton County Children, Youth and Families Division. She testified that Geraldine was the one "in the best position to provide care."

Judge Roscioli agreed. She noted that Jean-Michael chose not to be a part of his children's life before. If and when he requested a custody hearing, Roscioli said she would grant one, but in the meantime a decision had to be made that very day about Trystan and Annikah's care.

Geraldine said she didn't object to Jean-Michael seeing the children.

"You have an order that precludes him from taking them," the judge told her. "Now you don't have to be afraid of him coming and wanting to pay his respects."

Jean-Michael Merhi did indeed request a custody hearing, and just three days later they were all back in court.

He told Judge Roscioli he'd found out about Denise's death on Sunday and immediately bought a plane ticket

Monday to fly from Guadeloupe, the French Caribbean island where his family had lived for fifty years, to come to the Lehigh Valley, where he was born. Jean-Michael claimed he arrived Tuesday and was denied the opportunity to see his children, and he spent all day Wednesday working on his effort to seek their custody.

The hearing was the day of Denise, Dennis, and Alvin's funeral, so Geraldine wasn't in court. Her attorney told Roscioli that Geraldine didn't want Jean-Michael approaching his children at the funeral. The judge told Jean-Michael he could go if he paid his respects quietly.

Jean-Michael explained he had not kept up on his child support payments because he had been working for a company that went bankrupt. He had since worked odd jobs and made a child support payment of two thousand dollars earlier that year.

"When he had enough money, he sent enough money," said Ronald Clever, Jean-Michael's attorney.

Jean-Michael said he had recently moved from Puerto Rico back to his family's home in Guadeloupe. He had started working in a family-related business but had yet to be paid.

The judge told him if he paid four thousand dollars of the twelve thousand he owed in child support, she would vacate the bench warrant out on him. Jean-Michael asked if the amount could be one thousand, but Roscioli flatly rejected the request. She pointed out he could afford the plane fare to fly from Guadeloupe to the Lehigh Valley, so he should be able to come up with this amount of money.

Ultimately, both Trystan and Annikah remained in their grandmother's care. Their father filed another custody petition on August 13, arguing that Geraldine had no standing in the matter as a grandparent considering that the children's biological father was still alive.

Jean-Michael also argued that Geraldine's emergency

custody order had been awarded under false pretenses. Geraldine's original petition for custody said that she didn't know the whereabouts of Jean-Michael and that Trystan and Annikah were orphans. Jean-Michael's petition stated that he and Geraldine had spoken on the telephone the day before her petition was filed and that he told her he was at his family's home in Guadeloupe, a home Geraldine herself had visited.

Jean-Michael said he was permitted to see his children four times over his ten-day visit to the Lehigh Valley in July, but he had since been deprived of contact with them. He had been given their cell phone numbers but most or all of his calls to them had gone unanswered. He also pointed out that Denise, Trystan, and Annikah had lived with him previously in both Guadeloupe and Puerto Rico.

The matter would not be formally resolved for more than a month. On September 30, Roscioli filed the final order in the case of *Geraldine Dorwart vs. Jean-Michael Merhi,* which found that Geraldine did have standing as the children's grandmother. Trystan and Annikah were to stay in her custody.

Local forensic pathologist Dr. Samuel Land was tasked with performing autopsies on all four of Ballard's victims. Given multiple victims and their considerable number of stab wounds, it would prove to be a two-day process.

Land started off at eight o'clock the morning of June 28 with Steven Zernhelt. His most obvious injuries were on his neck and chest, where he had been stabbed multiple times, causing extensive damage. He also was cut several times on his face and head, including one long gash that stretched from his left cheek, down his jaw and neck, and into his chest.

Steve's arms and hands also bore cuts, which Land believed were mainly defensive wounds as he attempted to fend off the vicious knife strokes. The tip of his left thumb had been sheared off entirely. He probably raised that hand in an effort to ward off a blow, Land surmised.

The knife slashes had sliced three of his arteries and punctured his right lung. In all, Land observed more than twenty stab wounds.

Denise was up next, and her autopsy would be even more involved and even more horrid. If the police were correct, Denise was the object of Ballard's rage in this murder, and the severity of her injuries seemed to reflect that.

Land would determine that Denise had been stabbed forty-three times—more than twice as much as any of the other victims. In fact, it was almost the same number of stab wounds as was found on all of the other victims combined.

Denise had been stabbed on just about every part of her upper body: the top of her head, the back of her head, her left cheek, her left front chin, her neck, both sides of her upper back, her right shoulder. There were between four and five stab wounds in her chest cavity, several of which pierced her lungs. Her many stab wounds severed several arteries and veins, Land determined.

Her skull had been fractured due to the many knife cuts into the bone there. Her lungs, esophagus, and stomach were all filled with blood.

"She was basically breathing in blood while she was dying," Land would later testify. "[She] was alive when all of these wounds were inflicted."

The next day, Land conducted the autopsies of Alvin Marsh Jr. and his son Dennis.

The eighty-seven-year-old Alvin had been stabbed eight times, primarily on and around his neck and chest. Like his granddaughter, he, too, had breathed in a lot of blood, Land determined. Like Denise, his voice box had been severely damaged.

Alvin also had multiple wounds to both hands consistent with defensive wounds, Land found. On his right hand, the tip of his left finger had been sliced off. His left hand was wounded in a way indicating that Alvin had tried to grab the knife with it to keep it from striking the rest of his body.

Dennis Marsh had almost twice as many stab wounds as his father—Land would note fifteen in his report.

Dennis suffered stab wounds to his back, chest, neck, and collarbone. As with his father and daughter, his voice box had been slashed and there was blood in his lungs, indicating that he, too, was alive during most of his injuries and had begun breathing in blood. Dennis had actually been stabbed twice through the bone: in one of his ribs and in one of the bones shielding his spinal cord.

After adding up the number of stab wounds—a total of eighty-eight, Land would determine—he was finished with two days of tiresome and gruesome work.

"I would think there was a lot of pain involved with these injuries," he would later conclude. "Any time there's a defect of the skin, muscle, it causes great pain. We all have cut ourselves . . . even paper cuts are very painful. So this would have been a very painful process."

CHAPTER 10

Investigators, reporters, and members of the general public alike quickly began asking questions about Michael Ballard's past. What kind of upbringing, many wondered, would lead a man to commit such a horrific crime?

Ballard had only been living in the Allentown area for a short time before he killed Donald Richard in 1991. His formative years were spent in rural Arkansas. He was born on August 14, 1973, the first and only biological child of Wilhart "Mickey" Ballard and Wauneita "Nita" Mae Ballard, although Nita had a ten-year-old daughter from a relationship before Ballard was born. Ballard's father was an accountant and bookkeeper for the city of Fayetteville, while Nita was a licensed practical nurse who worked at various hospitals and nursing homes during Ballard's upbringing.

Mickey's family owned a good deal of farmland near West Fork, Arkansas, which is outside Fayetteville. Although Fayetteville is the state's third-largest city and home to the University of Arkansas, the city of West Fork—located about ten miles to the south—was a completely different world. It had a population of about one thousand residents when Ballard was born in 1973 and hasn't grown much since—the city had an estimated 2,317 residents in 2010.

West Fork has always been small, with most of its residents being descendants of the original settlers. Most of the residents worked in the Fayetteville area, as West Fork itself had very little industry. The school district in 2005 served 1,158 students spread over a 131-square-mile area. The region's significant backcountry lands included the area where Ballard grew up—about eight miles outside West Fork off Route 170. Even today, the area remains very rural.

When Ballard was growing up, everybody referred to him by his middle name, Eric. His paternal grandmother, Hilma Ballard, lived just down the road from his father's house, also on farmland owned by the Ballard family. Years ago, the family had raised crops, but by 1973 the land had been split up and the family no longer performed any commercial farming other than hay baling for themselves and a select few others.

The family still kept farm animals, which they relied on as their main source of food. They also canned fruits and vegetables and went to the grocery store only for a few items.

Although both of Ballard's parents had respectable jobs, the family lived in circumstances akin to poverty. Ballard's childhood home had no electricity or running water. The family went to the bathroom in a bucket and, on one occasion, went to a local state park to bathe. The family reportedly never visited a doctor, even when Ballard was run over by a car at age five and feared dead. He owned only one pair of jeans as a youth.

"Life was pretty sparse," a court sentencing specialist would later say after interviewing Ballard's family and friends for his death penalty trial.

It was not a happy life for the Ballard family. When Ballard was about a year and a half old, Mickey came home from work to find his wife in a pickup truck with another man. Convinced they were having an affair, Mickey threw Ballard's mother off the property and later filed for divorce. His suspicions seemed to be confirmed when, shortly after the divorce, Nita moved to Hawaii with the man she had been caught with, and the two got married.

Mickey Ballard filed for sole custody of his son and, in his court testimony, said his wife didn't take good care of Eric. Mickey claimed he would often find his son unbathed and wearing dirty diapers that she had not changed for hours. The Chancery Court of Washington County, Arkansas, ultimately agreed with Mickey and found that Ballard's mother failed to provide proper care for her son. Temporary custody was awarded to Mickey in February 1975, and he received permanent custody when the divorce was finalized four months later.

But Mickey Ballard didn't really want full responsibility for his young son, according to court documents. Harboring a great deal of bitterness and resentment over his ex-wife's infidelity, Mickey considered his son a reminder of that pain, so he sent him to live with his own mother. Shortly after his custody hearing, Mickey brought Eric directly to Hilma's house and said, "Here, I guess you see what your job is now."

Mickey visited his son occasionally, but the relationship was strained because he continued to harbor ill feelings toward Nita for years. One day, when Eric was about three years old, Eric was singing the popular children's tune "Baby Bumblebee." But when he sang the lyrics "won't my mommy be so proud of me," Mickey screamed at his son and told him never to mention his mother in his house again. The incident greatly frightened young Eric.

Eric also had mixed feelings about his grandmother, who could be kind to him, but was also nasty toward him on a regular basis. Still, as with his father, their time together did not last very long. Already quite elderly when Eric came to live with her, Hilma Ballard had also long before lost one of her legs to illness. Taking care of an active toddler proved overwhelming for the old woman.

When Eric was four, he went to live with his grandmother's aide, Lavern Cook, who lived in town in West Fork. Psychological experts would later say being constantly displaced and moved around created major abandonment issues for Ballard, particularly when it came to female figures in his life.

Nevertheless, his time living with Cook may have been the happiest years of his youth. With two sons of her own about Eric's age, named Jonathan and Justin, Lavern provided a type of care the often-neglected boy was not accustomed to, and he genuinely enjoyed living with her.

One day, when they were watching television together, Eric leaned in close to Lavern and asked whether he could ask her a question.

"Honey, you can ask me anything you want to and I will answer you honestly," she said.

"Well, Jonathan and Justin have you for a momma and I don't have one. Can I call you momma?" Eric asked her.

"You sure can," replied Lavern, who said Ballard continued to call her momma many decades later.

Eric's mother was living in Hawaii at the time. His father, while still in the area, may as well have lived across the country based on how little he appears to have been involved in his son's life.

Lavern later testified that when Eric contracted the measles, she immediately called Mickey Ballard, who disregarded the news as unimportant. And Mickey would regularly fail to show up after making plans to visit Eric, even during holidays and the child's birthday. On those occasions, Eric would wait for hours at the front window.

Lavern later recalled one specific day when, after waiting at the window for a father who was not coming, Eric sighed and said, "Well, I know he's not coming, so I'm going to quit watching."

After about a year or two, Eric went back to living with his grandmother. His father had started dating a new woman named Thelma Jeanine Richardson, who went by Jeanine. The two were married in November 1978.

The couple first lived in a motel together while Mickey Ballard was building a new house on his property. The one-room motel home wasn't an appropriate place for a child to live but Eric did come over on Christmas that year, according to Jeanine.

Once the house was built, Eric lived with his father and Jeanine during at least part of their marriage. Jeanine considered Mickey Ballard a hard worker. He liked to drink beer in the evenings but never missed a day of work, and he baled enough hay on the weekends that it essentially was a second job. Despite Mickey's treatment of Eric in the past, Jeanine felt he was a good father who would put his son's feelings before both his own and those of his wife.

"I can't find any fault in his fathering during the time I was with him," she would later say.

Jeanine described young Eric as "starved" for a mother, but said she was not really a mother figure to him. She had children of her own and thought of Eric more as her "buddy" than her son. She preferred to do fun things with him, like going swimming and driving around together looking for yard sales.

At a later trial, a psychologist testified that some of Eric's cousins had described Jeanine Richardson as a "barfly" who often was seen around the town half lit.

There are reports of sexual assault against young Eric during this time in his life, according to the various therapists who would later analyze Michael Ballard. According to multiple reports, Ballard was molested by both a male and female relative when he was five years old. He never received treatment for this childhood sexual abuse, and it is a subject he discussed as little as possible, both as a child and later in adulthood.

Additionally, when Eric was seven, another relative also lived at the house with the family. She would occasionally share a bed with Eric so they could both stay warm in the night. On at least one occasion, according to reports from sentencing specialists, she allegedly performed a sexual act while they were in bed together.

These traumatic events in Eric's childhood prompted him to beg his mother to come back from Hawaii and take care of him, though it is unclear whether she knew specifically about the sexual abuse. Nita returned to Arkansas in 1980 and, upon hearing that Mickey was drinking excessively and not caring for her son, successfully sought custody of the seven-year-old Eric in October of that year.

Ballard would later say that life seemed to get better when he was living with his mother. She worked a lot and was not home very often, but his stepsister Arlene cared for him in his mother's absence. Nevertheless, Ballard claimed he never felt a bonding or love for his mother. He was always suspicious and fearful that she would leave him again.

His father was not doing much better. According to reports introduced in Ballard's trial, his father was charged with making terroristic threats to kill another man in March 1981. He was fined and ordered to receive counseling.

Despite their many problems, once Nita Ballard was

back in town, she and her ex-husband reconnected. Mickey and Jeanine divorced after two years of marriage; Jeanine later said that she had suspected he still had feelings for his ex-wife.

Mickey and Nita Ballard were remarried in 1984, but that did not seem to give Eric any more stability in his life. Several people said the couple drank and fought on a regular basis, and Ballard himself later told the sentencing specialist that his parents had drunken brawls where his father threatened to kill his mother. On at least one of those occasions, Eric had to physically intervene to protect his mother.

Ballard also told Louise Luck, the sentencing specialist, that his parents had inappropriate boundaries—they lived in a very small house yet they would have loud sexual relations. He also said he was never shown any affection, never given a hug or kiss, never told he was loved.

"There's just so many levels of dysfunction in the home," Luck said during a later court hearing.

There were witnesses to some of the family's violent episodes. Lavern Cook later testified that when Eric was older—long after he had lived with the Cooks—Lavern Cook said Mickey Ballard was drunk every time she saw him and was often an angry drunk. One time, Mickey came to her house drunk and brought a pistol with him. He sat down at her table, playing with the gun and saying, "One of these days I'm going to own the whole town of West Fork." Then the gun accidentally went off and shot out one of Lavern's windows.

In 1981, the Washington County Sheriff's Office had to be called to the Ballard house. A call came into the county dispatch center that Mickey Ballard had threatened his stepdaughter, Arlene. When Sergeant James Acker arrived at the Ballard home, Arlene informed him that Mickey had threatened her with an iron fireplace poker.

Arlene explained that Mickey had run off to his mother's house about a mile down the road. When Acker went to investigate, he found an intoxicated Mickey standing in the front yard. Mickey ran into the house upon seeing the officer, so Acker went around to a screened back porch adjacent to the house.

Suddenly Mickey appeared in the doorway clutching a fireplace poker and yelled, "You're going to be dead!" He charged toward Acker, whose first instinct was to draw his gun and shoot Mickey, but he resisted that inclination. Instead, Acker hit him on the head with his flashlight as Mickey charged toward him. That knocked Mickey to the ground, where Acker was able to handcuff him after some struggle.

A terrified Eric Ballard watched the whole thing, hugging his grandmother's hips and hiding behind her apron as his father was arrested.

Mickey was charged with making terroristic threats once again and received a two-year suspended prison sentence and two years of probation in addition to counseling and a thousand-dollar fine.

Some in town also thought Mickey Ballard was violent toward Eric. Several of his childhood friends remember him coming to school with bruises, welts, and black eyes, which they believed came from his father. One time, Eric had a group of friends waiting for him outside his house—Eric was not allowed to have friends over—and one of the friends, Rhonda Maples, heard Mickey Ballard call Eric a "no-good worthless bastard."

"You're good for nothing," she also heard.

Ballard said that while his father hurt him emotionally and mentally, he never hurt him physically. With his rough-and-tumble personality, he would often fight with his friends, and he said that's where the bruises and black eyes came from, not from his dad.

"My father never hit me," he later said. "I personally wouldn't term it as being overly abusive. Were there abandonment issues? Absolutely."

Mickey Ballard taught his son how to fire a gun at age six, but according to friends and family, that was just part of the culture in rural Arkansas. Eric's cousin Joseph Bearden, for example, fired his first gun at age three.

Mickey Ballard apparently introduced a lot of things to Eric at an early age. When Eric was eleven, Mickey gave him a motorcycle so he would stay away from the family house as much as possible, according to Lavern's son Justin.

And when Eric was thirteen, his father got him drunk for the first time. Several of Eric's childhood friends said he was a heavy partier from then on, drinking regularly as well as doing drugs.

"Marijuana, meth, cocaine, acid—I mean, anything we could get our hands on," friend Russell Drake later testified.

Between the ages of thirteen and seventeen, Eric was drinking at least two beers a day and regularly using marijuana and cocaine, he would later tell a psychiatrist. LSD was a summer hobby for him and his friends; he said he probably used LSD about one hundred times in his summers during high school and once got so high that they got lost and ended up in Texas.

In addition to physically fighting other teens, Ballard also exhibited violence toward animals in his early teenage years. Once when drinking with friends, they found an opossum, which they tortured and set on fire. On his own, Ballard put one cat in a clothes dryer and another in a microwave oven.

He would later say he had more remorse for the animals he had hurt than the people he had killed.

As with drinking and drugs, Ballard also experimented with sex from an early age. He had been sexually active since age thirteen and once was chased by two cars full of guys because he had slept with one of the guys' girlfriends. They waited for him at the end of his driveway and chased him up to his house, where they jumped him. When Ballard's mother and father heard the fight, Nita Ballard encouraged her husband to get a tire iron.

During another fight that his father witnessed, Mickey cheered his son on, then threatened to shoot the teens who were fighting Eric.

"This was the environment I grew up in," Michael Eric Ballard later said.

Mickey Ballard always told his son to stand up and fight like a man. After that, he never wanted to be picked on or thought of as a loser.

"He always wanted to be better than others and win his father's favor," a psychiatrist would later note.

With more interest in drinking, drugs, and girls than in his education, Ballard skipped a lot of school. His high school transcripts indicate that he failed most of his subjects; by the second half of tenth grade, he was failing all of them. His school records also indicate he had trouble with language comprehension and oral expression in reading, as well as suffering from overall emotional problems.

When he was in the eleventh grade, three of his friends were killed in a car crash. Ballard had been riding with them earlier that night, and was dropped off only minutes before the fatal accident. The traumatic experience made him value his life even less, according to later reports. He started taking more risks, and by the second half of eleventh grade he had dropped out of high school altogether.

But by age seventeen, it started to look like Ballard's life might turn around.

On February 7, 1991, not long after dropping out of school, Ballard went to Springdale, Arkansas, and enrolled in the US Army. He was quickly transferred to Fort Jackson, South Carolina, where he underwent basic training and was schooled in heavy-wheeled vehicle maintenance. He began training to become a "tank catcher," using the massive M88 recovery vehicles to recover tanks and other heavily armored vehicles stranded during battle.

Ballard found that he loved working with heavy machinery and vehicles, and the farther into his basic training he got, the more he felt right at home in the military.

Coming from a home with so little stability, Ballard loved the structure and discipline of the life in the army. He was well liked by his superiors and became a leader during drills and exercises, even being permitted to lead his fellow trainees and carry the flag during runs. Ballard took particularly well to shooting and earned the distinction of a sharpshooter badge with an auto rifle bar.

"I was an expert in everything I did," Ballard later said. It was a much-needed boost of confidence for a teen who, throughout his childhood, never received any attention that was not negative.

But Ballard's newly found happiness was not going to last.

In August, Ballard was called into his superior's office and informed he was to be "cycled out" and discharged from the army because his enrollment was fraudulent. Unbeknownst to everyone, including Ballard, he had been on probation at the time that he enrolled. When he was fifteen, a lot of Ballard's friends had been purchasing large sound systems for their car. Ballard could not afford one for his Jeep, so he stole one of his grandmother's checks and filled it out so he could buy one. His grandmother would often give him her Sears credit card so he could buy things, and he felt taking the check was no different.

"She spoiled the shit out of me, so I didn't think it was a big deal," Ballard later said.

However, shortly after Ballard had purchased the sound system, the police came to his part-time job and removed the stereo equipment from his car. What Ballard did not know was that he was charged with writing a fraudulent check and placed on probation. According to Ballard, he never went before a judge, nor did he receive a letter or any kind of notice that he was on probation. When he joined the army, he had no idea.

But that excuse mattered little to the military. Ballard was discharged on August 27, 1991, not even seven months after he had joined. And, because he was discharged, he was not eligible for any of the benefits he would have received otherwise. Worse than that, the structure, confidence, and sense of purpose that he had finally discovered, that he had lacked all his life, was gone.

Looking for a fresh start, and a way to escape the rejection and bad memories of his home, Ballard decided to move out of Arkansas and head north to live with his father's cousin in Allentown, Pennsylvania. But the contentment that he was seeking continued to elude him.

"I was still lost as hell," Ballard later said. "I had no direction, I had no goals, I had no ambitions, nothing. I wasn't living, I was just existing day to day."

CHAPTER 11

In the days following the quadruple homicide, Trooper Raymond Judge was tasked with retracing Ballard's steps on the day of the killings. Ballard had obtained a job at Monarch Precast, an Allentown concrete company not far from the community corrections center. Judge interviewed one of Ballard's co-workers there, James Shankweiler, who said that on June 25, the day before the killings, he had heard Ballard say over the phone, "Think about me, baby."

Judge also interviewed several of Ballard's fellow residents at the Allentown Community Corrections Center, the local state-run halfway house where Ballard had been living since he was paroled in April. A bland, nondescript building made entirely of brick, the corrections center has no exterior clues to indicate what is inside; the only visible window is a large reflective one that is impossible to see through from the outside.

Several of the residents there had also observed Ballard's phone interactions. One claimed Ballard had told him that Denise hadn't been calling him recently. He said Ballard referred to Denise as his wife, and to her kids as his children. During one phone conversation, the resident heard Ballard yelling into the phone, "What are you saying? What's going on?"

The morning of the killings, Ballard stayed in the area of the halfway house's telephones from 8:39 to 11:41 a.m., constantly making calls or, it seemed, waiting for calls. Several residents and staff members told Judge they saw Ballard pacing up and down the hall, appearing anxious and upset. One of the residents claimed Ballard told him he was waiting for a call from his girlfriend, with whom he was having problems. Another said he saw Ballard slam the phone receiver several times.

These accounts offered Judge a glimpse into Ballard's state of mind that morning. He had called Denise and Marilyn Rivera multiple times in the twenty-four hours leading up to the murder—to the point of obsessiveness— and he seemed to grow more and more restless and furious with each call.

Next, Judge used footage from the corrections center's extensive system of surveillance cameras to review Ballard's activity on the morning of June 26. Little of it was particularly alarming, although at one point Ballard appeared to grow agitated when he tried to check out of the facility and a staff member refused to let him leave with his paycheck. But then, just as quickly as Ballard's temper had risen, he appeared to calm down.

The trooper continued monitoring the tapes until 11:48 a.m., when Ballard checked out of the Allentown Community Corrections Center. Signing out at the lobby, Ballard was carrying a green backpack and a radio, and wearing a pair of jeans, brown boots, a blue-green baseball cap, and a light blue short-sleeved T-shirt with a Superman emblem.

As it turned out, it would help police very much that Ballard wore that particular shirt. Not only was it obviously the same article of clothing they later recovered, folded neatly on an armchair next to Dennis Marsh's corpse, but it made Ballard stand out to several witnesses whom he encountered in the hours before the killings.

After Ballard checked out, surveillance footage showed him walking west on Hamilton Street, a main thoroughfare in downtown Allentown where the corrections center is located. Judge followed that path and discovered two pawnshops just three blocks to the west. With the security staff and metal detectors, Ballard would not have been able to have a knife at the corrections center, so the trooper suspected one of the pawnshops was the most likely place for him to have acquired one.

Indeed, by reviewing city surveillance cameras, Judge found that Ballard had entered a pawnshop called Pawn America around noon, where he looked over the store's collection of samurai swords and decorative daggers but didn't buy any. Next Judge went to A-Town Pawn, just three doors down the block. A store employee explained that Ballard had pulled at least three separate knives out of the display case to look them over. He had been extremely deliberate about it, testing each knife for sharpness and balance.

Ballard eventually settled on a Ruko Muela-brand knife. Judge now knew where Ballard had obtained the murder weapon, and the fact that he was so meticulous in studying the knives before the purchase only further spoke to the premeditated nature of the crime.

"He seemed like an ordinary, average, everyday guy," store manager David Toolan would later say. He remembered Ballard's distinctive Superman T-shirt, but nothing else struck him as the least bit suspicious.

With his pawnshop business completed, Ballard headed for the local bus station, first stopping to make a call at a pay phone outside of a 7-Eleven convenience store about two blocks from the pawnshop. When Judge later checked the phone records, he learned those calls were made to Marilyn Rivera, in addition to the several Ballard had made to her earlier in the day at the corrections center.

After he had hung up the pay phone, Ballard bought a bus ticket from Allentown to Northampton borough, the scene of the killings. But as Judge learned from reviewing various retail surveillance cameras, he didn't go straight to Denise's house. First he stopped at Boxers Bar and Grille, a local watering hole next to the bus stop, and ordered a Long Island Iced Tea. It was a drink well known for its high alcohol content, but Ballard downed it in a matter of minutes.

Ballard left the bar and headed closer to Denise's neighborhood, but instead of going directly there, he stopped at the nearby Assante Ristorante Italiano and had another drink. From there, he walked to Ridge Alley, a narrow backstreet that runs parallel to Denise's street, and spoke to Karl and Cynthia Swankoski, who own a house on the side of Ridge Alley just opposite Denise's home.

Judge questioned the Swankoskis, who explained Ballard had asked them if he could cut through their yard to reach the alley, and they agreed. From their yard, Ballard had a clear view of Denise's house. To the Swankoskis, it appeared Ballard was conducting surveillance of sorts on the house. But he must not have seen what he was seeking, they later told Judge, because he quickly turned away from the house and walked back toward Main Street.

By now it would have been 2 p.m., just hours before Denise and the others were murdered. Judge reviewed yet more security footage from the neighboring stores, and learned that Ballard had gone to the nearby State Liquor Store and purchased a 2.25-pint bottle of vodka.

Questioned later by Judge, the clerk claimed he noticed Ballard's distinctive light blue Superman shirt and was tempted to ask, "Where's your cape?" But there was something disturbing in the customer's eyes, and the clerk decided against making the joke.

"He looked distant," the clerk told Judge. "Like he was here, but not here."

Judge also later learned that Ballard visited another bar where he drank another Long Island Iced Tea and his entire bottle of vodka mixed with Mountain Dew. Ballard had consumed a lot of alcohol in a short amount of time, especially for a man who seldom drank otherwise, having lived most of his life in prison and his recent months in a halfway house.

Judge suspected Ballard was trying to calm himself before committing his crime, and Ballard himself would not dispute that interpretation.

"I don't know if I was numbing myself from what I was going to do," Ballard later said. "I'm out there getting shitfaced because maybe I can't deal with the decision I've made but I can't stop myself."

Surveillance camera footage showed Ballard stopping in at a convenience store and a pharmacy up until 2:20 p.m., when the cameras lost any further trace of him. A later check of phone records revealed Ballard called Denise's cell phone twice. The calls lasted three and a half and five minutes. What words the two may have exchanged in those calls might never be known.

It took Judge a great deal of time to retrace Ballard's steps, but it gave him a good idea of the man's movements that day, as well as a glimpse into his state of mind. The obsessive calls he made from the community center, his meticulous testing of the knives, the drinking to still his nerves: To Judge, it was clear that Ballard started June 26 with just one goal in mind: to kill Denise Merhi.

On June 29, a few days after Judge had finished retracing his steps, Ballard was released from St. Luke's Hospital. He was taken directly to the Northampton County

Prison, where District Judge Jackie Taschner arraigned him via video. Although he had already been arraigned in Lehigh County, it had to be done a second time now that he was being brought back to the county where the murders took place. The police, the victims' families, and many in the community breathed a sigh of relief upon learning that Ballard was out of the hospital and back behind bars.

CHAPTER 12

Violently slain together in the home they shared, Denise Merhi, Dennis Marsh, and Alvin Marsh Jr. would also be buried together.

The joint funeral service for the three took place on July 1, five days after the murders, at Faith Evangelical Lutheran Church in Whitehall Township. Denise had been a member at the church, a large building with tan and gray stone, a black pitched roof, and a modern-looking cross made of black metal rods. Three white hearses lined up in front of the church, where more than three hundred friends and family members came to pay their respects.

Among those in the crowd was Marilyn Rivera, who was stunned by the sheer number of people who had come out to remember her friend. As she approached the church, she saw a huge line of people stretching out of the building and toward the parking lot. News crews were set up a few yards away, with reporters trying to talk to mourners as photographers and video cameras captured images of the scene.

Marilyn didn't want to wait in the line, so she walked up ahead and saw that Denise's cousin Bubba was monitoring the crowd as people filed into the church. She asked whether she could cut ahead, and Bubba nodded, motioning for Marilyn to walk past the line into a small, dimly lit room within the church building.

The three caskets were set up next to one another, almost in a half circle. Denise was in the middle, her father and grandfather on either side of her. Chairs were set along next to Dennis and Alvin's caskets, where friends and members of the family sat. The line of mourners, almost all wearing black, snaked silently across the room, allowing them to pass each of the caskets before greeting Geraldine Dorwart and other family members as they left.

Geraldine was sitting next to some of the empty chairs, which allowed the mourners to sit and speak with her for a few moments before leaving the room. She hugged, kissed, and shared a few words with everyone who came to see her. Marilyn looked forward to speaking with Geraldine. She had only briefly spoken with her once since Denise died, when Geraldine called looking for one of Denise's scrapbooks.

Their relationship had been a bit strained in recent months after Denise and Marilyn got into a fight a few months before Denise's death. The two reconciled, as they always did after a fight, but Marilyn felt that Geraldine was concerned about the reconciliation because she feared Marilyn would hurt Denise again. Otherwise, Marilyn had always gotten along with Geraldine. In fact, at one point Marilyn and Geraldine were so close that Denise had even become jealous of their relationship.

Next to Geraldine were Denise's children, Trystan and Annikah. Marilyn noticed that Trystan wasn't crying, and was trying to be very brave for his mother. Marilyn felt she couldn't have been more proud of him if he were her own son.

As the line moved forward and Marilyn got closer and closer to Denise's casket, she passed two tri-fold boards with photos of Denise, Dennis, and Alvin. Marilyn noticed several pictures of herself and her children along with Denise, Annikah, and Trystan.

When Marilyn was finished paying her respects, she approached Geraldine. While she had sat down and spoken with everyone else who approached her, Marilyn was surprised when Geraldine immediately stood up as Marilyn approached.

"I don't have time for you," Geraldine said, with such a look of disgust on her face that Marilyn felt like she wanted to throw up. In that moment, she could tell that Geraldine blamed her, at least partially, for Denise's death.

"It's not my fault," Marilyn said. "Denise had a mind of her own."

"Well, things could've been avoided," Geraldine said, looking away.

Marilyn was mortified.

"It's not my fault Denise decided to date a psychopath," she said. "You know Denise. You know how strong-willed she was."

Geraldine looked back at Marilyn.

"This could've all been avoided," she repeated.

"Denise was going to do what Denise was going to do," Marilyn said.

Geraldine again looked away and said, "Well, other people are waiting to give their condolences."

Marilyn didn't know what else to say, so she walked away. She was so upset that she couldn't even stay for the service itself; she just rushed back to her car and drove away. Marilyn tried to give Geraldine the benefit of the doubt—she had just lost her daughter and must be hurting beyond belief. But Geraldine's words had hurt Marilyn, and she knew she would never forget them for as long as she lived.

The service itself was held in the church sanctuary, where rows of maple-colored pews faced an elevated altar area set against the backdrop of a brown and tan brick wall with a huge golden cross. The room was lit by a handful of cylindrically shaped light fixtures that hung from the ceiling, each of which also had crosses on them. The three caskets were sprinkled with holy water and covered with white palls.

The Reverend Jared R. Stahler, Denise's cousin, traveled from New York City to preside over the joint funeral of Denise, Dennis, and Alvin. His voice echoing throughout the high-ceilinged sanctuary, Stahler reflected on how the four brutal murders had stunned the local community.

"There is no sensible way to explain this horrific act, the killing of three generations of a family and a heroic neighbor," he said, as reported by the *Express-Times*.

"No measure is enough to gauge the tears shed at these deaths," he continued, according to the *Morning Call*. "Family and neighborhood, community and valley—we are astounded by these events. Trying to understand how this happened is all consuming."

Geraldine spoke on behalf of the family. Still shaken five days later, she had lost the remarks she had prepared for the service and said she would have to instead speak from her heart.

She described Dennis as a car enthusiast with an even greater passion for spending time with his grandchildren. Geraldine also recalled her former father-in-law Alvin's military service and his affinity for telling stories about the old days.

"He was more to me than most fathers could have been

to any child," the *Express-Times* reported she said. "He was a loving, caring, giving man."

It was an emotional speech for Geraldine, but it was even more difficult for her to talk about her daughter. Denise had a generous nature, Geraldine explained, which served her well both as a nurse and as a mother. She spoke about Denise's love of scrapbooking, spending time with friends, and, most important of all, caring for her two young children.

"She was well mannered . . . and always caring for others," Geraldine said. "She was always there when I needed her."

Geraldine finished her comments by reciting a poem from a condolence card.

"One day we will all meet again," she said. "That's what I believe."

A handful of the family's neighbors also gave their remembrances. One recalled how Alvin Marsh once skated on the streets following an ice storm. Another, Nancy Birosik, relayed how Dennis Marsh loved to sit in the shade on the deck that he built.

"If I heard him say it once, I heard it a million times," she said. "This was the best neighborhood he ever lived in."

Shelly Youwakim, Denise's cousin, spoke about the dozens of family photos on display at the church that day, especially those of Denise, whose eager smiles brought tears to the eyes of many mourners. Denise had been known for taking numerous photos at gatherings and events. But, Shelly said, for some inexplicable reason Denise did not take any photos during a gathering of family mere days before her death.

"Maybe she wasn't supposed to take pictures," Shelly said to the reporter from the *Express-Times*. "Maybe we were supposed to remember."

Among the mourners were two of Denise's former romantic partners, Brian Miller and Peter Hoff. Brian, Denise's two-time former fiancé, had actually had a chance encounter with Denise the day she died, he would later testify. He had been doing some computer troubleshooting side-work at an auto repair shop where Denise happened to be picking up her car. The two seemed to hit it off once again, and Brian offered to take Denise to a concert he had tickets for in July.

Shortly after she left the auto shop that afternoon, Denise sent him four messages, each of which said, "It was nice seeing you again." He didn't write back. They would prove to be the last contact he ever had with her.

Peter had also seen Denise the day she died. Denise had called him the night before she got home from her trip to the New Jersey shore and asked to get together with him. Peter later testified that they had gone out to two local clubs, and he stayed over at her house that night. He left at seven o'clock the morning. Only a few hours before four people were murdered in that very house, he later recalled.

Denise and Peter had arranged to get together later that same day, but she never returned the calls he made to her. He went to another Phillies game without her the next day, and on the way home he received a call from his sister that the police wanted to speak to him.

"I really didn't want to believe it a hundred percent for sure until I got home and I actually went on my computer, typed her name in and it popped up in front of my face," he later said in court.

After the funeral service ended, the caskets were taken outside to the three white hearses awaiting them. A color guard of uniformed veterans, carrying the American flag, stood at attention in honor of Alvin Marsh Jr.

The three generations of the Marsh family were buried

all together later at the Cedar Hill Memorial Park in nearby Hanover Township.

Steven Zernhelt's funeral, held the next day on July 2, was a smaller affair with no media coverage. The family held calling hours beginning at one o'clock; the funeral began at three o'clock at the local Schisler Funeral Home, just around the corner from the Zernhelt and the Marsh/ Merhi homes. Reporters and news vans had come out but, at the request of the Zernhelt family, they maintained a respectful distance down the street and did not bother any of the mourners.

A large crowd came out for the service, which flattered Janet Zernhelt, but did not surprise her. Even before the funeral, she had experienced a tremendous outpouring of love and affection from people, including some who were total strangers to Janet. She received hundreds of condolence letters after her husband died, including one from an elderly couple Janet hadn't known who were clients of Steve's workplace and explained that, when they were having trouble with their air-conditioning, Steve stopped by the house on his own time to help them fix it.

That was the kind of man Steve was, Janet knew. He was a kind, modest man who would do anything for anyone, especially his children.

The funeral reminded Janet of so many memories of her late husband. His love of his favorite drink, Mountain Dew. The enormous collection of Steve's how-to books in the basement. The time that Steve and Ryan rebuilt a truck together, which was later featured in a truck magazine. The hours Janet and Steve would spend together on their boat—a boat she now intended to sell, knowing she couldn't bear to be in it again without him.

And then there was all the work that Steve had done on the house they had shared for more than three decades.

Steve hadn't known anything about home improvement in the beginning, but he didn't want to pay a handyman for that kind of work, so he taught himself. In their time in that house, Steve completely renovated their kitchen, enclosed their porch to add more indoor space, and installed new masonry and landscaping to the backyard. It looked beautiful, like it had been done by a professional.

It made Janet sad to think of all the work Steve had still planned to do, but now never would. He had wanted to refurbish the hardwood floors, bury a drainpipe in the side yard, clean up the backyard after having removed a pool that had once been there.

But Janet never gave thought to leaving the house. Some asked her if the memories were too painful for her to stay, and Janet knew if Steve had been killed inside the house, rather than next door, it would have been different. But to Janet, this was still their home together, and she knew she didn't want to be anywhere else.

Steve's funeral brought back many memories for Jaime Zernhelt as well. She recalled how her father had paid for both her college education and that of her brothers, yet never spoiled them. She remembered how he would drive three hours just to help them fix something. And she recalled how he was like a father not only to her, but to her friends as well. One time, he picked up Jaime and her friends at college in the middle of a snowstorm just to take them grocery shopping.

"He was a loving, caring person, he always took good care of me," Jaime said. "Every moment with him was a good moment. He was always our hero."

It was too painful for Janet to speak at the funeral, so Jaime served as the spokesperson for the family. She read a poem she had written about her father, one filled with inside jokes about King Kone, the ice cream shop down the street from the Zernhelts' home, a place he always loved to take them when they were growing up:

"If there's King Kone ice cream cones in heaven, Lord feed my dad a few, but remember, he wouldn't want a cherry, especially not two. Tell him that I love him and miss him. And when he turns to smile, place a kiss upon each cheek and hold him for a while. Remembering him is easy, I'll do it every day, but there's an ache within my heart that will never go away. Husband, father, friend, hero. Always in our hearts."

About a week after the funeral, the Zernhelt family announced that they had set up a memorial fund to help with Steve's burial costs and also to financially assist his family in the future.

Soon, other benefits were organized, for both the Zernhelt and Merhi/Marsh families. In just a few weeks after the slayings, friends and family put together an event called the Merhi-Zernhelt Community Benefit, which drew one thousand people and raised seventeen thousand dollars in its first year. It has since turned into an annual event, expanded to help the families of other murder victims in Northampton County.

Once the immediate shock of the grisly quadruple murder had started to wear down, media outlets and members of the public alike began to ask the same question: How could it be that Michael Ballard, who had already committed a brutal murder more than eighteen years earlier, had been walking the streets a free man?

As the local newspapers turned their attention to this question, the details about the circumstances of Ballard's parole quickly began to emerge.

As the conclusion of his fifteen-year minimum sentence approached, Ballard was first granted parole by the Pennsylvania Board of Probation and Parole on September 18, 2006. In its notice to Ballard about its decision, the board cited several factors that led to its ruling, including Ballard having expressed remorse for the crimes he committed, a positive recommendation by the state Department of Corrections, Ballard's completion of institutional programs, and a review of all his mental health reports and behavioral evaluations.

Also among the factors that went into Ballard's release was the inmate job he had held for two years at a hospice unit for elderly prisoners. Although all inmates were required to have a job within the prison, this particular one was among the toughest and most unpopular. Ballard had nevertheless volunteered for it. Similar to nursing home professions outside of prison, it involved interacting with the elderly and sick inmates, writing requests on their behalf, serving them meals, and cleaning up after them. Ballard received average work reports, demonstrated no problems during his time with the patients, and spoke regularly to counselors throughout his two years on the job.

In Pennsylvania, the parole process begins eight months prior to the end of the prisoner's minimum sentence. Staff members from both the parole board and the Pennsylvania Department of Corrections, as well as counselors and other employees of the prison, prepare a case file about the inmate for the parole board to eventually review. This case file includes information about the inmate's crime, criminal history, emotional stability, history of family violence, prison misconduct records, and status of institutional program completion. The file also includes testimony notes from the sentencing hearing and any recommendations by the judge, prosecuting attorneys, institutional counselors, and prison warden about the prisoner and his possible parole. That file is then sent for consideration to the parole board, which interviews the inmate four months prior to the end of their minimum sentence.

Two people who did not share the state's enthusiasm for Ballard's chances at rehabilitation were Gloria Sieber and Elaine Keim, the sisters of Donald Richard. After their brother was killed, members of his family swore that they would do everything they could to ensure that Ballard never got out of prison again. When the time came for his parole hearing, Gloria and Elaine wanted to address the board directly, but were denied that opportunity because of the amount of confidential, sensitive information about Ballard that would be discussed at that hearing. Instead, they wrote a letter to the board strongly encouraging them to deny Ballard his freedom.

One group that did not oppose Ballard's release, however, was the Lehigh County district attorney's office. As was common practice, the parole board submitted a letter to the office seeking any opinion about Ballard's possible parole, and warned that a failure to respond would mean an assumption that there were no objections. The district attorney's office did not reply.

"I wish to hell I could say to you I have a letter that says, 'We strongly object to his being paroled,'" Lehigh County District Attorney Jim Martin told the *Morning Call* after they reported the failure to respond. Martin, who was not district attorney at the time of Ballard's 1991 murder, told the newspaper his office would review every parole case involving a violent crime. But he said he did not know whether he would have objected to Ballard's parole anyway, given his young age at the time of the murder and lack of other criminal record.

On November 27, 2006, Ballard was released from the SCI–Laurel Highlands state prison in Somerset County and placed into the custody of the Allentown Community Corrections Center halfway house. He was officially paroled on March 1, 2007, and released from the halfway house, although he was still required to follow an ongoing post-release plan.

But barely more than a year later, Ballard would be back in prison.

He was taken back into custody on April 23, 2008—almost a year after he had started dating Denise Merhi—for failing to complete a mandated anger management program under the terms of his post-release plan. This violation of Ballard's parole made him a "technical violator," according to the state. Most such violators are sanctioned an average of five times before they are sent back to prison.

Then came the claims that Ballard sexually assaulted an underage girl during his brief time out of prison. The authorities investigated the claims and determined they did not have enough to file criminal charges against him. Nevertheless, Ballard's parole was formally revoked on June 2, 2008, due to the technical violation, and he was returned to SCI–Laurel Highlands. There he was ordered to participate in another institutional program and not to receive any reports of misconduct, after which the board would review his case again in another six months.

This time, after those six months passed, the board opted to deny his parole. During a November 25 notice about its decision, the board indicated that Ballard had failed to demonstrate any motivation for success, continually minimized or denied the seriousness of his crimes, and refused to accept responsibility for his actions. According to the board, Ballard was still in need of continual treatment from the prison's institutional programs, and was too much of a risk to the community to go free.

Just over a year later, however, that same board would reach a very different conclusion altogether.

On December 30, 2009, Ballard was granted parole a

second time. The board's reasons for this decision mirrored those of its first parole decision, such as good institutional behavior and a positive recommendation from the Pennsylvania Department of Corrections. It now also stated that Ballard showed remorse for his crimes and demonstrated a strong motivation for success, points that were completely opposite of those cited in its 2008 decision to deny parole.

Ballard was once again released to the Allentown Community Corrections Center on April 19, 2010, a little more than nine weeks before he murdered four people in Northampton borough.

As is often the case after a paroled criminal commits a violent crime, the Pennsylvania Board of Probation and Parole came under harsh criticism following the quadruple homicide. The local newspapers were flooded with letters and Internet comments condemning the board and questioning how Ballard could possibly have been granted freedom.

In one such letter that ran in the *Express-Times,* Bath borough resident Brian Smith wrote, "If Michael Ballard had committed a murder similar to the one he did in 1991 while living in Russia, China or any Arab country, he would have been rightfully executed within two months and given no second chance to murder again." In another, Barry Willever of Wilson Borough wrote, "The people who let this man out should be charged as accomplices to four murders."

The *Express-Times*'s editorial board was almost equally reproachful. In a June 29 editorial titled "State's Prison System Failed Us All," the paper claimed that the system had failed with both of its decisions to grant Ballard parole: "Ballard scammed the system to get out, behaving while he was locked up and convincing prison officials to write recommendations that members of the Probation and Parole Board looked upon favorably. Someone needs to explain how that happened."

One of the most vocal critics of the parole board was John Morganelli himself. Long before the four Northampton murders in June 2010, Morganelli had strongly and vocally maintained that parole should be abolished altogether for those convicted of violent crimes like murder, rape, armed robbery, kidnapping and crimes committed with a gun. While the *Express-Times* called Ballard's case an unfortunate failure of the parole system, Morganelli called it an inevitable result of the way that system was designed.

And the more he reviewed Ballard's case, the more Morganelli became convinced that his position was correct.

Although the parole board reviewed Ballard's behavioral evaluations while considering their parole, and the Pennsylvania Department of Corrections issued positive recommendations on his behalf, Morganelli's review of Ballard's records revealed that he had committed several infractions throughout his time in prison.

Ballard's first reported violation was on November 24, 1993, less than one year into his first prison term. On that day, Ballard refused to cooperate with a corrections officer who had ordered him to return to his cell, shouting, "Don't touch me." When the officer ordered Ballard to place his hands behind his back to be handcuffed, Ballard shoved him, and then took a swing at him with a closed fist when they tried to further subdue him.

Ballard was written up for the assault and refusal to obey orders, the first of several similar violations. He was written up on the latter infraction twice more that year, on December 15 and December 22, for separate unrelated incidents. On August 9, 1995, he was written up again for violating prison rules and illegal possession of a controlled substance.

Ballard continued to display resistance to authority over his next several years in the prison. On August 31, 1996, he was written up for fighting, refusal to obey orders, and presence in an unauthorized area of the prison. He was issued the last two violations again on separate incidents in 1998. On March 6 of that year, after a corrections officer found him in an unauthorized area, Ballard ignored several calls issued via a PA system to clear out. On September 27, he was written up again when he was found in another unauthorized area, hiding underneath a towel in the corner. He ignored several verbal commands to come to the door.

On June 24, 1999, Ballard was written up once again for possession of a controlled substance. On December 11 of the next year, he received another infraction for violation of rules, this time after giving a corrections officer trouble as he tried to inspect his cell. Ballard became furious with the guard, who repeatedly tried to calm him down. When he asked Ballard to remove the tape that was holding pictures against the cell wall, Ballard ripped the pictures down altogether and became aggressive with the guard, forcing him to exit the cell and lock the door before the situation escalated any further.

Ballard's violations became less frequent as time passed, but they did not end altogether during his final prison years. He was written up for another violation on May 26, 2005, barely a year before his first parole, this time for failure to cooperate with prison staff as they were attempting to do an inmate count and make sure all the prisoners were accounted for.

The Pennsylvania Board of Probation and Parole, no stranger to public criticism after a paroled inmate commits another high-profile crime, defended itself when reports of Ballard's parole history began to emerge. When questioned by the *Express-Times,* a parole board spokesman pointed to the positive recommendations Ballard received as part of his case file when questioned by the board.

They also noted the board considered a total of 1,713 parole decisions the month Ballard's parole was considered. If you factored in other matters before the board such as recommitments, references to prior actions, and court assignments, they considered a total of 3,595 decisions that month alone, according to the board.

Although the extent of Ballard's misconduct violations had not yet been made public, Morganelli, in the course of his pre-trial preparation, eventually spoke to one of Ballard's former correctional counselors from SCI–Laurel Highlands. Penny Lynn Sines, who now worked as a social worker at the women's state correctional institution at Muncy, had been one of several people who interviewed Ballard and made a recommendation for his 2006 parole as part of his pre-release case file.

Sines explained that many of Ballard's misconducts were informal resolutions, meaning they were referred to the prison's unit manager for disciplinary sanctions rather than going through the more formal process before a hearing examiner. In an eleven-year period prior to his parole, all but one of his violations were informal resolutions, according to court records. While he had some official misconducts on record from his time at other prisons early in his term, he had none during his time at SCI–Laurel Highlands at the end of his term.

During his time at that prison, Ballard was found to have a health stability rating of B, which indicates that he had a mental health history but did not require any mental health services in the prison. His psychiatric history was reviewed before he started working in the hospice unit, and he showed no signs of problems during his sessions with counselors during that time, Sines told Morganelli. As his case file was prepared, Ballard was deemed a low risk to reoffend.

A parole board spokesman told the *Express-Times* that a review of the process that led to Ballard's parole would be conducted, and any deficiencies identified would be reported and addressed. However, the spokesman said this report would be made available only to the Pennsylvania Board of Probation and Parole and its staff, and would not be publicly released or discussed.

Report or no report, family members of the four murder victims and many others were infuriated to learn that Ballard had been released despite a history of past infractions.

"He wasn't a good person in jail, and he got out anyway," Jaime Zernhelt later said. "He should have still been in jail, and none of this would have happened. If he'd still been in jail from the first time, our lives wouldn't have been ripped apart."

CHAPTER 13

The week preceding Denise's death was an emotional one for her and Ballard, judging by the text messages they exchanged with each other.

As part of their investigation, the state police had checked Denise's text messages in the month leading up to her death. Between May 20 and June 26, Denise had exchanged 561 text messages, 86 of which were with Ballard. All those messages were exchanged in the five days immediately before her death.

As a halfway house resident, Ballard was not allowed a cell phone, so he would often call Denise on the house's pay phone immediately after getting back from work at Monarch Precast. If he was even just a few minutes late, he would often be greeted by a message next to the phone reading: "Mikey, your wife called. Call her." Without a cell phone, Ballard had no ability to call Denise during the day, but a co-worker at Monarch regularly allowed him to use his phone during work hours to send text messages.

Ballard's text to Denise at 12:15 p.m. June 21 was about a pressing matter. He had just spoken to his parole supervisor, who had warned him that he might be sent back to jail because of outstanding issues with Forensic Treatment Services, the counseling group he had been required to attend as a parolee. He had hired a lawyer to help with his case, but it would cost $750 for her to file a petition on his behalf. He asked Denise if she could contribute $250 toward the fee.

"I dont want 2 go back baby . . . If i do, i want u 2 know i will always love you denise!!" he wrote. "I am scared. And i am having a hard time with this . . . My fucking heart is breaking."

Denise tried to call him, but they couldn't connect, so she texted him back at 1:31 p.m., writing: "Baby I would give u the money if I had it. I've been crying since this text came to me. I'm soooo soooo very sorry baby."

At 1:33 p.m. she texted him again: "I want u to know I took the mirena out a month ago." Mirena is a birth control device.

Ballard was overjoyed to hear Denise speaking once again about having a baby with him. His return text came about an hour later.

"I Love you . . . For all the right reasons," he wrote. "And I'm glad 2 know u feel the true love u have 4 me again . . . Thank u!! You make me feel like i really am superman!!"

The texts began again the next morning, when Denise and Ballard continued their conversations about one day having a baby together.

"I can't wait to feel this baby grwoin inside me. Havin a part of u!!!!! God I so love u michael," Denise wrote at 11:37 a.m.

Ballard appeared equally excited.

"We're really gonna have a baby," he wrote at 11:50 a.m. "i mean try 2 anyway. I'm so nervous, overjoyed, but still nervous! Thank u!! Thank u!! Thank u!! God be with us through this i pray!!"

But their happy plans were not without some anxiety. Just three minutes later, Denise texted that she feared what others would think if she and Ballard had a baby.

"I'm so fuckin stoked!!!!!!!" she wrote at 11:53 a.m. "But scared as hell. What the hell do I tell people. I mean seriously."

"Wow!" Ballard replied at 12:05 p.m. "Um, well lets just become pregnant first, ok? Then we'll look at the ppl who we can be honest w/ and make decisions then. Ok?"

But Denise was not so easily calmed.

"Well I cannot tell my mom or kids or even my dad," she wrote at 12:15 p.m. "I'm gonna look like a fuckin whore."

Ballard's message at 12:25 p.m. was the last in the conversation.

"No u wont look like a whore!" he wrote. When some small portions of the text messages were later read in court, this particular line struck a chord with many newspaper readers. They were reminded of the message written in blood on Denise's wall: DENISE IS A WHORE.

Ballard's text message continued: "And u know u can tell ur dad and as far as the kids are concerned the talk we were having last night needs 2 take place between u and her trystan u can tell and slow ur mind down thats whats making ur head hurt!"

Ballard's shift at Monarch ran from 7 a.m. to 3 p.m., but in his exhilaration over the idea of having a baby with Denise, he must have arrived early specifically to contact her, as his next text message to her arrived at 6:37 a.m. And while he expressed love for her and excitement over the baby, he also indicated a concern that Denise might turn her back on him.

"Get up and get the day going!! I love u denise!!" he wrote. "Plz dont ever again think of wanting 2 put someone in my place . . . U know the love u have 4 me well my love 4 us is 1,000,000 times stronger and the idea of u wanting a man buddy fuckin sux and makes my heart hurt plz just always keep in mind ur my wife and soulmate even when we r apart :) love u!!!"

Denise wrote back right away to reassure Ballard of her affection for him.

"Micael. I don't want sex with anyone but u baby," she wrote at 6:41 a.m. "Remember how I talked about dealin with fts and I made u cry. Baby remember this stuff when u get fucked up. I am ur wife. I want no one else."

Later in the morning, Denise wrote, "I wish u weere goin to seaside with me."

"I want 2 go with u 2 i am so sad about not being a bigger part of ur life it makes me so mad 2 think about sometimes," Ballard responded at 9:09 a.m. "And I do want 2 think about what u told me when u made me cry but it's a contradiction 4 u 2 tell me what u did and then ask me if id have any problems with u going out with other guys . . . Ya know?? I want 1 clear path that i know u r on."

It was not clear to the police reading the text messages whether Denise had explicitly asked Ballard for permission to see other men, or if Ballard was making accusations. Regardless of which was true, Denise had immediately responded to Ballard with yet another reassuring text message.

"I'm on my way baby," she wrote. "I love u and that's what u need rto know. I will make u proud."

"Thats good enough 4 me :) I love you muffin!" Ballard responded.

"Love babny," Denise wrote.

"Love me? Mrs. Ballard! Miss u. U think of me at all?" Ballard wrote.

"Of course," Denise replied. " I love u mr ballard as a wife loves her man."

Her response cheered Ballard, but his mind was still obviously on their previous conversation about her involvement with other men.

"Thats y u 99% of the time fucking rock!!!!" he wrote at 12:08 p.m. "Of course there is that 1% that i want u 2 work on. Then i wont be such a paranoid jealous mess either! :) I love the response u gave me though!!!! Thank u!"

As the day progressed, most of the text messages were from Ballard, with Denise responding less and less frequently.

"I Know u think deb wont approve if u contact me but id like 4 u 2 think about how much i miss u and y ur thinking about me is cuz u love me and miss me 2," he wrote at 1:37 p.m., referring to Denise's cousin Debbie.

Ballard sent another off two messages in a row at 2:45 p.m.

"Almost 3 pray u have a safe trip have fun just not 2 much fun :) I love u denise make 2day special 4 pooter," he wrote, referring to Denise's daughter's birthday trip the next day.

"Ur a good mom, and i hope u r carrying our baby soon!!" he added in his second message.

Denise responded to this one, writing, "Awww. Me to baby. Love u." But her attempts to reassure Ballard didn't totally end his obsession over Denise's involvement with other men.

"Out of all the men youve tried 2 replace me with u know i was meant 4 u and u 4 me . . . Dont u???" Ballard wrote at 2:49 p.m., followed by another message reading simply, "I love you!!!"

"I love u too. Yes I know :)" Denise wrote at 3:21 p.m.

It was their last text message for the day. Their texts didn't start up again until late the next day, and the tone wasn't quite so affectionate this time. Each had expected the other one to text earlier, but Denise had left her phone in her hotel room. When she hadn't heard from Ballard at nearly 3 p.m., she feared he had been sent back to jail.

"R u alive?????" she texted at 2:51. And then a minute later she sent: "Hello babe. I miss u!!!!!"

Ballard's response at 2:54 p.m. was far colder: "This is the first ive heard from u all day . . . Y?"

She fired off two messages in a row at 2:55 p.m.

"Sorry . . . I left my phone in the room." And then: "I thougjt u went back in."

Ballard responded with just one letter. "Y?"

"I didbt hear from u," Denise wrote back.

Ballard still was not pleased: "if u thought that y didnt this phone ring first thing this a.m.?"

With the end of Ballard's workday, the two were free to talk on the phone when he returned to the Allentown Community Corrections Center. It appeared the two cleared the air a bit during that phone conversation, because a text message Denise sent Ballard that night was much more conciliatory.

"I love u michael. I am$ laying in bed wishing I wouldn't have cut u short tonight when u said u wanted to marry me bfore u went back in," she wrote. "I don't really think ur goin back in. Why would they make u wait till July 1 baby. We will talk about all of this sometime over the weekend ok. Have a safe day today (when u get this message). Love and kisses. U r my superman :)"

"Thank u 4 the message . . . I love you denise," Ballard wrote back the next morning at 6:26 a.m. "Cant wait 2c u!! There is so much 2 talk about . . . All good. Anyway time 2 go 2 work . . . B safe coming home . . . I love you!!!!"

"Love u too," Denise wrote in response. "We may stay an extra night. Not sure though. I love u supermnan."

"OK let me know what u decide I miss u!" Ballard wrote at 8:42 a.m. Half an hour later, he: texted "Justice of the peace in Northampton 6102627422 love u!!!"

Ballard had sent the phone number for the nearest district judge's office as his way of telling her where they could quickly get married. But to the police reviewing the exchange of texts, that particular message was chilling for another reason: It was the same office where Ballard would be charged with his four homicides just a few days later.

Of course, there was no way Denise could have known that at the time, but even Ballard's suggestion about marriage seemed to cause some hesitation for her this time.

"Omg. Ur crazy michael," Denise wrote at 9:47 a.m. "We need to tal about the marriage thing ok?"

"u changing ur mind about marrying me?" Ballard wrote.

"I said we need to talk first that's all baby," Denise replied.

"Whew!!!!! U made me nervous!" Ballard wrote back, his relief followed again by suspicion of Denise cheating on him. "We should talk. Just so long as its not u wanting 2 b with other men while i'm in prison! Anyway. Hows the h20? I'm so bummed i'm here, and not with u. I love you."

The text messages went back and forth over the next two hours, but something seemed different this time. The two continued to assert their love for each other, but Ballard appeared unable to shake his concerns about Denise wanting to talk further about their future marriage.

"I love and miss u 2!" Ballard wrote. "What did u decide about stayimg? And what do u want 2 talk about about our marrying one another?"

"I'm goin back tonnight some time," she wrote back. Ballard could not help but notice that Denise ignored his second question altogether.

"OK, is something wrong?" he wrote at 2:36 p.m.

Getting no response, he tried again eight minutes later.

"Hello mcfly :)" Ballard said, a reference to a line in the film *Back to the Future*. "I asked if everything is alright??"

Again, no response. In fact, Ballard got no more text messages at all until after sending his last one before the workday ended.

"Almost time 2 go," he wrote at 2:51 p.m. "B careful on the roads coming home! I love you baby . . . :)"

"Ove u too," Denise responded. And although it was a positive ending to their conversation, anyone reading the texts could see that Denise had grown more and more distant, and Ballard had grown more and more suspicious.

It was the last text message the two would ever exchange.

In the early evening of July 6, almost two weeks after the murders, Ballard made a collect call to his father back home in Arkansas. Mickey Ballard was worried the authorities would use the recorded call against his son, but took the call anyway because he was desperate to hear from him.

"What in the world happened?" Mickey asked. "Can you tell me or not want to tell me?"

"I don't want to say it over the phone," Ballard responded.

"Well, that's probably a good idea," Mickey agreed. "Can you write me a letter?"

"Not yet," his son said. "They still got me under this big suicide watch thing." Then he asked if Mickey had been contacted by a lawyer Ballard had previously spoken with.

"Yeah, we talked a pretty good little while," Mickey said before quickly changing the subject back to his son's crimes.

"Well, I wished you could've stayed away from that old gal, and then what I said, it wouldn't have been too much longer, maybe you could've been outta there."

Mickey sighed, then spoke about the financial hardship it would cause for him to pay for a lawyer for Ballard.

"There ain't no way in hell I can ever do anything about this, you know," he said. "Everything I got couldn't make a drop in the bucket. I couldn't even sell it now anyway with the economy like it is," referring to his property.

"I'm not asking for none of that," Ballard said.

"I love ya, you know that, and I believe in ya and you don't have to worry about me standing behind ya," Mickey told his son. "If I can write to ya or send ya money I will, if they let me, and you can call me if you can and let me know what's going on."

Ballard had started crying. "Will you?" he asked, his voice cracking between tears.

"You're still with me. It's OK, you go ahead, you know I'm right with ya," Mickey said, trying to comfort his son.

"I did everything I was supposed to do," Ballard said, his sadness turning into anger.

"I know. I know you did, goddamn it," Mickey said, reinforcing his son.

"And she played me like a fiddle," Ballard said, fully angry now. "Played with my fucking heart."

"I tried to tell ya to stay away, boy," Mickey said, almost reprimanding him. "You know, I had a feeling about that woman and you shoulda just listened to your dad."

Mickey softened his tone, speaking pragmatically now: "When it comes up, you explain that to everybody about how you tried and about how the treatment centers and how they fucked you around, harassed you every damn second. You put all that effort into trying to do the best you could, so that should be taken into consideration."

Mickey's voice continued to grow calmer as he thought about his son's future trial.

"Of course, this may go up to trial pretty fast, but whatever the outcome is, it will take a long time," he said. "You know, if it's a bad one, you know it will take years if it rolls around to that. I'll get up there to see ya if I'm able, just don't know when and all that."

"They want to do all four of 'em, they want all four of 'em," Ballard said.

"What do you mean all four of 'em?" his father asked.

"They want all four death penalties," Ballard said.

"Well, hell, they can't kill ya but one time," Mickey said.

"They brought me back once—I died there," Ballard said. Ballard was convinced this was the truth, even though the doctors had told him otherwise. He strongly believed that he had died during the car crash and that the paramedics had brought him back to life.

"Well, how are you physically now?" his father asked.

"I'm a fucking wreck. My ribs are kicked in, part of my back is broke," Ballard responded. "Some of my fingers are broken."

"Have they given you any medicine?" Mickey asked.

"They're just now starting to give me stuff, the last couple days," Ballard said.

"Well tell 'em to give you something for the pain. You don't have to damn suffer. This ain't Guantanamo."

"They gave me Tylenol," Ballard said.

"Yeah, hell, that helps a hell of a lot," Mickey said, letting out a half laugh.

"Yeah, I'm not entitled to nothing," his son responded.

During a pause in the conversation, Ballard's mind drifted back to Denise.

"You got [to] know, Dad, of all people, you have to know how much I loved that woman," he said, becoming emotional again.

"Well, I know you did," Mickey said in a comforting tone. "I just wish ya took my advice, but I done all I could do and you can't change the past."

"Maybe if I get lucky and win the lottery," he said, his thoughts returning to his inability to pay for Ballard's defense. "The only way I could do anything would be to win the lottery, big damn chance of that, but I pray every night for ya and that something good will happen.

"All I know to tell you is I love ya and just keep hanging in there, OK?"

"Yeah," his son responded glumly.

"But if it comes down to it, you know, when it's all over and done with, you ask the Lord to forgive ya and you'll be with your mommy and gramma and grandpa and I'll be there along."

Mickey continued rambling: "We'll be together in the afterlife, you just ask the Lord to forgive ya. Oh, hell, there's been people who kill people before and they didn't go to hell for it. Hell, they pin medals on soldiers' chests for it, so I guess in some instances it's not even considered bad. Of course, it's not considered good—it's a shame, it shouldn't [have] happened, but I know that you can't change the past."

Mickey said he shouldn't talk much longer because the collect call would be getting expensive.

"But I had to hear ya, had to hear your voice," Ballard told his father.

"Well, I'm glad you called, I wanted to hear yours, too. I've been worried to damn death," he told his son.

"I want you to know that I ain't turned my back on ya," Mickey said, his tone turning serious. "I know you tried to do right and I know how the system just horse-assed you around like this and drove you to it, and given the opportunity, I'll damn sure let 'em know about it. It may not do any good, but given the opportunity I will."

There was a short silence between father and son.

"You know what really just fucking kills me is when all this happened, I actually did die from the wounds that I've got," Ballard said again. "I died on the side of the road, and they brought me back. Some point in time between there and the hospital. Now I don't even feel like me again. Like I don't know who the fuck I am. Like I woke up to somebody that I don't even know."

"Yeah, well you tell them that," Mickey replied. "When they talk to you, just try to be strong and pray to the Lord and stuff. I want you to know that I'll be here and I'll help ya if I can in my prayers. Like I say, money wise, I couldn't do nothing, social security check and you know, the only way is if I was to get luck and win the lottery or something like that, then I'd definitely go rocking their damn boat," Mickey said, dreaming again.

His son was again in tears. "This couldn't have been the hand that I was dealt in life, Daddy. Couldn't have been . . ."

"Yeah, I don't know . . . hell," Mickey said, unsure of what to say to his son. "Some people, it just seems like the way it goes. Hell just seems to follow ya, you know? I don't know what to tell ya son, other than . . ."

Ballard cut his father off and asked, "Am I that bad?"

"Huh?"

"Was I that bad?"

"No, no, you just, maybe you made some of the wrong choices along the way. And I guess a whole lot of people do things bad that they shouldn't, you know. Just, it's not that you're bad, you know, not basically. I mean, I know you tried to do good."

"Everybody betrayed me, though," Ballard said, his despair giving way to anger again. "Everybody looked in my face and swore to me, 'Yes, we love you, yes, we're behind you, yes, we're one-hundred percent.'"

His voice growing furious, he nearly shouted. "And I turn to find out, you know, there's pictures of them on their cell phone, of them fucking other guys."

"Well, hey, you didn't need her then, did ya?" Mickey responded.

That did little to calm his son, who was now having trouble focusing his thoughts. "How am I supposed to . . . I'm told one thing and I live my life accordingly . . ."

"Yeah, I know," Mickey said.

"You know, I get up, and I go to work and I pay my bills and I do what I'm supposed to do."

"Yeah, I know," Mickey said again.

"And I expect a woman that's going to be good, true to the heart that I've given her," Ballard said, his anger growing and growing.

"Well, you tell, you tell the lawyers," Mickey suggested. "You tell the lawyers this and everybody else. Let all that shit be known, OK?"

"All I've got left is my story," Ballard said flatly.

"Well, you go ahead and you tell it, by God, tell every damn bit of it when the time comes."

"I begged him. I begged him to get the phone and the computer and all that other shit," Ballard said, speaking about his lawyer. He believed if his attorney would just find those photos of Denise with other men and show them in court, everyone would understand why he did what he did. "I begged him to, like, subpoena and get her phone, and you know, like her home computer."

"Yeah, well, you tell him to confiscate that stuff and check out your stories and stuff, by God," Mickey encouraged his son.

"That's what I did," he responded.

"Well, son, I can't keep running this bill up," Mickey said.

Before Ballard let his father go, he passed on to him the name and number of his public defender, a Bethlehem-based lawyer named Michael Corriere. Mickey said he would call him in the morning.

"I want to call him just as much as I possibly can," Ballard told his father. "The cell phone and the computer and the laptop, they're crucial for me to show that this fucking drove me nuts."

"Yeah, well did he tell you he should be taking care of all of that, confiscating all that stuff?" Mickey asked.

"I hope," Ballard said. "I hope, because if we lose it, or if somebody else gets it, or if a family member takes it and destroys it, then we're done."

"Well, son, keep your spirits up and I'll talk to you later," Mickey said. "And like I say, I'll do all I can, I'll stand behind ya."

"I know," Ballard said.

"I believe in ya, and I know you got a dirty deal. But we'll do what we can."

"I love you," Ballard told his father.

"I told you, too, boy," Mickey said. "I got your card. It was a beautiful card, Father's Day card and everything."

"Thank you," Ballard said. "I love you."

"I love you, too, boy. Just hang in there, don't give up."

"I won't."

"Well, we don't quit," Mickey said. "We'll keep, we fight 'til the last damn breath and we'll . . ."

"And then they'll friggin' bring me back to do it again," his son interrupted.

"Well, we'll keep fightin'. We'll keep fightin' 'em," Mickey asserted.

"All right, Dad," Ballard said quietly.

"All right. I love you. Try to get a good night's sleep."

CHAPTER 14

Having spent more than fifteen years behind bars, Ballard didn't find life at Northampton County Prison all that different from what he was accustomed to. But to the prison staff, Ballard was an abnormality. The 819-bed facility had certainly hosted its fair share of accused murderers before—even mass murderers—but Ballard's history of five vicious attacks frightened county prison officials.

Upon Ballard's entry into the jail, Warden Todd Buskirk issued a memorandum outlining the jail's special policy for dealing with the five-time murderer. Ballard was to be escorted by four guards—one a supervisor—every time he left his cell. A five-guard detail would be necessary when he took showers.

His cell would be searched during each of the day's three shifts. All guards would now carry Tasers for their own protection, something they had never done before.

Ballard didn't see what the big fuss was about. Other accused murderers were allowed to roam the halls without guard escorts. One fellow inmate who had shot two people had even climbed a razor-wire-topped fence in an attempt to break out of the prison while Ballard was there. So why should Ballard be viewed as the prison's biggest threat?

"They were just fucking terrified of me," he later said. "Like I'm fucking public enemy number one."

Everything Ballard drew was confiscated, including a picture of a female prison employee, who was later questioned about why Ballard would be drawing pictures of her. In a separate incident, while trying to choose a book from the jail's book cart, someone recommended to him *The Devil in the White City,* the true story of serial killer H. H. Holmes, who lured victims to their deaths around the time of the 1893 World's Fair. The mere fact that Ballard possessed the book later drew red flags among the prison staff.

Authorities seemed to take a particular interest in Ballard's reading material. The state police seized two other books that he had left behind at the Allentown Community Corrections Center on June 26: *Angel of Darkness,* a true crime book about one of the world's most prolific serial killers, Randy Kraft, who was suspected of murdering 67 people, and *The 48 Laws of Power,* a Machiavellian how-to book on obtaining power. The laws include "never put too much trust in friends" and "crush your enemy totally." Both would later be among the items submitted as evidence for his trial.

Ironically, Ballard was able to use the prison's fear of him to obtain additional benefits from the staff. As incentive for staying in line, Ballard was allowed two visits a week instead of the usual one. He also eventually persuaded prison officials to forgo one of his three daily cell searches—the one during the 10 p.m. to 6 a.m. shift—so he could get a full night's sleep.

But despite the Tasers and additional restrictions, Northampton County Prison officials continued to feel

uneasy housing Ballard. County officials requested that
he instead be housed in one of the state prisons. In mid-
July, he was transferred to State Correctional Institution–
Frackville, a state prison about seventy miles northwest
in Schuylkill County, and he was only transported back
to Northampton County Prison when he had to make a
court appearance.

The first of those appearances was Ballard's preliminary hearing, where the prosecution had to prove that
enough evidence existed against him for the case to proceed to trial. While normally held in the small satellite of-
fices of locally elected district judges, the hearings for
more serious crimes were sometimes held at the Northampton County Courthouse in Easton, where sheriff's deputies could provide better security. This was the case for
Ballard's preliminary hearing, which was held August 31
in the county courthouse before District Judge Diane
Marakovits.

The hearing marked the first time Ballard had been
presented to the public since his arrest. The only image
most people had ever seen of him was his widely publi-
cized mug shot, taken while he was still in the hospital.
Dressed in a hospital gown, Ballard appeared severely disoriented in the photograph, as if drugged. His eyes seemed
to convey no sense of feeling or emotion whatsoever.

During his preliminary hearing, Ballard appeared far
less dazed as he was led into court, his hands and feet
shackled, wearing a prison-issued orange jumpsuit, sport-
ing short-buzzed hair and a small mustache. But much of
his stoicism remained. Testimony about the grisly details
of his crime caused multiple gasps and cries from friends
and family on the prosecution side of the courtroom, but
Ballard remained entirely emotionless throughout the
ninety-minute hearing.

Troopers Raymond Judge and Mark Rowlands testified about their discoveries of the crime scenes, and Judge spoke of Ballard's confessions during his stay at the hospital. Emily Germani, Denise's fourteen-year-old neighbor, testified about spotting a blood-soaked Ballard on the front porch of Denise's home the day of the killings, trying to "shake [the blood] off himself," according to the *Morning Call*.

But perhaps the most noteworthy testimony came from Northampton County Coroner Zachary Lysek, who painstakingly detailed the number of times Ballard had stabbed each of the four victims. Lysek particularly highlighted the many defensive wounds found on Steven Zernhelt.

"This individual, it appeared, fought very vigorously to defend himself and protect himself from being stabbed," Lysek said, according to the *Morning Call*.

The bloody details—as well as the shocking revelation that Ballard had written DENISE IS A WHORE in blood on the wall—would lead news reports the next day. As expected, Judge Marakovits determined that enough evidence indeed existed for the case to go to trial. Ballard's two publicly appointed defense attorneys, Michael Corriere and James Connell, declined to speak to the press afterward, as did the family members of the victims who attended.

By now the newspapers had reported that Ballard had lived with Denise for a period of time, and many suspected that the two had dated and that the murders may have resulted from their relationship. But Ballard's motive for the quadruple homicide did not officially become publicly known until September 7, when John Morganelli submitted court paperwork laying out that the stabbings were a premeditated effort by Ballard to get revenge against Denise for her infidelity.

That court paperwork was Morganelli's filing to seek the death penalty against Ballard.

"[Steven] Zernhelt was in the wrong place at the wrong time, interrupted Mr. Ballard's revenge killing and was most likely killed because he was a witness to what Ballard had done," Morganelli told the *Express-Times*.

To win a death penalty verdict, prosecutors had to prove only one of the state's eighteen aggravating circumstances that permit a death penalty finding. Examples of such circumstances include the killing of a police officer, and the torture of a victim. In Ballard's case, two aggravating circumstances applied: There were multiple victims, and Ballard had already been convicted of a murder in the past.

And while Morganelli had a long-standing practice of taking the death penalty off the table for murderers if they accepted life imprisonment without parole and agreed to waive their appellate rights, he made it clear to Ballard's attorneys that no such offer would be made in this case.

"You're not getting an offer of life," he told them. "Even if the guy would come in tomorrow and say I'll plead guilty to murder one, four counts, give me life. I would say no to that."

Michael Ballard's case was not the first to draw questions about the effectiveness of Pennsylvania's parole system.

One of the state's most notorious cases was that of Reginald McFadden, who was convicted in 1969 of the murder of his sixty-year-old neighbor, Sonia Rosenbaum. McFadden, then sixteen, broke into her Philadelphia home along with three accomplices to rob the place. After Rosenbaum revealed the location of her valuables, they tied her up, pushed a desk onto her legs so she couldn't move, and stuffed a washcloth into her mouth. The elderly woman suffocated as a result.

McFadden was sentenced to life in prison without the possibility of parole. However, after serving twenty-two

Police found a bloody and disoriented Michael Ballard after he crashed his car alongside Route 329 in rural East Allen Township, PA. *(Courtesy: WFMZ-TV)*

Officers investigate the home of Denise Merhi in Northampton, PA, where four bodies were discovered. *(Courtesy: Chris Post / East Coast News Photo – www. NewsPhoto.tv)*

Pennsylvania State Police troopers investigate the back of Denise Merhi's property. *(Courtesy: Chris Post / East Coast News Photo – www. NewsPhoto.tv)*

Denise Merhi (*right*) embracing her best friend, Marilyn Rivera. *(Courtesy: Marilyn Rivera)*

Marilyn Rivera and Denise Merhi. Marilyn received phone calls from Michael Ballard the day of the murder. *(Courtesy: Marilyn Rivera)*

Steven Zernhelt, Marilyn's neighbor, who was killed after hearing the other victims' screams and running next door to help them. *(Courtesy: WFMZ-TV)*

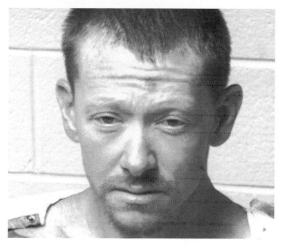

Michael Ballard, who told a doctor he cut himself while he was "stabbing some dude." *(Courtesy: Northampton County Prison)*

More than 300 people attended the funeral of Denise Merhi, Dennis Marsh and Alvin Marsh Jr. at a church in Whitehall Township.
(Courtesy: WFMZ-TV)

Raymond Judge, the 15-year veteran Pennsylvania State Police investigator who handled the Michael Ballard case.
(Photo by the authors)

A young Michael Ballard after his arrest in 1991 for the murder of Donald Richard. *(Courtesy: WFMZ-TV)*

Michael Ballard, then 18, was sentenced to 15 to 30 years in prison for the 1991 homicide. *(Courtesy: WFMZ-TV)*

Michael Ballard was paroled after his minimum sentence and released in 2006. *(Courtesy: WFMZ-TV)*

The Allentown Community Corrections Center, a halfway house for state prison inmates, where Michael Ballard stayed during his parole. *(Photo by the authors)*

Geraldine Dorwart, the mother of Denise Merhi, speaking with reporters outside a court hearing. *(Photo by Tim Wynkoop)*

Northampton County District Attorney John Morganelli, who prosecuted Michael Ballard.
(Courtesy: John Morganelli)

James Connell, one of the two defense attorneys who defended Michael Ballard, along with Michael Corriere.
(Photo by the authors)

Steven Zernhelt's daughter Jaime (*left*) leaves the Northampton County Courthouse along with other family members, including her mother Janet.
(Photo by Tim Wynkoop)

A 2011 prison mugshot of Michael Ballard after he pleaded guilty to four counts of first-degree murder and was sentenced to death by a jury.
(Courtesy: Pennsylvania Department of Corrections)

years of his sentence, the Pennsylvania Board of Probation and Parole considered the possibility of early release
for McFadden. During its monthly meeting on August 27,
1992, McFadden was one of twelve cases the board considered in a two-and-a-half-hour period, according to the
New York Times.

They spent only a few minutes reviewing the case and
never met with McFadden personally, according to the
newspaper. Instead, they took into consideration his good
psychological evaluations, favorable behavioral reports
from prison, and a letter from his sentencing judge claiming he believed McFadden had been rehabilitated.

The board voted four to one to commute McFadden's
sentence, but under the condition that he spend two years
of supervised release in a halfway house to ensure a safe,
gradual transition back into society.

But everything went wrong.

The commutation papers went before Governor Robert
P. Casey Sr. to be signed, where they lingered on his desk
for a year and a half before he finally signed them. State
officials later said that the documents from the Pennsylvania Board of Probation and Parole were so poorly written that parole officials mistakenly believed McFadden
was to be freed immediately, with no halfway house or
any other supervision whatsoever.

McFadden walked free on July 7, 1994, and moved to
New York. Over the next three months, he was accused of
killing two people, raping a third, and possibly killing
other unknown victims.

On October 6, McFadden was arrested for the September 21 kidnapping and rape of a fifty-five-year-old woman
in South Nyack, Rockland County. After abducting the
woman while she was taking out her garbage, McFadden
raped her three times, beat and tortured her for five hours,
and stole all her cash and jewelry. The woman survived.

Shortly after McFadden was arrested, authorities realized he was responsible for even more heinous crimes.

He eventually admitted to raping, strangling, and stabbing to death a seventy-eight-year-old woman named Margaret Kierer while she was walking home from a railroad station in Floral Park, Long Island. McFadden later told a Nassau County judge that he'd stumbled upon Kierer after he had gotten lost after leaving the same train station.

"I got kind of frustrated and my history of when I get frustrated is I develop, I guess, rage, anger," he told the judge, according to the *New York Times*. "Something came out of the shadows [and] I just went off. Just when I realized it was this little old woman, it was too late. To be quite frank with you, she wasn't responding, it was just like I was throwing a rag doll around and I wasn't getting any response from her."

McFadden was convicted of the Kierer murder, the South Nyack rape, and the murder of Robert Silk, a forty-two-year-old computer programmer from Long Island. Police claimed Silk was murdered after he pulled over to help McFadden when his car broke down. Silk's decomposing body was found in Rockland County six months after he went missing in September. Authorities alleged that McFadden may have been responsible for at least two other murders, though he was never charged with them.

McFadden's release, and the apparent errors the Pennsylvania parole system made in the process, drew harsh criticism for the state. When asked whether McFadden would serve his full sentence in New York before possibly being extradited back to Pennsylvania for violating his parole there, Rockland County District Attorney Michael Bongiorno told the Associated Press, "We don't want him going back to Pennsylvania. They didn't do the job the first time. We'll see it's done correctly this time." The scandal torpedoed the 1994 gubernatorial campaign for Democratic Lieutenant Governor Mark Singel, who served on the parole board and cast one of the votes for McFadden's release.

Another famous case that crossed state lines was that of Robert "Mudman" Simon, a member of Warlocks motorcycle club. Originally from Upper Darby, Pennsylvania, Simon had been in and out of prison since age eight. He was already serving time for an armed robbery in 1982 when he was charged and convicted for the 1974 murder of his former girlfriend, Beth Smith Dusenberg.

Simon had wanted the nineteen-year-old Dusenberg to have sex with other members of the motorcycle gang. When she refused, Simon pulled a gun and shot her in the head, then dumped the body into a sixty-foot strip mine. It would be eight years before her remains were discovered, allowing police to trace the murder back to Simon.

When confronted with evidence of the crime, Simon spoke of having sex with the corpse and told police he wanted to decorate his cell with evidence photos of her mummified remains, according to the Associated Press.

Simon was sentenced to ten to twenty years in prison for second-degree murder. His time in prison did not stop his violent tendencies: He fatally stabbed another inmate during a fight, but was acquitted after it was determined to be self-defense.

Although Simon became eligible for parole after ten years, he was rejected for release three times before he was finally paroled in 1995 and released to Williamstown in Gloucester County, New Jersey. The parole board was impressed by Simon's promises to leave the Warlocks behind and stop using illegal drugs, and they determined that, despite the stabbing incident, he had been a model prisoner.

The parole decision came despite objections by members of Dusenberg's family, as well Carbon County Judge John Lavelle, who first sentenced Simon.

"I consider him one of the most dangerous individuals who ever appeared before me," Lavelle wrote in a letter to the parole board. "This man has no respect for human life and I believe that it would be only a matter of time before he would kill again."

As it turned out, the judge was correct.

On May 6, 1995, just eleven weeks after Simon was released, he was the passenger in a car that was pulled over in Gloucester County's Franklin Township. It was 10:25 p.m., about half an hour from the end of the police sergeant Ippolito "Lee" Gonzalez's shift. Gonzalez approached the car and asked for the license and paperwork from the driver, also a member of the Warlocks.

As Gonzalez reviewed the papers, Simon fired a shot into the forty-year-old sergeant's neck. After the officer went down, Simon fired a second shot into his head. Gonzalez died a few hours later. Simon and the driver were apprehended later that night after a brief car chase.

The incident led to the expected cries of outrage against the parole system and, as with McFadden, finger-pointing across state lines. The killing resulted in hearings by the Senate Judiciary Committee as well as an investigation into the parole system by Pennsylvania Governor Tom Ridge. But Pennsylvania officials also blamed New Jersey for not properly monitoring Simon and ensuring that he followed a parole condition that he no longer associate with the Warlocks.

For her part, New Jersey Governor Christie Whitman claimed Pennsylvania did not properly alert them about the conditions of Simon's release. She questioned why Simon was released in the first place, let alone released to Williamstown, which, as it turns out, was a hotbed of Warlock activity.

Simon pleaded guilty to murder in 1997 and was sentenced to death. Although he was scheduled to die by lethal injection, the matter was rendered moot in 1999, when Simon was brutally beaten to death by another inmate at the state prison in Trenton, New Jersey.

Another case slightly closer to home for the people of Northampton County was that of Raymond Edward Webb, who went on to commit attempted murder in neighboring Bucks County after getting released on parole.

Webb had previously been convicted of a home invasion murder in August 1971. He and two other people had traveled from Pennsylvania all the way to Jefferson County, Missouri, to rob a couple whom Webb's two accomplices claimed owed them money. Police discovered their bodies three days later: Thirty-year-old William "Tex" Redden was found dead in a garage covered with a green tarp, and his twenty-two-year-old wife Joyce was found in a bedroom with a butcher knife in her back and two bullet wounds to her head.

Webb fled back to Pennsylvania after the murder, where a Bucks County couple picked him up hitchhiking along Route 309 near Montgomeryville on August 17. Once inside the car, Webb drew a .45-caliber revolver—one of three guns he was carrying at the time—and forced the couple to drive him to a rural area of Bucks County.

Along the way, he bound the man's hands with rope, forced him out of the car, then continued on with the nineteen-year-old woman, whom he eventually raped at gunpoint.

Webb was eventually arrested and convicted for both

crimes. He was sentenced to two concurrent life sentences in Missouri for the murders and a separate five-to-fifteen-year sentence in Pennsylvania for the rape. At the time, first-degree murderers were eligible for parole in Missouri. That changed in 1986 when the state parole law was revised, but Webb was grandfathered in under the old law and still legally eligible for parole.

Citing his good behavior in prison, the Missouri parole board shortened Webb's sentence to seventeen years in 1988, which made him immediately eligible for parole. He was extradited back to Pennsylvania to serve his time for the rape conviction, but was released after six years, less than half the maximum sentence. Officials told the *Philadelphia Inquirer* that Missouri's decision to release him early likely played a role in Pennsylvania's decision to do the same.

Webb went free in 1994 and, for a time, seemed like he might have indeed been rehabilitated. Over the next nine years of parole he had only one minor infraction, when his urine tested positive for alcohol, which he was forbidden from drinking. Otherwise, parole officials told the *Inquirer,* Webb met regularly with his parole officer, registered as a sex offender as required by law, attended Alcoholics Anonymous meetings, and stayed out of trouble.

But that all changed on August 18, 2003, when the fifty-nine-year-old Webb met a woman at a Quakertown bar. After she was injured in a bar fight with another woman, Webb offered to accompany her to the hospital. Along the way, he directed her to a deserted stretch of road, forced her to pull over, dragged her into a field, and attacked her. Wrapping a leather belt around her neck, he threatened to kill the woman as he raped her.

"I'm going to drown you in the swamp if you scream," Webb told the woman, according to police reports.

The woman was saved after a passing newspaper carrier saw them and informed two state troopers, who found Webb on top of the woman and arrested him. In 2004, Webb was sentenced to life without parole for kidnapping charges. To ensure that he never left prison again, Bucks County Judge David Heckler also gave him an additional forty to eighty years for attempted murder, rape, and aggravated assault.

But for his rape victim, the damage had already been done. Although she survived the attack, she was emotionally traumatized. Not long after the attack, she attempted suicide by leaping into the Schuylkill River from the Green Lane Bridge in Philadelphia. She also purchased a handgun for protection, which one night she pointed at three men after they tried to drive her home from a bar, concerned that she'd drunk too much. Terrified, she had believed those men wanted to rape her, too.

"If he doesn't get the death penalty, I want him to have to go to church in prison, so he can tell God he's sorry for what he did," the woman said at Webb's sentencing hearing, according to press accounts.

She then turned directly to Webb and shouted: "But you're still going to burn in hell! Because that's what you deserve!"

While most of these incidents had long since fallen from the public's memory by the time of Michael Ballard's alleged murders, a more recent case had drawn such an intense public uproar and so many calls for reform that it led to a temporary halt for parole releases in the state altogether.

Daniel Giddings was charged with his first violent crime at age ten, when he was convicted of beating and robbing a mentally disabled man in his home neighborhood in North Philadelphia. Over the next seven years, Giddings fathered three kids, was shot twice, and had been arrested several times for assault, some of which involved a handgun. He freely spoke to authorities about selling drugs on the corner, raising pit bulls, and gambling throughout his youth.

In August 1998, during a botched carjacking, the seventeen-year-old Giddings shot a man in both kneecaps and robbed him of a hundred dollars. After he was convicted of robbery and aggravated assault in a Philadelphia court, Assistant District Attorney Joseph Coolican sought the maximum sentence of twenty-two-and-a-half to forty-five years, which would have kept Giddings in prison until at least 2020.

"From what I have seen in the four years of prosecuting violent crime, I have never seen an individual who presents a higher risk of reoffending," Coolican told the court, according to the *Philadelphia Inquirer*.

Instead, Judge Lynn B. Hamlin sentenced Giddings to the mandatory minimum of six to twelve years.

During his time in prison, Giddings was written up for thirteen misconduct violations between 2001 and 2006, according to the *Inquirer*. Those allegations included fighting, stealing from cellmates, and, on one occasion, passing a sharpened metal object to another inmate. He spent 498 days in solitary confinement within the prison as a result of these infractions, and served four years longer than his minimum sentence due to the pattern of misbehavior.

Although Giddings was twice denied parole before getting released, he appeared to show more promising signs of possible rehabilitation by the latter part of his prison term. He underwent extensive counseling; took courses in anger management, violence prevention, and victim awareness; and had no reported misconducts after 2006. Giddings was paroled on August 18, 2008, having served ten years of his twelve-year sentence, and was sent to live in a halfway house in Philadelphia starting August 25.

Just under a month later, on September 23, Giddings was a passenger in a car that was pulled over by Philadelphia Highway Patrol Sergeant Patrick McDonald. It was 1:20 p.m. in North Philadelphia. As McDonald spoke with the other occupants of the vehicle, Giddings slipped out of the car and fled, prompting McDonald to run after him. After a three-block chase, McDonald caught up with Giddings and the two got into a physical struggle.

In the midst of the fight, Giddings pulled out an illegally owned .45-caliber Taurus semiautomatic pistol and fired.

The round entered McDonald's shoulder and struck his heart. As he fell, the officer drew his service revolver and fired one shot, but his injury was too severe and he missed. Giddings stood over the fallen McDonald, prone and helpless on the ground, and shot him several more times, killing him execution-style.

Giddings himself was killed shortly thereafter. After stealing a bicycle and attempting to ride away, he encountered two other police officers and exchanged gunfire with them. One of the officers, Richard Bowes, was non-fatally shot in the hip, but Bowes returned fired and gunned Giddings down. The shooting was later determined by prosecutors to be justified.

The death of Sergeant Patrick McDonald at the hands of a recent parolee provoked wide feelings of anger not only in Philadelphia, but also across the state of Pennsylvania and beyond. And with Giddings dead and many in the public looking for someone to blame, much of the criticism was levied against the Pennsylvania Board of Probation and Parole.

Members of the media and the public began to ask how it was Giddings had been paroled at all, given his long history of violent crime. Philadelphia District Attorney Lynne Abraham placed the blame squarely on Judge Lynn

Hamlin for imposing a minimum sentence against the suggestion of prosecutors. Philadelphia Mayor Michael Nutter and Police Commissioner Charles H. Ramsey publicly expressed outrage that Giddings had been freed and demanded an inquiry into the parole board.

Among the strongest voices against the parole board was that of Larry McDonald, Sergeant McDonald's father. He spoke publicly in favor of a bill proposed by Pennsylvania state representative Brendan Boyle calling to lengthen sentences and eliminate parole for second- and third-time violent offenders.

"I will not insult the heroic actions of my son Patrick and Ricky Bowes by accepting validations of procedures that dearly need to be completely revised," McDonald said of the parole system during testimony before the Pennsylvania House of Representatives, according to court documents. "Experts may disagree, but I believe that some people can not be rehabilitated, and therefore, should never be released."

CHAPTER 15

Several hearings for Michael Ballard were held over the next couple of months. On September 18, Ballard appeared in the courtroom of Northampton County Judge Edward Smith, where the attorneys discussed tentative trial dates and their time line for filing motions in the case. A county judge since 2001, the forty-nine-year-old Smith had a kind face and a bright smile and always spoke very politely in a gentle tone of voice. But his appearance and manners were sometimes deceiving to the accused criminals who came before him. A former US Navy man and military judge, Smith had earned a reputation as a tough but fair jurist during his nine years on the bench, despite his friendly demeanor.

Wearing an orange prison jumpsuit and shackles on his wrists, Ballard was taken before Judge Smith again on October 15, this time for a discovery hearing and a discussion about future scheduling for the case. District Attorney John Morganelli was still waiting on some information, including autopsy reports and state police lab results, but he had a trove of other evidence, which he had already shared with Ballard's defense attorneys.

Among the evidence discussed before Judge Smith were cell phone records, a transcript of Ballard's prison phone call with his father, and surveillance videos of the various places Ballard had been before the murder, including the Allentown pawnshop where he bought the knife. Morganelli also briefly discussed the allegations that Ballard had sexually assaulted a girl during his previous parole. That information had never been publicly released and, despite the fact that charges had never been filed, it led many of the newspaper stories and television news broadcasts the next day.

Nobody from the victims' families was in attendance, so the benches were relatively empty behind Ballard. He sat calm and unmoving throughout the hearing, showing no sign of emotion. However, once the proceedings were finished and the guards began to escort him out of the courtroom, he glanced at a woman sitting in the second row behind him and winked. She smiled and blushed, delighted at the bit of attention he had afforded her.

Her name was Danielle Kaufman, and she had been exchanging letters with Ballard for the past several weeks.

The twenty-seven-year-old was a lifelong resident of the Northampton area. A 2000 graduate of Northampton Area High School, she was now living in a mobile home in Allen Township, about two miles north of the borough itself. Now married, with a three-year-old daughter named Katrina, Danielle had been writing to prisoners since she was fifteen years old.

It all started when she did an Internet search about finding pen pals and read about people who regularly wrote to inmates in prison. Her parents hated the idea. In fact, when she was a sophomore in high school, her father once brought her to Lehigh County Prison, hoping the gritty reality of prison life would scare her straight. Instead, the plan backfired, leaving her even more fascinated with the people she was writing to.

By her estimate, Danielle had written to hundreds of inmates over the years. Not everybody wrote back, and with many the correspondence was brief. Some were too busy working on their defense cases to write, and others only wanted money, after which Danielle would quickly end all contact.

She decided who to write to based solely on mug shot photos she found online. The men had to have a "friendly face," according to Danielle, and she was usually drawn to those with blue eyes. She didn't pay attention to the crimes they committed, and in some cases didn't even bother to look up their criminal history before writing.

"If it doesn't affect me, I don't care," she said.

It was a kind of emotional detachment Danielle experienced in other aspects of her life. For example, she was working at the gift shop of the Lehigh Valley International Airport near Allentown during the terrorist attacks of September 11, 2011. Everybody around her was crying, running to get out of the airport, scrambling to call family and friends. But Danielle didn't understand what the commotion was about.

"I mean, I was excited because I got to go home early, but I didn't care," she said. "Everybody was crying and stuff, but if it doesn't affect me personally, I don't care."

Danielle had written to several murderers over the years. There was Leif Bothne, who was convicted of killing a teenager in Austin, Texas. And Richard Borjerski, the Florida man who decapitated his landlord and hid the body in the trunk of a car. There was Stanley Elms, who raped and murdered a Kansas woman. And Glen Burton Ake, who shot a Baptist minister and his wife to death in their Oklahoma home. Danielle stopped writing to Ake after a short while because, she said, "he creeped me out."

She had even sent Christmas cards to famous serial killers Dennis Rader—also known as the BTK Killer, which stood for "Bind, Torture, Kill"—and David Berkowitz, better known as the Son of Sam. Neither responded to her.

"It takes a degree of insanity to do what I do, I guess, but I'll be the first to admit I'm nuts," Danielle said with a laugh in a later interview. "I love these fellas, and I really believe that no matter how damaged a human being might be, if they have someone standing behind them, they can change for the better. I'll never stop reaching out to the fellas, and I really don't give a shit if society ever understands why or not."

Despite having written to several killers, Danielle claimed she was not drawn specifically to murderers.

"I can't help that the faces I seem to like to talk to are murderers or something," she said. "It's not like I dig the murderers. I would've talked to Michael even if he was in for tax fraud or whatever."

Danielle claimed it was also a common misconception that she was in love with the people she wrote to. Although married for five years to the father of her child, Danielle claimed the marriage was more of a friendship than a romantic relationship. Nevertheless, she insisted her letters to inmates were strictly platonic. While she admitted to harboring some feelings toward Stanley Elms, Danielle said that she never developed any major romantic feelings for any of the men she wrote to.

Except for Michael Ballard.

Ballard was different from the beginning. Danielle wrote to inmates all around the country—she usually went with the states that had the best prison websites and easiest access to mug shot photos—but Ballard was the first man she had written to from her local area. In fact, she wanted to write to him immediately after seeing news footage on television right after the Northampton murders. The broadcasts showed videos and photos of Ballard both from the present day and from his first murder charges in 1991, and Danielle was immediately captivated by his bright blue eyes and the intense look of hatred in his face.

"Whoa," she said while watching the news.

"Is that a friend of yours?" her father asked in response.

"No," she said. "But he might be soon."

Danielle didn't write to Ballard until late July, about a month after his arrest, because it took time before his information was registered in the prison system. To her excitement, he wrote back right away. Ballard claimed he had received lots of letters in prison, but most of them were from religious people who wanted to "save" him. He did not bother writing back to most of them, but told Danielle he had picked her letters out from all the others to respond to. It made her feel extremely special.

Soon they were exchanging letters on a regular basis, and she was accepting collect calls from him from prison. By September, she was visiting him at the Northampton County Prison whenever he was brought up from SCI–Frackville for a hearing. They spoke in a room much like the type you would expect from a police television drama: all-concrete walls and floors, and rows of booths where visitors could speak to inmates through Plexiglas walls via tiny holes at mouth level. She came to see him about a dozen times, as often as she was allowed.

Some questioned how Danielle's husband must have felt about the close relationship she appeared to be developing with this accused killer, but according to Danielle his biggest concern was the amount of gas money she was spending during her visits. After all, gas prices had reached around $3.59 a gallon.

Danielle found Ballard to be funny, charming, and very intelligent. Contrary to the public opinion that was rapidly forming about him, she never believed him to be crazy or evil. He was, however, very intense, which was something Danielle found appealing. His moods shifted drastically and very quickly. One moment he'd be calm and mellow, the next angry and animated. The same would occur in his letters, and Danielle quickly found his handwriting would actually differ depending on his mood.

If it turned out he had multiple personalities, Danielle thought, *I wouldn't be surprised.*

Ballard also struck Danielle as a very creative person. He loved to read and would talk to her about books he particularly enjoyed. Some of Ballard's letters to Danielle were written in a secret code that she had to decipher, a game that she reveled in. They came to call their shared language "Rascality," named after a word used in *The Devil in the White City,* which Ballard read in prison.

Ballard also drew pictures for Danielle, and she found him to be a fairly decent artist. Some of the pictures were light and serene, sketches of wildlife or nature settings. Others were much darker. One time he sent her a drawing of a horrifying man with no mouth and his eyes cut out. Danielle thought it was just a sketch, and didn't believe the man was supposed to secretly represent Ballard or anybody in particular.

"I thought that one was pretty cool," she said.

The Northampton County Prison guards started to refer to Danielle as Ballard's girlfriend. It was a classification she felt perfectly comfortable with. In fact, Ballard even referred to Danielle as his wife in some of his letters, just as he used to with Denise Merhi.

Ballard and Danielle talked freely about harboring feelings of love for each other, and at times some of their letters turned sexual as well. She affectionately referred to Ballard as "Blue," and he wanted Danielle to get MI-CHAEL tattooed on her forearm.

Danielle even let her three-year-old daughter speak to Ballard during some of their phone calls. Katrina spoke of Michael often, and would tell him she missed him when they spoke on the phone. Ballard referred to her as "little Kat."

But one thing that became very clear to Danielle during their correspondence was that Ballard had indeed committed the murders.

Ballard spoke candidly and in vivid detail about his crimes from early on in their relationship. At one point, he told Danielle that he had killed Denise to save her from herself. According to Danielle, Ballard told her that Denise was becoming so promiscuous, he had to kill her to ensure she would get into heaven before she got worse.

In one letter, he told a story about killing four spiders that had wandered into his cell within the prison. He explained that one of the spiders wouldn't die right away, so he had to kill it twice. It was obvious to Danielle that he was really speaking about his four murder victims.

Once, he went so far as to draw a picture of the crime scene. It was a sketch of Ballard standing in Denise's kitchen, standing over her dead body, a bloody knife clutched in his hand. He had even pricked his finger and let his blood drops fall over the drawing of Denise to illustrate all the blood after he stabbed her. The drawing was so vivid in its details that he had sketched a candle that sat in the kitchen windowsill the day of the murder, complete with the label of exactly what scent it was.

It wasn't a fit of rage, Danielle realized of his murders. *He remembers. He knew what he was doing.*

In some letters, Ballard appeared to feel remorse for his crimes. Or, at the very least, he felt shame about the kind of person he had become. In one such letter, he wrote that his father had a monster for a son, Danielle said, and that while Ballard kept killing people, the person he really wanted to kill was himself. Like the crime scene drawing, this letter also included dried stains of Ballard's own blood.

Some letters were even more disturbing. In one, Ballard told Danielle that he had indeed molested the girl that he had been accused of sexually assaulting during his first time out on parole.

Ballard even went so far as to claim in his letters that not only had he molested the girl, but the girl's mother was aware of it and was present when it happened. Danielle did not believe this was the truth. In one of Ballard's drawings to Danielle, he depicted himself sitting alongside the girl, who was naked, except that in his drawing she was depicted as a teenager much older than she had been in real life.

In a different drawing, Ballard drew an image of Denise Merhi's daughter, Annikah, with the words "Should have raped her" written in their Rascality code in the corner of the page, Danielle said.

These drawings, and Ballard's claims that he had sexually assaulted a little girl, were the only ones from their many letters that disturbed Danielle, since she had a daughter of her own. But they did nothing to dampen her romantic feelings for him; nor did they make her consider ending their correspondence. The two went on to exchange hundreds of letters.

"There's just something about these men that compels me to want to talk to them and hear what they have to say about things. I love it," Danielle later said of her tendency to write to inmates.

"You ask any 'normal' person what color the sky is, and they won't even look at it. They'll just reply, 'Blue,'" she said. "You go up to one of these men, these beautiful deviations of society, and ask them what color the sky is and they'll stop and look up at it and end up telling you a story of something they dream of or something they've done in the past. They'll never actually tell you what color the sky is but that part doesn't matter.

"With Michael, the sky was never blue," she added. "I loved that about him. I still do."

CHAPTER 16

Ballard appeared in court again on December 10 for a pre-trial hearing to discuss evidence that was being gathered for his upcoming trial. At this stage, it was unclear how many of the items provided during the discovery process would actually be used during the trial, as some of them had little value as evidence.

For example, among the items was a photograph of Ballard and Denise Merhi at a Halloween party, where Denise dressed up as a witch, and Ballard dressed as Jason, the famous killer from the *Friday the 13th* movies. While the pictures were unsettling in hindsight—with Ballard wearing a hockey mask and a clutching a plastic machete—they weren't evidence fit for a trial.

Michael Corriere indicated during the hearing that he would be seeking MRIs and CAT scans for Ballard so they could determine whether an insanity defense was appropriate. The trial was tentatively scheduled for March, but Corriere asked for more time to allow for the medical tests. District Attorney John Morganelli tried to argue against this, claiming the trial was nearly ready to commence and should occur as soon as possible. Judge Smith asked Ballard what he thought, since the defendant was the one who had a constitutional right to a speedy trial.

"I agree with my attorney on this. There's still a lot of things that need to be taken care of," Ballard said. Judge Smith agreed to postpone the trial to May 9.

Corriere also argued for a change of venue, meaning he wanted the trial to be held outside of Northampton County. The four murders had gotten a tremendous amount of press attention, the attorney explained, and he felt it would be nearly impossible to find a jury of twelve men or women who could act neutrally or impartially. At the very least, Corriere said, if a change of venue was not approved he would request that a jury be brought in from outside the county for the trial in Easton. Judge Smith said he would take the requests under consideration and rule at a later date.

The next month, Danielle Kaufman was approaching her home after having helped shovel the snow at her father's house. It was a freezing, snowy day as she approached her front door, and she was surprised to find a business card placed under the door knocker. Picking it up, she was startled to find the Pennsylvania State Police logo on it. Trooper Raymond Judge had stopped by and, having missed her, scribbled a note asking her to give him a call.

Without hesitation, Danielle opened the door, entered her house, and called the trooper, making arrangements to meet with him at a later date.

Danielle still harbored strong feelings for Ballard, of course, and was still writing, calling, and visiting him on a regular basis. She felt terrible speaking to the police behind his back—although she would let him know she was doing so at her earliest opportunity—but she never for a second considered not cooperating with them.

I don't mess with cops, she thought. If they wanted her help, she would give it.

Ballard, less than thrilled upon learning that she would be meeting with Judge, later wrote to Danielle and insisted she didn't have to tell the police anything she didn't want to, but she planned to go ahead with the meeting anyway. She loved Ballard, but she still felt cooperating with the authorities was the right thing to do.

By now, Danielle had gotten a bit of publicity from the newspapers herself. At one of Ballard's October court hearings, a man had approached her during a recess and started asking how she knew Ballard. She happily responded at first, but after he identified himself as *Morning Call* reporter Riley Yates, she was a bit nervous. After all, Ballard had warned her that the reporters were having a "feeding frenzy" on his case and that she should avoid them at all costs.

Nevertheless, she spoke to Yates, and felt the story he later wrote about her quoted her fairly and accurately.

"He's a real sweet guy," she had said of Ballard in that story. "He's got a great sense of humor. I don't think he's a vicious guy."

The story had gotten Danielle a lot of attention, though it wasn't exactly positive attention. Her own mother hated the fact that she was visiting this accused killer, though Danielle and her mother had never really gotten along in the past anyway.

Danielle's mother was sick with cancer, and whenever Danielle spoke of visiting Ballard, she would say, "I can't believe you would spend time with that murderer instead of me." She never referred to him as Michael, as Danielle asked her to, because she claimed, "He doesn't deserve a name."

In fact, the backlash from her name appearing in the newspaper was so bad that shortly after the story ran,

Danielle received a piece of hate mail. Although it had no return address, she was quite sure it had been sent by a member of Denise Merhi's family. For one thing, the author had referred to Denise by her maiden name—Denise Marsh—and they also referred to Ballard as "Red," seemingly a reference to his red hair.

"I'm a sweet guy from the Marsh/Zernhelts and you're a sweet woman of the devil Ballard," the letter read. "What if Red had done this to your family, you dumb jerk?" It was signed, "A human," a clear indication that the author felt Ballard and Danielle were less than human.

But the letter didn't bother Danielle. In fact, she saved it, keeping it in the same place she kept all her letters from Ballard.

If this guy sleeps better at night yelling at me, then that's good, she thought.

The newspaper story mentioning Danielle surely did not escape the attention of the Pennsylvania State Police, but what really prompted Trooper Judge to reach out to Danielle was a specific letter Ballard had written to her, in which he threatened to harm one of the guards at the Northampton County Prison.

Some time before December, Danielle had tried to visit Ballard at the prison, but she wasn't able to see him because he had already been taken back to SCI–Frackville. While she was sitting there at the prison, disappointed, one of the uniformed men from the prison sat down next to her.

His name, he explained, was Lieutenant Conrad Lamont. He was very friendly to Danielle, with no trace of judgment in his voice, but explained that he had seen her several times during her visits to Ballard and felt she should reconsider her relationship with him.

"You have a nice heart, but it's misguided, and you

should put it to better use," he said. "You shouldn't waste your time with this guy."

Danielle later mentioned what Lieutenant Lamont had said to her in one of her letters to Ballard, and he was furious. In his response letter to Danielle, Ballard said he was going to find Lamont and make him pay for what he had said. He vowed to head-butt him so hard in the face that he would break his nose, and said he would "kick him so hard between the legs that his nuts will pop like grapes."

In January, when Ballard was due to be brought back to Northampton County Prison for another hearing, Danielle visited the prison with her daughter Katrina in tow and asked to speak with Lamont. "I just wanted to tell you to stay away from Michael when he comes back, so nobody gets hurt," she said.

At first, Danielle didn't want to talk about why she feared for Lamont's safety, but when he gently pressed she admitted what Ballard had said and handed over a copy of the letter to show him. Lamont thanked her for her concern but assured her there was nothing to worry about, and that the prison staff was well trained to handle altercations from prisoners if Ballard was to try anything. However, he explained, he would have to keep the letter and turn it over to his superiors so they could write up an official report.

That letter eventually made its way into the hands of Trooper Judge, which prompted him to arrange a meeting with Danielle. She visited him at the state police barracks in Bethlehem a few days later, carrying a large three-ring binder in her arms. As they sat down to talk, Danielle was visibly nervous and obviously conflicted, but Judge gently assured her that the best thing for her to do would be to help the police with their investigation.

"I have two orphans here," Judge said. "I have a widow. We have to do the right thing."

Danielle nodded. *That makes sense,* she thought. *After all, Michael did do it.*

She started to tell the trooper about her correspondence with Ballard. By now, she said, they had exchanged hundreds of letters, which she had compiled in the three-ring binder that she called her Michael Book.

She opened the book for Judge, revealing a collection of Ballard's handwritten musings to her, all of which she kept preserved in clear plastic sheets, arranged in chronological order. His drawings of himself standing at the crime scene, holding a knife over Denise's bloody corpse. His sketch of Denise's daughter, alongside the words "should have raped her." His letters suggesting that he had sexually assaulted a minor while on parole. They were all there.

The value these letters could hold for Judge's investigation was immediately obvious to the trooper. In fact, it was even possible for the police to pursue separate charges against Ballard based on his admissions that he molested the girl, since there would be no statute of limitations in that case, although that hardly seemed necessary at the moment with Ballard safely imprisoned without bail.

"You're not leaving with that," Judge said, pointing at the binder. "We'll either get a warrant, or you can just give it up, but you're not leaving with that."

Judge kept his tone polite and not unfriendly—like Lamont, he was not at all judgmental or condescending toward Danielle—but she could also tell from his voice how serious he was. She agreed to give over her Michael Book voluntarily.

CHAPTER 17

As part of their efforts to determine whether Michael Ballard was competent to stand trial, Michael Corriere and James Connell arranged for a wide range of psychiatrists and experts to meet with their client. Ballard had already spoken to several over the past few months.

There was James Garbarino, a developmental psychologist and an expert on family and adolescent development issues. And Gerald Cooke, a forensic psychologist and consultant at numerous Pennsylvania state prisons. There was Robert Sadoff, director of the University of Pennsylvania's Center for Studies in Social-Legal Psychiatry. And Frank Dattilio, a clinical psychologist and expert in cognitive behavior therapy.

But of them all, Ballard spent the most time with Susan Rushing, who met with him for more than seven hours over the course of two February visits at Northampton County Prison. An attractive woman with fair skin and dark blond hair running just past her shoulders, Rushing was a psychiatrist, an attorney, and a professor at the University of Pennsylvania's Perelman School of Medicine. She earned her bachelor of science at the Massachusetts

Institute of Technology, her MD at Yale School of Medicine, and her JD at Stanford Law School.

For both visits, Rushing was led into a private room, where Ballard sat across from her enclosed behind a metal mesh and glass divider. Two or three armed corrections officers were present at any given time throughout the interviews, and Rushing noted that they appeared particularly vigilant, even considering the fact that they were guarding an accused multiple murderer. Ballard himself, however, appeared well groomed and neat, despite his orange prison jumpsuit and the shackles around his wrists.

Ballard started off one of the interviews apologizing for smelling like macaroni and cheese. But despite that unusual icebreaker, Rushing noted that the man seemed otherwise calm and demonstrated good behavioral control. His speech was fluent and articulate; he made excellent eye contract and spoke at a regular rate and normal volume; his thoughts appeared linear and logical.

Rushing began asking some of the standard questions, and Ballard responded in kind. No, he was not experiencing any auditory or visual hallucinations. No, he had harbored no suicidal or homicidal intent during his time in prison. No, he had not experienced any psychotic symptoms. Rushing wrote it all down in her notebook, and Ballard watched her pen closely as she jotted down the notes.

As the questions continued, Rushing noted that Ballard seemed absolutely determined to be found sane. He appeared pleased with himself when he answered the questions to what he believed was Rushing's satisfaction, at one point commenting, "I'm not giving you much to work with, am I, Doc?"

But Ballard appeared more unsettled when Rushing began to discuss his upcoming MRI and PET scans, scheduled for later that month. Like a sick patient afraid to visit the hospital for fear of finding something wrong with him, Ballard dreaded the neuropsychological testing because, if they uncovered any brain damage, he wouldn't be able to deny it to himself anymore.

"Those results would be final," Ballard said. "Indisputable."

But for all of Ballard's assurances that he was completely sane and normal, Rushing noted several symptoms of psychosis, anxiety, and features of mania during their interviews. Despite his clean appearance and coherent speech, Ballard seemed overly attuned in his observation of the guards and any other activity around him. He jumped at the sound of loud noises and constantly checked the positions of the corrections officers behind him. Rushing believed this was a sign of hypervigilance, an enhanced state of sensory sensitivity where the mind and body stay instinctively and intensely alert to potential threats, whether real or imagined.

As with the police, Ballard had no hesitation in admitting to Rushing that he had killed his four victims—five, if you include Donald Richard. He spoke about the murders with a kind of cold detachment, as matter-of-factly as if he were talking about any given memory from his past. He also spoke of Debbie Hawkey, Denise's cousin who came into the house the day of the murders, and freely admitted he would have killed her, too, if he had caught her.

"I butchered four people with a knife, there's no getting around it," Ballard later said.

Nevertheless, Ballard steadfastly refused to discuss specific details about what happened during the specific moments of the killings. Words were exchanged between him and Denise, as well as some of the others, he admitted, but Ballard would not discuss them.

"It doesn't do any good to put those actions and that

gore out there," Ballard later said. "It's not going to change the end result."

Just as Ballard flatly confessed to his murders, he was equally forthcoming with the fact that he no longer really cared whether he lived or died. His only concern in that regard was for his father, Mickey Ballard. If he was executed, his father would feel lost, Ballard explained. That was his only concern, and he mentioned several times during his conversation with Rushing how badly he felt about disappointing his father.

Ballard admitted to a long history of depression and anxiety throughout his life, as well as a tendency to engage in impulsive behaviors, but he insisted he was no longer feeling sad. In fact, Ballard claimed he was generally devoid of feelings altogether anymore. He could still take pleasure in some activities like reading, writing, or drawing, the last of which he had never bothered with until his recent incarceration. But for much of his life Ballard said he found it difficult to feel sad or cry, and he had no ability to cry for Denise Merhi.

Ballard also admitted he didn't sleep much: only two or three hours a day, and sometimes not for several days in a row. But he insisted this was normal for him, and that he'd never gotten more than a few hours of sleep at a time since his childhood. Ballard denied having nightmares or feelings of re-experiencing the murders, although that directly contradicted what prison psychiatrists had reported about him.

It also conflicted with a letter Ballard had written to Louise Luck, his mitigation specialist, just a few months earlier in December. In that letter, Ballard described a nightmare in which he was "blowing away" people with a shotgun at Denise's house and "laughing hysterically knowing the number of people I've killed that day" before waking up.

"It was just a horrible, horrible dream; so goddamn vivid," Ballard said, visibly unnerved.

Ballard claimed it wasn't Denise or the others he was killing in that dream, but rather one of Denise's neighbors. It wasn't Steven Zernhelt, either, he said, but someone else who lived on that block that he didn't know very well. Ballard insisted he didn't have nightmares about his actual murder victims, although with prodding he admitted their deaths were in his waking thoughts every single day.

"All I do in life is destroy things," he said.

Ballard told Rushing he had low levels of energy and concentration, which again conflicted with prison records indicating he had been active and even hyper during his incarceration. Ballard acknowledged that his thoughts moved very quickly and that it felt like his mind was always racing, and sometimes he wrote furiously for hours on end just to get those thoughts out of his head.

Despite all of this, Ballard unwaveringly insisted he was not suicidal. Rushing brought up his attempted suicide from September 2008, after his arrest for parole violations, when Ballard was discovered in his cell with a bedsheet tied around his neck. Ballard shrugged it off, insisting that hadn't been a suicide attempt at all.

But, he admitted, he probably had been suicidal in the past, and had always tended to live his life a bit recklessly. Growing up, Ballard said, he would take unnecessary risks and do stunts by himself just for the thrill of it, like the time he drove an all-terrain vehicle off a bluff and fell fifty feet before landing in the water below. He used to ride his motorcycle and slide underneath eighteen-wheel tractor-trailers just to see if he could do it.

Ballard never feared getting hurt, he told Rushing. In fact, most of his life, he felt invincible.

Returning to the day of the murders, Ballard claimed

he felt justified in killing Denise because she had betrayed him. While his voice had been calm and relatively quiet for most of the interview, Rushing noticed that Ballard's speech was becoming louder and more emotionally charged once they reached this topic.

Ballard angrily recalled what he claimed were repeated adulteries Denise had committed, both when he was back in prison for his parole violation and afterward.

"She was sneaking out in the middle of the night and driving two hours to Philadelphia to give it to some stranger, sometimes literally on the side of the road!" Ballard later said. "This was my house. This was my wife. This was my family she brought this filth into."

Ballard said that after speaking with Marilyn Rivera on the phone and learning that Denise had gone to a baseball game with another man, he removed the wedding ring Denise had given him and instead started wearing it on a chain around his neck.

Ballard claimed he deliberately wore that chain when he went to Denise's house to kill her. He also purposely wore the Superman T-shirt that authorities later discovered neatly folded on a chair next to Dennis Marsh's body. Ballard explained that he was wearing it when he stabbed Denise to death, a sickly ironic reminder that she had nicknamed him Superman in reference to his sexual prowess.

Rushing noted that even now, with Denise gone, Ballard's anger over her cheating had not appeared to diminish. Ballard told Rushing that after he had killed Denise, he grabbed what he believed was her purse—it had in fact belonged to Debbie Hawkey, who'd left it behind after fleeing the house—and tried to check the calls on her cell phone to confirm her infidelity.

Rushing asked what purpose confirming such a thing would serve, considering that Ballard had already killed

Denise and members of her family. Ballard didn't seem to comprehend the question, and could offer no explanation.

What about the others he'd killed that day? Rushing asked. Dennis and Alvin Marsh, and Steven Zernhelt? Even if Denise did betray Ballard, weren't those three men innocent?

But Ballard didn't see it that way. He did regret that Steve ever came to the house that day, but Ballard insisted the man shouldn't have interfered with what was going on, and that he'd still be alive if he hadn't.

"It's like the quote on the first US penny," Ballard said. " 'Mind your business.' "

Indeed, the first design for the penny, designed by Benjamin Franklin and known as the Fugio cent, did include the inscription MIND YOUR BUSINESS along the bottom. But Ballard seemed to mistake the quotation as a message from the Founding Fathers that you should, in present-day parlance, "Mind your own business." Rushing knew that in fact, most historians believe it to be a more literal reference to business as an enterprise. She did not bother to correct Ballard's misinterpretation.

But while Ballard considered Steve Zernhelt an innocent bystander, he refused to regard Dennis and Alvin Marsh as blameless victims. Instead, Rushing noted, he exhibited a similar rage toward them as he had toward Denise, although on a lesser scale. This was especially the case for Denise's father, Dennis, whom Ballard said lived in Denise's basement and did nothing, living basically a worthless existence. While Ballard at times wished Alvin hadn't been home the day of the murders, he felt no such wish for Dennis.

Ballard claimed both men were father figures in Denise's life, so he believed they were responsible for controlling her behavior, and that therefore, in a way, they allowed her to cheat on him.

"They are the males of the house; they allowed her to do that shit," Ballard said. "They had ultimate control over Denise's actions. They were culpable for her sins."

Ballard insisted he wasn't alone in feeling this way, and that anybody would agree with his views about an adult woman's subordination to the men in her household. His voice rising louder and louder by the second, he asserted, "You are still your father's daughter. He still has an influence in your life."

Rushing countered this, arguing that most American women in their thirties lead lives fully independent from their fathers. But Ballard shook his head and remained adamant, claiming that his views on the sexes were governed by God's law. He paraphrased the story of Adam and Eve from the Bible, pointing out that man was created first and that woman was created from man to be his helper.

"Religion guides the male–female interaction," he said. "The male is the head of the household."

Ballard repeatedly returned to the issue of God and religion throughout the interview, so much so that Rushing believed him to be suffering from delusions of grandeur. She found it fascinating, especially because his thought content and cognitive abilities were quite remarkable for someone suffering such delusions. His upcoming neurological tests would shed more light on this, but Rushing was well aware that these kind of delusions can arise from traumatic brain injuries.

Ballard insisted he had been killed at the scene of the car accident shortly after his murders, and had later been brought back to life by the emergency responders. Rushing knew this was a claim Ballard had repeated before, and she also knew it to be false: Medical records clearly dispelled it. But Ballard insisted he had been saved because a higher power had some reason for wanting him to remain alive.

"I should have died, but God didn't want me to," he said.

Rushing also knew that many of Ballard's manic writings from prison were filled with religious quotes and explorations of the mythical and magical, as were some of his letters to Danielle Kaufman. The disturbing sketch Ballard drew of himself holding a knife over Denise's body at the crime scene—the one smeared with his own blood—was titled "The Dead Are Free from Sin."

In another of his letters to Danielle, Ballard wrote that he killed Denise because he had to "cleanse that house (our home) of the sin she brought into it." He claimed he "spoke to each victim in turn and gave them respite and absolution" before their deaths, although Ballard would later deny having done this.

He wrote that he had judged Denise to "God's standards" and that "God's laws are infallible and eternal." Now, Ballard wrote, Denise was awaiting God's final judgment because, in murdering her, he had released her from sin.

He also quoted Romans 7:6, "But now, by dying to what once bound us, we have been released from the law so that we serve in the new way of the Spirit, and not in the old way of the written code."

While staying at Northampton County Prison, Ballard also drew a picture depicting himself as Jesus hanging on the cross at the Crucifixion. At the base of the cross were five skulls, one for each of his victims, as well as the caption "Golgotha," the hill upon which Christ was crucified to ensure sinners would reunite with God in heaven.

"Mr. Ballard believes that he has been chosen to act as a warrior of God," Rushing wrote in her notes. "He believes that God has allowed him to purge the world of sin; so that the sinner's souls can face God's judgment in heaven. He also seems to think that he has the Christ-like power to bring a wayward sinner back into God's graces."

Beyond his religious delusions, Rushing found it interesting that Ballard continued to refer to Denise's house as "my home," and to her kids as "my family," even now after everything that had transpired. He spoke in detail about conversations and interactions with Denise, Dennis, and Alvin from three years ago as if they were recent events that somehow still held relevance.

Ballard said he believed that, upon dating Denise in 2006, he replaced Dennis as the leading male of the household. But he did not seem to understand that his two-year incarceration for a parole violation would have changed his role in that relationship; nor did he comprehend that Denise's family members, like Dennis and Alvin, might have perceived him differently than they had before his return to prison.

"This was my house," Ballard insisted. "My house."

CHAPTER 18

In late January, John Morganelli received a phone call from Jim Martin, the district attorney in Lehigh County, which was Northampton County's neighbor to the west. Martin had some interesting news, to say the least: He had received letters from two different inmates serving time in SCI–Frackville with Michael Ballard.

In those letters, they claimed that Ballard had described in detail for them not only the Northampton murders, but also other murders he had committed that authorities were not even aware of.

The letters came from Wilfredo Riddick and John Patrick McClellan. Riddick had previously served time for drug-related charges and was now back in prison on a technical parole violation. McClellan had been convicted in 2004 of theft and impersonating a public servant. Authorities said he claimed to be an undercover police officer and demanded the wallets of his victims, then pocketed their cash.

Morganelli was a bit skeptical of the letters—after all, they had been written by two convicted felons—but felt they were worth investigating, especially because the letters were consistent with each other. There was also the fact that both men wrote that Ballard killed Dennis and Alvin Marsh because they were witnesses to Denise's murder, and killing a witness was another aggravating factor for the death penalty that Morganelli could pursue.

The district attorney immediately reached out to Raymond Judge, who on January 25 took the ninety-minute drive over to SCI–Frackville, along with Corporal Paul Romanic, to meet with the inmates.

Located in the low-populated Ryan Township, SCI–Frackville was one of two state prisons located in Schuylkill County. The other, SCI–Mahanoy, was a medium-security facility located just a few miles northwest. As a maximum-security prison, the thirty-five-acre Frackville was smaller than Mahanoy and much more imposing. A population of about eleven hundred inmates lived behind its uninviting walls of thick concrete brick of a drab tan color.

Upon arrival, Judge and Romanic spoke with Timothy Clark, a captain with the prison's security office who was personally familiar with Ballard, Riddick, and McClellan. Clark told Judge that Riddick was probably a credible source and might be honest with them, but McClellan was another story. The forty-one-year-old man was a delusional paranoid schizophrenic. Nothing he would say could be trusted as accurate, and he would probably report anything the troopers told him immediately back to Ballard anyway.

Judge took the captain's advice and decided against interviewing McClellan, but Wilfredo "Dro" Riddick was brought into the prison's security office to speak with him. The thirty-four-year-old light-skinned black man had short-cropped black hair and stood about five feet ten inches tall. He had two teardrop tattoos under his right eye—a symbol often associated with the number of victims killed by a gang member—as well as tattoos of Japanese symbols on both sides of his neck.

Riddick told Judge that he had been placed in Frackville's restricted housing unit along with Ballard from November 16 until December 30. During that time, the two inmates communicated via a method called flicking, where they used toothpaste to attach notes on the ends of threads taken from their jumpsuits and literally flicked the letters from cell to cell.

Riddick didn't have physical copies of the notes Ballard supposedly sent him, which Judge knew would hurt the credibility of his claims in the eyes of a jury.

Riddick claimed that Ballard told him he had killed his girlfriend, and that she had "deserved it." Ballard also told him, according to Riddick, that he killed Denise's father and his grandfather—"the old man"—because he didn't want to leave any witnesses, and then he subsequently killed Steve Zernhelt because he was "being nosy" when he ran into the house to investigate their screams.

Riddick also said Ballard repeatedly spoke ill of Denise, and that he claimed she would still be alive if she had just been honest with him. Ballard also claimed that he deliberately stabbed himself in the leg and severed his artery in an attempt to commit suicide after the attack, Riddick said. Ballard had told Riddick that he had, in fact, died shortly after the murders, but was brought back to life by the doctors.

Riddick said that Ballard bragged about the people he killed, claiming he was "good at what he does." According to Riddick, he claimed responsibility for seven total killings: the four in Northampton, Donald Richard back in 1991, and two other people in the Poconos—a mountainous region in northeastern Pennsylvania—when he was paroled for the first time. The police didn't even know about those two, Ballard had allegedly boasted to Riddick.

Ballard told Riddick that he always used a knife when he killed somebody, not a gun, because, "I'm not a pussy," the inmate told Judge. He said that Ballard also claimed he liked to write on the walls using his victims' blood. In some of his letters, Riddick said, Ballard wrote that he "hates faggots" and "kills faggots and rats."

Once the interview was finished, Judge took a written statement from Riddick, and then retrieved all of Ballard's medical, psychological, and psychiatric records from the prison. Upon his return to Northampton County, he immediately shared all of Riddick's statements with Morganelli.

It would be several weeks before Ballard himself learned of Riddick's and McClellan's letters. According to him, there was no truth to them whatsoever.

McClellan—or "delusional boy," as Ballard called him—was considered something of a joke around SCI–Frackville. Many of the inmates enjoyed mocking him, including Ballard. McClellan was always mumbling incoherently to himself and constantly believed others were out to get him.

After he was placed in the prison's restricted housing unit wing near Ballard's cell, McClellan became convinced that the guards were giving Ballard information about him. He started writing letters to people all over the state that Ballard was going to tell all his "motorcycle buddies" on the outside to burn down McClellan's house and rape his mother. McClellan even started asking the other inmates to sign an affidavit—or a "fadvit," as McClellan misspelled it—claiming Ballard had repeatedly threatened him.

According to Ballard those claims were all nonsense,

but he still used them as an opportunity to give McClellan a little hell. After one of the other inmates slipped McClellan's affidavit to Ballard, he mailed it to Danielle Kaufman and had asked her to make copies of it for him. He also asked her to look up any information on McClellan that he could use against him.

"Dig up whatever you can get on this piece of shit and mail it to me," Ballard said.

Danielle dutifully responded to Ballard with information she had found on the Internet, as well as half a dozen copies of the affidavit. On each copy, Ballard placed a stamp he had gotten from his father of Mother Teresa—because McClellan's mother was named Teresa—and started passing the copies around to the other inmates so they could laugh at McClellan.

That stunt got him into a bit of trouble with the prison staff, who, unbeknownst to Ballard, were monitoring his mail in response to McClellan's claims that Ballard wanted to kill him. Ballard was called down to Captain Clark's office to discuss the matter, but according to Ballard, Clark took one look at McClellan's "fadvit" and released Ballard, realizing there was nothing credible in McClellan's rantings.

McClellan committed suicide just over a year later, hanging himself inside his cell at SCI–Cresson near Altoona, Pennsylvania, in May 2011. Ballard had little sympathy for the man. *Just deserts, in my opinion,* he thought.

As far as Wilfredo Riddick was concerned, Ballard knew of him, but claimed he had never even seen his face, let alone confided details about the murders to him.

"I wouldn't know him from a can of paint," Ballard later said.

Ballard first came to know "Dro" after he was placed into the restricted housing unit for a prison misconduct. Riddick was placed a few cells down from Ballard and directly across from McClellan. Riddick and McClellan exchanged letters from time to time, which Ballard believed explained why McClellan wrote nearly the same exact letter to Lehigh County District Attorney Jim Martin as Riddick did.

According to Ballard, Riddick learned some details about Ballard's crimes because he received some of Ballard's mail by mistake. After reading it, Riddick—unaware that Ballard himself was only a few cells away—started talking to the other inmates about how Ballard had killed a bunch of people while he was living in a halfway house on parole, and how that was going to make it harder for anybody else to get parole.

What Riddick did not know was that, besides McClellan, most of the other inmates in the restricted housing unit were friendly with Ballard, and one of them let him know what Riddick was saying. After Ballard called down to Riddick's cell and demanded his mail, Riddick came back at him with what Ballard described as "tough guy shit."

"Fine then, sign up for yard block," Ballard responded. "We'll trade on the fence."

"Trading on the fence" was, according to Ballard, a common way that inmates inside SCI–Frackville fought with each other. Two inmates looking to settle a score would request the same period of outdoor time in the prison yard. Once they got there, the inmates would go up to one of the chain-link fences and "trade shots," according to Ballard.

One would place his face against the fence, and the other would punch him as hard as he could. Then the other would place his face on the fence and allow the other inmate to punch him. This continued until one of them couldn't take it anymore and gave up, and the other was declared the winner.

According to Ballard, after he suggested trading on the fence, Riddick quickly reversed course and wanted to be friends with Ballard. The two didn't talk much and Ballard claimed that, contrary to Riddick's statements, they never exchanged letters with each other. But it didn't surprise Ballard to learn that Riddick claimed they had.

Riddick was only sent back in prison for a technical parole violation, but according to Ballard he was nervous because he had another parole board meeting coming up. Riddick knew they wouldn't grant him parole if he was in the restricted housing unit for a prison misconduct.

So, Ballard claimed, Riddick was looking to inform on anybody he could to get back into the general population. Ballard heard Riddick claim that he knew which prisoners were dealing drugs, and which prisoners were having affairs with prison staff, and that he'd give them all up. Now, it appeared, he was trying to give up Ballard as well.

According to Ballard, all of Riddick's knowledge of Ballard's crimes came from the mail he read, and that the rest of it—including the two supposed murders in the Poconos—was pulled out of thin air.

"He just pulled that out of his ass like a Cracker Jack toy," Ballard later said.

John Morganelli didn't place much credence in Riddick's statements, either, but for different reasons. First of all, the word of a convicted criminal wasn't worth much, especially when he didn't actually have Ballard's supposed letters to back up what he was saying. But even if Riddick's statements were true, and Ballard did say those things to him, that didn't necessarily mean anything significant as far as Morganelli was concerned.

To the district attorney it sounded like a lot of tough talk, just posturing on Ballard's part to make himself more intimidating to the other inmates. It wasn't very uncommon behavior among inmates. In fact, the district attorney surmised, perhaps the greatest value these comments had for Ballard was that they made pursuing an insanity defense that much more difficult because, if he'd really made those statements to Riddick, it proved he'd had an intent to kill. The claims about killing witnesses also gave Morganelli another aggravating factor with which to seek the death penalty, so he filed notice in court that he planned to seek that factor.

But when it came to the claim that Ballard killed two people in the Poconos, Morganelli doubted there was any truth to it based on the simple fact that Ballard wouldn't have had time to commit these murders.

Ballard was only out of prison for just over a year after his first parole, and for almost that entire time he was under the supervision of the Allentown Community Corrections Center. Ballard's movements were pretty well accounted for during that time, and there was no evidence he had gone anywhere near the Poconos.

Nevertheless, Morganelli shared the information with authorities in Monroe County and elsewhere in the Poconos. They were investigated, according to the district attorney, but no evidence of any such murders was ever uncovered.

CHAPTER 19

Ballard appeared in court again on February 8 for a hearing on the various pre-trial motions that had been raised by the attorneys on both sides. Danielle Kaufman came out to support him, sitting in her usual spot: Ballard told her to always sit on the aisle of the second row on the right side, right behind Ballard, so he could easily turn his head and see her whenever he wanted.

Danielle found the six-hour hearing to be a pretty grueling process. She had always enjoyed watching court scenes on television, but after attending a few in real life, she was quickly learning they weren't as interesting as they are on *Law & Order*. But still, she loved any opportunity she got to see Ballard.

"It's hard for me to even tell you how happy you can make me in such a short amount of time," Danielle once wrote in a letter describing how she felt watching Ballard get brought into the courtroom for a hearing. "Seeing you, for me, is like getting a B_{12} injection. Instant euphoria."

Various pieces of evidence were discussed during the hearing, including Ballard's alleged statements to Wilfredo Riddick, his various confessions at St. Luke's Hospital, and whether his 1991 murder of Donald Richard should be admitted into evidence. Raymond Judge testified about Ballard's purchase of a Ruko military-style knife, upon which the blood of both Ballard and Steven Zernhelt was found.

Little new information came out of the hearing except that Judge Smith formally responded to the prosecution's request that the trial be held in another county. The trial would remain in Northampton County, Smith ruled, but a jury would be brought in from outside to hear the case. It would later be decided that the jury would come from Wayne County, a rural area located about two hours north of the Easton courthouse.

Ballard, as usual, remained calm for most of the proceedings, except when John Morganelli mentioned a copy of a letter Ballard had written from prison that might be submitted into evidence. Upon hearing this, Ballard jolted upright, a look of shock on his face, and he turned around to face the audience.

"Fuck!" Ballard said. "Fuck!"

Danielle cringed. Ballard wasn't looking at her when he muttered those expletives, and it was far from clear whether he was directing them at her or somebody else. But she felt horrible nevertheless. She remained desperately conflicted about cooperating with the police, feeling as if she had betrayed Michael, and she knew the statements Ballard had made in her letters were damaging to his case.

Throughout the hearing, Danielle had tried to get Ballard's attention, leaning over and smiling at him whenever he looked her way. But every time she tried, the guards surrounding him would step in her way and shake their heads. She was growing more and more upset as the hearing went on.

It breaks my heart that we live in a world where smiling

at someone warrants you be treated like a terrorist, she thought.

During a recess, after Ballard was temporarily escorted from the courtroom, one of Ballard's lawyers—she couldn't remember this one's name—approached her.

"Do me a favor and move back a row and sit all the way over next to the wall," he said. "Michael wants to see you but he can't because of the cops."

Danielle frowned. She did not like the idea of being put in a corner, out of the way. *But,* she thought, *Michael wants me to sit there, so here I will sit.*

A few moments later, Ballard was brought back into the courtroom and seated back at the defense table. Before the proceedings started again, he turned his head to the left and glanced at the audience behind him. Watching him intently, Danielle was horrified: She believed that Ballard was looking for her where she had been sitting earlier.

Her jaw dropped in shock. Danielle was absolutely convinced that Ballard hadn't asked her to move at all, and that his attorney had simply wanted her out of the way, perhaps so the guards would no longer be bothered by her. Her mind was racing. She was so upset she could no longer even hear what was going on or see anyone else around her besides Ballard. Everything else looked like a blur.

Micahel probably thinks I left him! she thought. *DO something, Danielle!*

She started focusing her eyes intently on the back of Ballard's head. As she later described it, she was "hoping that I stumble on the right channel" and that Ballard would somehow sense her and turn to look back at her. He didn't. Tears started to form in her eyes, and she started pinching her hand and arm, a nervous habit she falls back on whenever she starts feeling like she might lose control of herself.

At one point, Ballard started to turn his head slightly. *He's going to look at me!* she thought. But then he just glanced at his lawyer, the same lawyer who had made her move! Danielle tried to slide over slightly in her bench, trying to get Ballard's attention, but the two guards standing over him started making signals to each other. She was sure they were on to her. She just knew it.

By now, Danielle's hand and arms were bruised from all the pinching, but she was finding it harder and harder to keep from crying. She felt as if everybody in the courtroom—the audience, the lawyers, the judge—was staring at her. Everybody was looking at her. Everybody but Michael Ballard.

They don't see a person, she thought. *They see a piece of trash.*

Danielle finally couldn't take it anymore. She slipped out of the courtroom and, unable to fight back her emotions, ran back to her car in tears. She sobbed all the way from the courthouse back to her home in Allen Township. Once she arrived, she took a razor blade and cut eight slits across her arm until she was bleeding. They weren't deep cuts, and she wasn't trying to kill herself. She was just trying to numb the anguish in her mind. It was, she called it, one of the worst days of her life.

Danielle wrote several letters to Ballard in the days following that court hearing, and visited him twice over the next two weeks. If Ballard had been mad at her for having cooperated with the police and giving them the letters he had written to her, he didn't show it in his most recent letters and during her first prison visit with him. In fact, Ballard sang to her during that visit, and the sound of his voice had a soothing effect on Danielle.

But the second visit, on February 17, was totally different. By now Danielle was more than familiar with Ballard's shifts in mood, but this time his manner was completely cold. As she sat down and looked at him through the Plexiglas wall, he was absolutely silent. Instead of speaking, he handed a letter to the nearest guard, who passed it through the booth over to Danielle.

It was written by Ballard, but didn't at all resemble his usual way of writing or speaking. Instead, in a very technical tone, it stated that Danielle could no longer speak about him or their previous letters to each other, or he would take legal action against her.

Although it was written in legalese terms and Ballard was obviously trying to make it sound like an official document, Danielle knew there was nothing legally binding about it. Nevertheless, she felt simultaneously hurt, surprised, and annoyed.

"Michael, are you serious?" she said in an exasperated tone, holding the letter up.

"Visit's over," Ballard said, then walked away.

But if Ballard was really cutting off communications with Danielle Kaufman, it didn't last very long.

Within a matter of days, the two were again exchanging letters and phone calls. Danielle learned that on Sunday, March 6, Ballard would be brought in to Northampton County Prison from Frackville so he could later be transported to Philadelphia for a brain scan.

As always when Ballard was back in Easton, Danielle had arranged to visit with him. Wanting to look her best for him, Danielle dressed up in some of her nicest clothes, let her hair down, and wore her high heels for the visit. It was pouring rain when she drove over to the prison that evening.

Danielle knew there was a chance she wouldn't be allowed to see him. Sundays were always tricky because the prison was usually understaffed, and a lot of corrections officers had to be on hand for in-person visits. That was especially the case for Ballard, who was being kept in the isolation cell and—as always—was under very close watch by the guards.

When Danielle finally reached the prison doors and identified herself to the guards, her fear was confirmed.

"It's not going to happen today," one guard said. They just didn't have the staff.

Danielle was extremely disappointed. But when Ballard received the news, he was downright livid.

Ballard was always upset when he was denied something he felt entitled to at the prison—when he didn't have control. But in this case it was worse, Danielle later said. He felt that, by having this visit denied for him, it was as if a promise had been broken.

"He said he was tired of being made promises that weren't ever being kept," Danielle later said. "It was the same way with Denise Merhi, too. If you make a promise to Michael, it has to be kept."

From Ballard's perspective, his anger had little to do with getting to see Danielle and everything to do with his feelings that the prison staff were harassing and disrespecting him.

Ballard called out to one of the lieutenants—a man named Jason—and pointed at an imaginary watch on his wrist, indicating he had a visit coming. But Jason told him Michael Bateman, the deputy warden, had not approved any visits for Ballard that day.

Ballard was frustrated. It was a direct violation of what he believed was an unspoken truce with the prison staff: You give me two visits, I don't turn your prison into a war zone. But Jason called Bateman at home and the deputy warden confirmed that Ballard had not been approved for any visits because he had just had one Saturday. Ballard thought this was unfair because the schedule for visits restarted on Sundays.

"Jason, that's not the deal," Ballard said from behind his cell door.

"Bateman made the call," the lieutenant replied with a shrug.

Fine, Ballard thought as Jason walked away. *If you're not going to abide by your end of the bargain, I'm not going to abide by mine. Let's have a party.*

Ballard grabbed a pencil and one of the pieces of paper he usually used for his drawings. After a few seconds of furious scribbling, Ballard attached some of his toothpaste to the edges of the paper, then stuck it to the wall right outside his cell. The makeshift sign read:

COSTUME PARTY
BRING A FRIEND
FUN FOR ALL
HAVE A RIOT

After that, Ballard wet one of his towels in the sink and shoved it against the lower crack of his cell door. He knew that, for what he was about to do, the prison staff would try to pump pepper spray into the cell. Ballard then lifted one of the two mattresses in his cell and shoved it against the door, essentially barricading himself inside.

The corrections officers ordered Ballard to remove the mattress, but he refused. There were no other points where the guards could engage Ballard besides the entrance, as solid concrete walls encased the rest of the isolation cell.

Ballard clogged the sink and toilet drains with the rest of his towels, then left the water running and kept running the sink and flushing the toilet until the cell was flooded with about two inches of water. As the guards continued knocking on the door outside and ordering Ballard to remove the mattress, he picked up his toothpaste tube and squeezed it into his mouth, hoping that when the guards finally did break in, he could spit the paste into their faces and perhaps temporarily blind one or two of them.

By now, the prison was placed on lockdown, which meant inmates had to be kept in their cells and nonessential movement was strictly prohibited. The water was shut off once the guards realized Ballard was flooding his cell. Next, they called in the prison's Corrections Emergency Response Team to perform what they called a "cell extraction." They seldom had to call for such measures, so the process was new to several of the guards.

Half a dozen CERT members got into position outside the cell door, but Ballard was ready for them, after the warnings shouted by inmates in the surrounding cells. Those "wannabes" that Ballard had so little respect for were yelling out a play-by-play account of the guards' movements for him.

"Mike, there's six of them out here!" one inmate shouted. "One's got a battering ram!"

As if on cue, the guard with the battering ram started shoving the heavy instrument against the door. Ballard pressed his arms against the mattress, and the battering ram only succeeded in pushing the mattress out slightly before Ballard pressed it back up against the door. After ten or fifteen attempts at this, Ballard rolled his eyes.

Are you guys bored with this yet? he thought. *Because I already am.*

The shouts from the inmates continued, most of which Ballard had tuned out, except for one particularly startling warning.

"They've got a shotgun," an inmate shouted.

Ballard's eyes widened . . . *What?*

By now, the guards outside had cracked the door slightly, and indeed what appeared to be the long barrel of a shotgun came through the cell door. With the mattress still blocking the entranceway, the guards had no way of telling where they were pointing the weapon as they blindly worked it into the cell.

But Ballard could tell: It was pointing right at his face.

Ballard grabbed the barrel and shoved it against the wall, pointing it away from himself. As it hit the wall, the shotgun went off, making such a loud noise that Ballard staggered back, clasping his hands against his ears and letting out a moan, which was stifled by the toothpaste still in his mouth.

Feels like I'm inside a bell . . . , he thought, his head feeling completely shattered, his equilibrium lost. The non-lethal shotgun had fired off a diversionary device, a flash-bang that made an extremely loud noise meant to incapacitate a subject without permanently harming him.

As the CERT members finally knocked down the mattress and entered the cell, Ballard tried to regain his composure and squatted down in a position like a defensive lineman, ready for a fight. Two guards entered the room and split up, coming toward Ballard from opposite ends. They wore masks with plastic face guards and body armor from head to toe that reminded Ballard of the Teenage Mutant Ninja Turtles.

Ballard looked back and forth between the two guards. One looked about six feet eight inches tall and carried a large shield. The other was a man Ballard spoke with almost every day and genuinely liked. In fact, as other CERT members began to funnel in through the door, Ballard found that he recognized and liked most of them.

Nevertheless, he felt almost obligated to put up a fight. *We're committed to this little party . . .*

The tall guard, the one holding the shield, lunged toward Ballard, but he dropped low and the huge man barreled right over him. The second guard rushed forward next, but Ballard jumped back up and spit the wad of toothpaste he had been saving in his mouth directly into the man's mask, obstructing his vision. Ballard started barraging the man with a series of fast, wild punches, well aware that the guard would barely feel any of them through the body armor.

Hey, it's a party, Ballard thought as he kept punching. *This is what's expected.*

By now, the tall guard was back on Ballard, hurling him to the ground, but Ballard struggled back up. Another guard who had entered the room—a sixty-year-old man whom Ballard recognized—was shouting, "Lay down, Mr. Ballard! Stay down, Mr. Ballard! Lay down, Mr. Ballard! Stay down, Mr. Ballard!" Ballard had heard this guard had a heart condition, and he worried the old man would keel over from the excitement any moment.

By now, six guards had descended upon Ballard and one of them—whom Ballard recognized at the last moment as Jason—fired a Taser into Ballard's right leg. It was the first time he had been shot by a Taser, and he had seen men go down immediately after one blast, but to Ballard's surprise, he found it didn't hurt very much.

As he continued to struggle, another guard fired a second Taser shot at him, but once again it failed to take him down. By now he was mostly restrained by the half dozen armored men who had piled onto him, but his right arm was still free and he swung it wildly. His adrenaline was pumping so hard, Ballard felt like nothing could stop him.

Then he was shot by a third Taser blast. This time, it knocked him out cold.

Ballard, who was extremely proud of the fuss he had caused, suffered no serious injuries except for some bruising, including a large red mark on his right cheek. He appeared in court the next day for a pre-trial motion; he was fitted with extra shackles but otherwise appeared no different from usual. However, when the reporters noticed his injuries and inquired about them, the story of his prison exploits from the day before became prominently featured in their stories.

Danielle Kaufman was horrified when she heard the news.

"Oh my God babe! I just read online that you're hurt?!?" she wrote in a letter the night of the hearing. "Why would you do that babe? I can't deal with you getting hurt. Maybe I should leave you alone. Nothing good seems to come with you knowing me."

Danielle blamed herself for what had happened to Michael. In her letter, she explained that she believed in karma, and she felt that by dressing up nicely for Ballard in her high heels and "fruffy froo froo shirt," she somehow upset the balance of things for him and caused the incident in the prison. She even suggested that she intended to harm herself as punishment for what happened to him.

"You were burned, so I have to get burned now too . . . ," she wrote. The next day, she wrote in another letter, "I would die for you if I knew that it would take away your pain. I miss you Blue."

But Ballard was far from comforting in his responses to Danielle. Instead, he seemed angrier than ever with her for cooperating with Trooper Judge and the police, whom he regularly referred to as the "goof troop." Ever since learning Danielle had handed over her Michael Book, the tone of Ballard's letters seemed to fluctuate even more widely than usual. Sometimes he would say he loved her; other times he berated her and insisted everything that was going wrong with his case was her fault. During one previous court appearance, he had even turned to Danielle and mouthed the words, "This is all your fault."

His letters after the prison incident were along those same lines. Only this time, rather than apologizing or feeling guilty, Danielle became angry. She tore up and shredded some of the other letters she had kept from Michael. And in a letter she wrote to him on March 11, she angrily defended herself, insisting she was not going to risk getting charged with obstruction of justice and losing her daughter by refusing to cooperate with the police.

"I'm sorry to bruise your ego Michael, but I didn't know you in June last year. I didn't know her either," she wrote, referring to Denise Merhi. "I didn't twist your arm or force you in any way shape or form to do what got done, nor did I twist you to tell me about it. You done that all on your own. Your lawyers were even telling you to shut the fuck up and close your hole because they knew you were telling me too much.

"You're pissed because you want to control me and I won't let you have that power, which I'm really starting to realize was Denise's deal with you as well. You couldn't control her. Ohh you tried but in the end she obviously wasn't planning to settle with you, for whatever reason, and you couldn't handle that. 'If I can't have you then no one will.' And I dig that about you! Your intensity makes me so hot. But you're not going to control me either Michael."

CHAPTER 20

Throughout the month of April, Michael Corriere and James Connell began to receive the expert reports they had requested from their panel of psychiatrists and doctors: James Garbarino, Gerald Cooke, Robert Sadoff, Frank Dattilio, and Susan Rushing. Most seemed to paint a similar portrait of Michael Eric Ballard, and as the lawyers reviewed them, the possibilities and limits of their defense began to come into focus.

First of all, it was the unanimous consensus of the reports that Ballard was mentally competent to stand trial. He knew what he was doing at the time of the murders, understood that it was a crime, and knew that it was wrong and that it was a capital offense. He also fully understood how the legal system worked and was taking an active role in his defense.

It was obvious he did not suffer from the kind of impairments that rise to the level of an insanity defense.

However, the reports also claimed that Ballard's neurological testing indicated organic brain dysfunction stemming from the many head injuries in his past, and that this brain damage did contribute to the commission of his crime. Corriere and Connell had worked extensively to discover possible head injuries Ballard might have suffered and quickly found there was no shortage of such instances.

For example, there was a story the attorneys learned from Jack Gibson, who had been Ballard's close friend growing up. In ninth or tenth grade, Gibson and Ballard were outside a convenience store in Fayetteville when, all of a sudden, another high-school-aged boy jumped Ballard from behind, seemingly for no reason. The boy, whom neither of them knew, repeatedly punched Ballard in the head, then started bashing his head against the sidewalk before Gibson was able to pull him off.

"What is this about?" Gibson asked the boy after pulling him away.

"Look at his haircut!" the boy replied. Apparently, he had attacked Ballard because he didn't like his hairstyle.

Ballard refused to go to the hospital despite serious injuries to his head. In fact, Gibson recalled, he had never known Ballard to go to the hospital at any time that he was hurt. That pattern continued to emerge the more Corriere and Connell spoke to others.

The attorneys also talked to Russell Drake, a friend from Ballard's teenage days who admitted the two often abused drugs together, including hard drugs such as methamphetamine, cocaine, and acid. Drake also recalled that the two would ride their motorcycles together, and on more than one occasion Ballard would miss a corner and be sent flying. He hit his head several times—including one instance when he was knocked unconscious for several minutes when he was fifteen—but he always refused to go to the hospital.

Joseph Bearden, Ballard's first cousin, recalled a seventeen-year-old Ballard barging into his home at 3 a.m. with cuts and bruises all over his body and a softball-sized lump on the top of his forehead. As soon as he got into the house, Ballard passed out in front of their kitchen stove.

"He was beaten up pretty good," Bearden said. They later learned he had wiped out on his motorcycle on a dirt road outside Bearden's house. He had hit the ground so hard, he left a face imprint in the dirt. An emergency responder was called to the house, but, as usual, Ballard refused medical treatment.

"He didn't want any part of it," Bearden said.

Justin Cook Letwich, one of the sons of Ballard's former caretaker Lavern Cook, remembered another head injury caused by very different circumstances. When Ballard was sixteen, he was staying at a house with a girl he liked when that girl's boyfriend—or ex-boyfriend, Letwich could not recall which—had barged in and accused Ballard of being together with her.

Ballard was not in much of a state to defend himself— "We were tanked," as Letwich put it—and the man struck his head with a metal baseball bat, then hurled him off a second-floor terrace onto the ground below, where he landed headfirst. Ballard did not lose consciousness and, as with all the other injuries, he declined to go to the hospital. He instead simply dusted himself off and walked away.

Corriere and Connell worked to gather as many of these stories as they could. They eventually learned of as many as a dozen such serious head injuries, including at least three that rendered Ballard unconscious. The injuries, the fact that Ballard never received medical treatment for them, and the expert reports about brain damage still wouldn't allow the attorneys to seek an insanity defense, they knew, but they could serve as mitigating factors in the eyes of the jury when it came to the death penalty.

The neuroimaging from Ballard's MRI showed that

his overall brain volume was within normal limits, but that individual structures of the brain were severely damaged, specifically the regions crucial for regulating behavior. In other words, while Ballard could communicate clearly and outwardly appear to function properly, he had a great deal of trouble with impulse control, emotional regulation, and moral judgment.

Dr. Ruben Gur, the neuroimaging expert at the University of Pennsylvania School of Medicine who conducted Ballard's tests, identified abnormalities in several areas of Ballard's brain. For one thing, his damaged frontal lobe would diminish his ability to suppress socially inappropriate reactions to stress; nor would he be able to fully appreciate future consequences. Damage to this area could cause several of the behaviors that factored into his crime, such as hypervigilance, increased aggression, decreased empathy, impulsivity, grandiosity, and peculiar sexual habits.

Likewise, Ballard had damage in his cingulate cortex, which regulates conflict response and the ability to make decisions based upon emotions. This, Gur wrote, could explain Ballard's hostility, irresponsibility, disagreeableness, and emotional blunting.

Ballard had also suffered damage to his amygdala, which handles the processing of emotional reactions such as fear, anger, and pleasure, as well as perception of this information in others. Gur wrote that this damage was especially dangerous when combined with the abnormalities in his frontal lobe, which serves almost like a car's brakes to the primitive emotional impulses coming from the amygdala.

Without those brakes, Gur said, the resulting behavior would be disorganized, erratic, and unable to adjust to situational demands: "The situation is analogous to a car with weak brakes that are already engaged when it begins to race."

The more Corriere read in the reports, the more evidence emerged indicating damage to various parts of Ballard's brain. Damage to his temporal lobe could cause hypersexuality, disregard for social convention, and lack of respect toward authorities. Damage to his thalamus could have impacted the way he processed auditory, visual, and sensory information. Damage to his nucleus accumbens could have put him at a greater risk for hostility addiction.

Susan Rushing pointed out that much of the damage was to the right hemisphere. Religious delusions such as those she witnessed in her interviews with Ballard were usually associated with right-sided brain damage.

"It is my opinion to a reasonable degree of medical certainty that Mr. Ballard's head injuries predisposed him to psychosis, anti-social personality disorder and substance abuse," Rushing wrote. An insanity defense may be off the table, she said, but evidence existed that Ballard had "a psychotic disorder due to a traumatic brain injury with prominent delusions," which is a recognized psychiatric illness and an extreme mental disturbance.

As intimidated as Ballard was at first about learning the results of his MRI and PET scans, he now believed that the results made perfect sense. He felt they fully explained the enormous amount of rage he felt leading up to the murders, as well as his racing thoughts and erratic state of mind in the months afterward. He thought it even explained some of the things he had written to Danielle Kaufman and later came to regret.

I was in a total state of psychosis, Ballard thought.

The experts also indicated that Ballard's emotional problems from brain damage were exacerbated by the significant psychological trauma that he experienced early in his life, most prominently from the loss of his mother during a critical development stage, as well as the estrangement from his father.

Ballard's father and other members of his family openly discussed his mother's cheating in front of the young Ballard. That, combined with her absence in his life, formed a strong association in his mind between infidelity and abandonment, the reports indicated.

Dattilio in particular pointed out that Ballard had been abandoned by virtually every maternal figure in his life, whether through voluntary departure or death. He had been exposed to numerous female caretakers throughout his childhood—such as his grandmother and Lavern Cook—but they were all short-term, and in Ballard's mind their departures repeated the early abandonment he had suffered from his mother.

As a result of these past emotional injuries, Dattilio said that Ballard had great difficulty forming emotional closeness with others and harbored tremendous hostility and resentment, especially toward women. Garbarino echoed this analysis, and said these past traumas made abandonment a particular "hot spot" for Ballard.

Garbarino said Ballard suffered from "rejection sensitivity," where signs of rejection lead to panic, then rage, then aggression. In particular, women whom he viewed as having failed to nurture him threaten to unleash his rage to an uncontrollable degree. This, Garbarino said, is exactly what happened when he learned Denise Merhi was cheating on him.

"In many ways, Mr. Ballard might be described as a shell of a person who is not always in touch with his emotions," Garbarino wrote. Dattilio added that Ballard's angry outbursts might be a basic way of trying to control others, especially women.

The reports indicated that, in some ways, Ballard's

father was just as responsible as his mother for their son's traumas. Ballard himself adamantly denied that his father ever struck him, but the doctors nevertheless suspected there had been some physical abuse in their relationship, as well as a great deal of psychological abuse.

Whether Mickey Ballard hit his son or not, he certainly rejected him and neglected him emotionally, they wrote, throwing him out of his home at a critical time in his childhood when he was already reeling from abandonment by his mother. Garbarino wrote that the lack of a strong male role model in his life left him feeling particularly vulnerable, and thus susceptible to whatever negative influences surrounded him.

Garbarino said many individuals who commit homicides in adolescence, as Ballard did, exhibit childhood experiences that result in serious developmental damage, like severe abuse and neglect by the family, violently traumatic experiences in their home community, high levels of family disruption such as abandonment or rejection, and exposure to anti-social lifestyles. Ballard seemed to fit that bill all around, the doctor wrote, and it placed him at high risk for a lifelong pattern of anti-social behavior.

"Mr. Ballard was at risk for developing a social perspective characterized by extreme sensitivity to threat and a high probability of responding to perceived threat with aggression, including preemptive assault: 'Get them before they get you,'" Garbarino wrote.

"These two factors often provide the basis for rapid escalation of conflicts, even to the point of becoming lethal," he wrote.

Several of the reports indicated that the sexual abuse Ballard suffered in his youth at the hands of an older female relative further contributed toward his animosity and rage toward women. Dattilio said Ballard tended to confuse sexuality with aggression as a result of that abuse, and that made him prone to masochistic relationships in which he set himself up to be rejected, then acted out violently as a result.

In summary, the reports all seemed to indicate that Ballard had been suffering from major depressive disorder and anti-social personality disorder most of his life, with strong narcissistic paranoid and aggressive personality characteristics. Worse yet, Ballard's history of mental problems went essentially untreated for his entire life. Although he received some counseling and medication during his prison sentence for killing Donald Richard, it was nowhere near the type of in-depth psychotherapy he required.

This made Ballard particularly angry. If he had even a fraction of the kind of testing back then that he had now, Ballard felt he could have gotten the help he needed and maybe the other four murders would never have happened.

They dropped the ball on their end, Ballard thought.

The reports were helpful to Corriere and Connell, who well understood that they would need all the help they could get in providing Ballard with a defense. There was no arguing that Ballard didn't commit the murders, but the brain damage angle could at the very least keep him from receiving the death penalty. The reports indicated that the brain damage made Ballard more susceptible to the effects of alcohol, so they could couple that with Ballard's high blood alcohol content and testosterone levels on the day of the murders.

However, the defense had a major problem. And her name was Danielle Kaufman.

Most of the reports mentioned Danielle to at least some degree, and some went into greater detail about the letters Ballard had exchanged with her. That meant that if the defense introduced those reports in the courtroom, it would allow John Morganelli to raise questions about those letters, even some that might not be otherwise admissible during the trial. The legal term for this is *opening the door,* meaning the allowing of inadmissible evidence by the prosecution after the defense introduced that evidence itself, even indirectly or inadvertently.

The letters Ballard sent to Danielle were damning for his defense. His drawings of the crime scene, his claim that he "should have raped" Denise Merhi's daughter, the fact that he had pricked his finger so he would bleed all over the letters—all of these could work against him. Although they couldn't be considered physical evidence, they could only hurt him in the eyes of a jury. And when it comes to a trial, that's all that really matters.

CHAPTER 21

It was a chilly, cloudy day, with the threat of rain looming in the air, when *Morning Call* reporter Riley Yates arrived at State Correctional Institution–Frackville on April 8. Yates, a tall, lanky man twenty-nine years of age, had grown up in his native Petersburg, Alaska, as well as Seattle before coming to work for newspapers in Pennsylvania. The spectacled, soft-spoken reporter had been covering the courts in Northampton County for the *Morning Call* since 2008, and had reported on several homicide cases in that time.

Today he was about to speak with Michael Ballard, the first and only media interview the suspected five-time killer had granted up to that point.

Yates had been corresponding with Ballard since September, when the reporter sent him a letter requesting an interview, according to a report published later in the newspaper. The two had exchanged about half a dozen letters back and forth for months, and Yates had found in the tone of Ballard's writing a casualness that seemed rather cold, given the subject matter.

"On a personal note, I hope you're as excited to see

spring arrive as I am!" read one of Ballard's letters, a portion of which was later reprinted in the *Morning Call*. "Such a beautiful time of year. The electricity of life revving back up to full throttle after the dormant slumber of winter. Do you fish? Love springtime! I just love it!"

After a lengthy wait and vigorous screening process with the prison staff, Yates was led to a visitor's booth, where he came face-to-face with Ballard for the first time outside of a Northampton County courtroom. The prisoner sat waiting for Yates behind a pane of thick glass, wearing shackles and an orange jumpsuit. Correctional officers kept a watchful eye on Ballard, but this time his attorneys were nowhere to be seen; Ballard had agreed to meet Yates without them, no doubt against the advice of Michael Corriere.

According to the story Yates later wrote, Ballard spoke in a relaxed, matter-of-fact tone during the hour-long interview. Speaking to Yates with a phone cradled under his chin, Ballard did not expressly admit to killing Denise and the others, but he did not deny it, either, according to the story. He simply explained that it was something he couldn't discuss much before his trial.

But one thing that became abundantly clear from Yates's interview was that Ballard was very much aware of his perception by the general public.

"Popular opinion isn't necessarily in my favor," Ballard said. ". . . My side needs to be said."

While limited in what he could say before his pending trial, Ballard seemed to express little optimism about the pending verdict. He did not hide the fact that he expected to be found guilty, according to Yates's story, and said his best hope was that he would get life in prison rather than the death penalty.

"I don't want to die," Ballard told the reporter. "I don't have a death wish."

Portraying himself as a human being, rather than a monster, seemed to be one of Ballard's primary goals for the interview. He took exception to the way John Morganelli was portraying him in his statements to the public, according to the story, particularly the district attorney's description of him as a "rabid dog" who needed to be "put down."

"He's wanted to dehumanize me," Ballard said of Morganelli, whom he'd referred to as "Little Napoleon" in one of his earlier letters to Yates. "He's wanted to portray me as some vicious animal, and that's not the case. I'm flesh and blood. I'm human. I have emotions."

When asked whether he felt remorse about Denise and the other victims, Ballard responded: "You've got to understand, we're not even a year removed. Despite what the prosecutor wants to believe, there's still a lot of raw emotion in me."

In his attempt to humanize himself, Ballard spent several moments talking about things that had nothing to do with his murder, such as his past and his time outside of prison when he was paroled for the first time, according to Yates's story. Ballard seemed to light up when he remembered those days, talking with pride about how he was able to find work upon his release and the way he "hit the ground running" despite the "chips [being] certainly stacked against me."

"Even the ones that are close and involved in this . . . they don't know the whole story," Ballard was later quoted by Yates as saying. "They make assumptions, but that's the best they have."

Ballard spoke about the pain he experienced from his suspicions that Denise was cheating on him after he got out of prison the second time. He said that something inside him snapped after her friend Marilyn Rivera inadvertently confirmed his suspicions when he spoke with her on the phone.

"It was a constant deception, and when it was finally validated by her girlfriend, that's when everything came to a head," Ballard said. "That's when everything I was in fear of became truth."

Ballard seemed to be angry not only about his own public image, but also about the way Denise was being perceived by the public. Yates's story later quoted one of the letters Ballard had sent him in January, where he claimed Denise had a "dirty secret, skeleton cache," adding, "Truth is sometimes stranger than fiction!"

"The martyrdom she's been given makes me fucking retch!" Ballard wrote to Yates.

Although he could not speak freely about whether he killed Denise and the others, Ballard answered affirmatively when Yates asked whether he regretted killing Donald Richard back when Ballard was eighteen years old.

"I do. He's still human," Ballard was quoted as saying. "There are so many emotions that are tied into an event like that. It's hard to boil them down and say, 'Do you regret things?' There's a lot of things I wish I could have done differently."

Other than trying to humanize himself, Ballard appeared to use Yates's interview to set the record straight about a number of aspects of his case. He claimed he did not remember making the confessions at the scene of his car accident or in the hospital later—confessions his defense attorneys were now desperately trying to have thrown out.

"You have to understand the medical condition I was in," Ballard told the reporter. "I bled out . . . There's a lot I don't remember."

And then there was Danielle Kaufman, a subject that seemed to make Ballard fume. He insisted to Yates that "eighty percent" of what he told Danielle was "horseshit."

"She's a groupie, and with that said, she wants to be told certain things and she asks for them," Ballard said.

He also addressed the letters written to the district attorney's office by John Patrick McClellan and Wilfredo Riddick. Ballard claimed the two prisoners were "absolute liars" who were seeking preferential treatment. He seemed to view their actions as petty and selfish.

"What more despicable motive do you need, especially to involve yourself in something this serious?" Ballard was quoted as saying. "My life is what's hanging in the balance."

On April 14, just a few days before Yates's story was to hit the press, Judge Edward Smith issued an eighty-eight-page ruling denying Ballard's pre-trial motions. It was another blow to Ballard's defense, the most significant of which was the denial of Corriere's attempts to have Ballard's confessions suppressed, including his statement to emergency responders during the car crash: "It's obvious, I just killed everyone."

Corriere had argued that Ballard was severely injured and intoxicated at the time, so he could not be considered to have been speaking voluntarily. To allow those confessions, Corriere had argued, would violate both Ballard's constitutional rights and medical privacy rights. Smith, however, found that Ballard made a rational choice to speak with the doctors and emergency responders; and while his injuries were serious, they "did not negate his ability for rational thought or overwhelm his free will."

The defense had also tried to argue that authorities had improperly searched both Denise's car and the halfway house where Ballard was staying at the time of the murders. But once again, Smith was not persuaded, and he found the searches to be legal. The only question left unanswered by Smith's ruling was whether or not testimony about Ballard's past murder of Donald Richard would be allowed during the trial. That question would have to be answered before jury selection began in Wayne County on May 2.

On April 17, in the Sunday edition where it would be the most widely read, Riley Yates's story about his jailhouse interview with Ballard was published in the *Morning Call*. The public response was massive because it was the first time, short of his brief statements in court or reports of what he'd said to police, that Ballard's own words were directly conveyed to readers.

The story began: "Michael Eric Ballard casts himself as a man wronged by many. A girlfriend who started seeing someone else. A district attorney who is seeking his death. A parole system that treated him unfairly."

It was a lead that neatly summed up everything Ballard had said during his interview with Yates. But to *Express-Times* reporter Sarah Cassi, it said a lot more than that. It also represented what she felt amounted to Ballard's attempt at media manipulation to convey the exact representation of himself that he wanted conveyed.

What nobody outside of her newsroom knew was that the *Express-Times* had been corresponding with Ballard for as long as the *Morning Call* had been, also attempting to arrange the same prison interview. Cassi had been writing to him since at least October. She remembered the timing because in one of his letters, he had casually noted how much he was looking forward to Halloween, his favorite holiday.

In her letters to Ballard, Cassi said she knew that he would be limited in what he could say before his upcoming trial, but if he were willing to talk to her, she would come to Frackville to interview him. At first, it seemed the arrangement would come together and that Ballard was anxious to tell his story. But he also seemed guarded.

At the bottom of his very first letter, Ballard wrote a disclaimer: "Until otherwise directed by myself in writing, you do not have my permission to reproduce, in any form, quote, or paraphrase the contents of my correspondence with you." Cassi was surprised. She had had sources ask to speak with her off-the-record before, of course, but she had never gotten a letter or an email from anybody with such a statement, even from people used to dealing with the press on a regular basis. It struck her as a shrewd and calculating move on Ballard's part.

He's a quadruple murderer who's media savvy, she thought.

But it did not stop there. After two or three letters, Ballard started dictating requirements for the story and their prospective interview. He made it very clear that there would be certain questions and topics that would be off-limits, although he declined to specifically identify what they would be. The more he wrote, the more he tried to assert what could be included or excluded from the story. He also wanted a list of questions in advance so he could review them.

From those letters, it was obvious to Cassi that Ballard had a specific purpose in mind for her interview. He spoke about the reporter as if they were to have a mutual, symbiotic relationship: She would get to sell a lot of newspapers, and Ballard would get to tell his story the way he wanted it told. In Cassi's view, that wasn't the point of the interview at all. She was looking to tell *the* story, not *his* story.

Cassi took the letters to her editors for discussion, including *Express-Times* editor Joe Owens, managing editor Jim Deegan, assistant managing editor Nick Falsone, and Lehigh Valley editor Rudy Miller. After a group discussion, they decided they would not agree to any of Ballard's proposed restrictions. It was one thing for a source to decline to answer a question during the course of an interview. It was something else entirely to let the source dictate the terms of an interview.

"It's kind of like the cliché: You don't negotiate with terrorists," Cassi later said.

Cassi wrote back to Ballard explaining that she could not agree to his requirements as he had presented them, but if he was still willing to talk, she was still willing to make the trip to interview him. He never wrote back.

It was a fine line in journalism. Practically everyone who speaks to a reporter has a motive for doing so, and all sources try to convey themselves or their issue in the most favorable light possible. But in Cassi's opinion, there comes a point where it is less about the story and more about propaganda, and she felt Ballard had crossed that line; that he simply wanted a platform to express the perception he held of himself. Cassi believed it all came back to Ballard's obsession with control, something she had been observing with growing frequency as the case unfolded.

It wasn't just the fact that Ballard had allegedly taken four lives, exerting the ultimate control over whether somebody lives or dies—Cassi could see it in the smaller things as well. Always wanting to be in control, Ballard made Danielle Kaufman sit in the same place during each of his court appearances: right behind him on the aisle of the second row. Even when he was in prison for his parole violation, he constantly needed to know what Denise had been up to. And when denied a Northampton County Prison visit, Ballard's sense of control was so threatened that he barricaded himself into a cell and fought the guards so fiercely that he had to be shot with a Taser three times before he went down.

For Michael Ballard, Cassi surmised, it was all about control.

CHAPTER 22

Just as many had questioned why Michael Ballard had been able to make parole in the first place, others started to voice the opinion that parole should be abolished altogether. Some of the harshest critics of parole in the American criminal justice system have made that argument before, at least for violent offenders. But efforts to put that idea into practice have met with mixed results, at best.

The murder of Philadelphia Highway Patrol Sergeant Patrick McDonald at the hand of a recent parolee drew such a furious response from the public that Pennsylvania Governor Ed Rendell took an unprecedented step. On September 28, 2008, just five days after the killing, Rendell placed a temporary moratorium on all parole releases in the state.

It was such an extraordinary decision that some questioned whether he even had the legal authority to do it. In fact, four state prison inmates sued the governor, arguing he was illegally increasing the length of their incarcerations. Nevertheless, Rendell announced there would be no more paroles until a thorough review of the policies of the Pennsylvania Board of Probation and Parole could be conducted, and a determination could be made as to whether the handling of inmates returning to society could be improved.

The board agreed to the demand, and Rendell retained John Goldkamp, chairman of the criminal justice department at Temple University in Philadelphia, to conduct the study. Goldkamp, who had spent decades studying drug courts, inmate treatment, and alternatives to correctional confinement, was widely considered one of the nation's foremost experts on the subject of incarceration.

As Goldkamp began his review of the state parole system, one of his earliest findings was that Rendell's parole moratorium was a mistake.

The Pennsylvania Board of Probation and Parole attempted to continue holding parole hearings, even though there could be no releases, in anticipation of the moratorium eventually getting lifted. But the sudden halt of inmate releases was creating such a tremendous backlog of cases that Goldkamp grew concerned that the board would not be able to afford the time and attention required for major cases when and if the releases resumed. Promising parole candidates who had been nearing their release were now back to square one, and any arrangements that had been made for employment or housing on the outside were suddenly lost.

And the problem spread beyond the parole board itself into all of the state's prisons. Without parole releases, the already-crowded institutions were now under more pressure than ever, morale among the inmates plummeting. Goldkamp concluded that the difficulty in managing these growing prison populations would only become more difficult, and the parole system was at risk of losing credibility altogether.

At Goldkamp's recommendation, Rendell lifted the moratorium on all non-violent offenders in October 2008, keeping the freeze in place only for violent crimes. By December, those restrictions were also lifted as a result of Goldkamp's conclusions, and parole releases for all types of crimes resumed.

The rest of Goldkamp's review lasted about eighteen months. But if members of the public were thirsty for a major overhaul of the parole board, or an indictment of what they perceived as a heavily flawed or corrupt parole system, his results were bound to be unsatisfying. In fact, the study found both the Pennsylvania Board of Probation and Parole and the state Department of Corrections to be meeting or exceeding expectations, especially when compared with similar systems in other states.

"[They] are considered among the well-functioning corrections and parole agencies among their peer systems in the nation," Goldkamp wrote in his final, ninety-six-page report. "Our findings do not identify dysfunction or poor performance responsible for the tragic police killings motivating this critical review."

Some changes were made as a result of Goldkamp's review, particularly within the Pennsylvania Department of Corrections. But Goldkamp quickly found that the Board of Probation and Parole was far more resistant to any type of change whatsoever.

His suggestions for the parole board were relatively innocuous. He said the guidelines for making parole decisions should be reviewed and revised, training for parole agents should be improved, and post-release supervision should be strengthened as a way to minimize the risk of violent crime. The board's capacity to gather information for the decision-making process and supervision of parolees should be improved, Goldkamp found, and the board should strive for a greater understanding of the challenges facing long-term prisoners recently released into the community.

But while some of the people working on the board were very cooperative, Goldkamp found that others—especially the higher up the totem pole they went—were less inclined to heed his advice. Goldkamp felt most of his suggestions to the board fell on deaf ears.

"The parole board was much more a political animal," Goldkamp said, looking back years later. "I didn't get the impression the parole folks followed through with what we did."

In his final report, Goldkamp warned that the predictable knee-jerk reaction to high-profile violent crimes by parolees was to crack down on parole releases or, as some legislators had proposed, to do away with parole altogether. Goldkamp warned that this type of reaction ran a high risk of backfiring. It might lengthen the prison terms for violent offenders, he said, but once they were finished with their maximum sentences, they would be free to return into the community unconditionally, with no support or supervision.

"The likely effect of this approach is to increase the numbers of potentially violent offenders returned to the community with 'no strings attached' to inhibit or help them in their readjustment," Goldkamp wrote.

Some disagreed with Goldkamp's conclusions, including John Morganelli. In a December 2009 editorial in the *Express-Times,* he cited a Pennsylvania Department of Corrections report that analyzed recidivism—former prisoners who returned to prison after their release—in the state from 1995 to 2000. The report found that inmates released on parole were significantly more likely to return to prison than those who went free after serving their maximum sentence.

For example, according to the study, 51.6 percent of those paroled in 1998 returned within three years, where only 19.3 percent returned after serving their maximum.

That same study, however, noted that the majority of parolees returning to prison did so for a technical violation, as opposed to committing a new crime.

Morganelli, however, felt there are too many liberals on the Pennsylvania parole board. While Morganelli himself is a Democrat, he noted that recidivism rates dropped when Republican governor Tom Ridge was in office, then went back up once Democratic governor Ed Rendell took office. While tragic crimes such as the murder of Officer Patrick McDonald or the killings by Michael Ballard always resulted in a backlash and investigation into the parole system, Morganelli knew it was only a matter of time before things went back to business as usual.

"The combination of liberal parole policies and bleeding-heart do-gooders who believe even the most violent of criminals deserve a ninth and tenth chance, has resulted in the taking of hundreds of innocent lives," Morganelli wrote in the editorial. ". . . After each of these tragedies, we hear how the parole board, governor or pardons board will review its decisions. The reality is there is nothing to review. This is the result of the intentional design of the process. The fact is violent criminals shouldn't be out on parole or given clemency. They should be in prison, period."

But other states had gone even beyond Governor Ed Rendell's brief flirtation with the idea of revoking parole. Some had ended their parole systems altogether, and the results proved even more problematic than they were in Pennsylvania.

As of 2012, sixteen states have abolished their discretionary parole boards, most in favor of a determinate sentencing system. This method dictates that prisoners serve a certain percentage of their term and then be released, according to the Association of Paroling Authorities International. Many, however, still have some sort of alternative program that considers prisoner releases outside of the standard time frame, and many still have parole boards to handle old cases from the time before parole was revoked.

In the early 1990s, Michigan underwent major changes to its parole system, partially in response to offenders committing violent crimes after having been paroled. Stricter parole guidelines were adopted, and prison sentences were lengthened. In 1992, as part of a promise to get tougher on crime, Governor John Engler changed the parole board from one of corrections professionals to one made up of political appointees.

Parole release rates dropped from 68 percent to 48 percent, according to the Citizens Alliance on Prisons and Public Spending (CAPPS), and many more inmates were returning to prison for relatively minor technical violations. Critics said these tougher stances were keeping people in prison who could be safely released. Inmates sentenced to life in prison prior to 1992 by judges who had intended for them to be eligible for early release were now being categorically denied parole.

Michigan prison population swelled from 40,500 in 1994 to 51,550 in 2007, one of the highest per-capita incarceration rates in the nation, according to CAPPS. Correctional facilities were overcrowded and, at an average annual cost of nearly thirty-five thousand dollars per inmate, corrections spending soared. By 2008, the state was spending $2.1 billion on its prison system.

Eventually, the rising numbers in both population and dollars led the state to increase the number of parole releases and reduce the number of inmates serving more than their minimum sentence. By 2010, the prison population had dropped to around 45,500, and parole revocations dropped by 35 percent compared with eight years earlier.

And, perhaps more important, fewer people appeared to be reoffending. According to CAPPS, the state saw a 32 percent reduction in recidivism for high-risk parolees compared with 1998 thanks to enhanced supervision of inmates returning to society.

Similarly, Colorado abolished discretionary parole release in 1979, then reinstated it six years later. Elected officials, along with law enforcement and corrections professionals, lobbied to reinstate parole release and supervision after data suggested that the length of prison sentence served had actually decreased following the elimination of parole. They also found the ability to provide surveillance of treatment of high-risk offenders had significantly declined, according to the magazine *Corrections Today.*

Connecticut also abolished parole in 1980, the same year the state doubled and in some cases tripled prison terms for certain offenses. According to the Knight-Ridder News Service, those changes grew the state's prison population from thirty-seven hundred in 1980 to more than ten thousand in 1990. And, according to the *Hartford Courant,* Connecticut ended up spending more than one billion dollars on new or expanded prisons during the latter half of the 1980s.

By 1989, Connecticut prisons were so overcrowded that prisoners were being released early in supervised home release. About seven thousand offenders were released by 1989, according to Knight-Ridder, some of whom served as little as 5 percent of their sentences. In 1989 and 1990, there were at least ten homicide cases in which the person charged was prematurely freed from Connecticut prisons, according to the news service.

By 1990, legislators were already drafting bills to reinstate Connecticut's parole board. They had concluded that revoking parole altogether was not the answer after all.

"The apparent solution contributed to the worsening of the problem," William A. Carbone, chairman of the state's Prison and Jail Overcrowding Commission, told Knight-Ridder. "In 1980, I supported abolishing parole. Since then, I've come full circle."

Connecticut Corrections Commissioner Larry Meachum made a similar comment to the news service that sounded almost like a warning to anyone else who would consider following Connecticut's example.

"Any state that eliminates parole may one day look back and say, 'What have we done to ourselves?'"

CHAPTER 23

On April 20, less than two weeks before his trial was to begin, Ballard did something that, once again, sent shock waves through the region: He pleaded guilty.

Appearing in Northampton County wearing an orange prison jumpsuit and glasses, with a beard and a shaggy head of hair, Ballard appeared completely devoid of emotion as he admitted before Judge Edward Smith to the four counts of first-degree murder. The guilty pleas meant that Ballard faced a guaranteed sentence of no less than life in prison without parole. Since Morganelli had made clear that he would not offer a plea bargain that took capital punishment off the table, Ballard's pleas also meant the possibility of the death penalty was not excluded.

"Do you understand that your guilty pleas may put you one step closer on the path to execution?" Smith asked.

"I'm aware," Ballard responded in a monotone voice. Even as he pleaded guilty, he still maintained contempt for the whole judicial process and the "goof troop" state police, whom he felt did nothing impressive when it came to his case.

I'd given them a case even Stevie Wonder could solve, Ballard thought.

Thirty-five people were packed into the courtroom for Ballard's pleas, most of whom were friends or family of the victims. In order to create a clear and concise record, Smith questioned Ballard about what he did to all four of his victims, starting with Dennis Marsh.

"I intentionally killed him," Ballard said.

"How did you kill him?" Smith asked.

"By stabbing him repeatedly with a knife," Ballard replied.

"You admit that you knew what you were doing at the time you killed them, and you knew it was wrong?" Smith asked.

"I do, Your Honor," Ballard said.

Ballard made the same admissions when questioned about Denise Merhi, Alvin Marsh Jr., and Steve Zernhelt. Representatives from Steve's family sat listening, and it made Janet Zernhelt feel sick to her stomach for Ballard to describe his horrible crimes in such a nonchalant tone of voice.

It's so easy for him to say what he did, Janet thought. *It's so easy for him to say it.*

At one point during the hearing, Smith mistakenly referred to Zernhelt as the third victim, prompting Ballard to shake his head and raise four fingers to indicate that Zernhelt was, in fact, killed fourth.

The correction rankled some in the audience, but not nearly as much as when, during the same conversation, Smith accidentally mispronounced Zernhelt's last name. Ballard interrupted the judge and corrected the pronunciation, infuriating members of the audience who believed it was wrong for Ballard to speak for Zernhelt, especially in such an offhand manner.

Express-Times reporter Sarah Cassi, who was among

other members of the media in the crowd, felt it was just another example of Ballard's love of control. There was no need for Ballard to correct Smith's pronunciation, as there was certainly no chance anyone in the room failed to understand whom the judge was talking about. Ballard was simply reveling in the opportunity to correct a judge, Cassi thought, and thus trying to control him.

As Smith and Ballard continued their exchange, Ballard spoke in such a cold, monotone voice about his grisly crimes that some in the crowd couldn't take it. Shelly Youwakim, Denise's cousin, who had been sitting next to Geraldine Dorwart, dabbed at her eyes with tissues and tried to control herself, but it proved too difficult.

"Sick bastard!" she yelled out before standing and storming out of the courtroom, muttering several other obscenities as she left.

Those two words were the banner headline in the *Express-Times* the next day, a source of some controversy and discussion among the newspaper's readers. One reader, Easton resident Karen Smith, wrote a letter to the paper calling the headline insensitive, inappropriate, and offensive, particularly for young people who might see the front page.

Others felt the headline perfectly conveyed the grief and contempt of those touched by Ballard's crimes. Some compared it to the famous "Bastards!" headline that ran in the *San Francisco Examiner* the day after the terrorist attacks on September 11, 2001, which was meant to convey the visceral feeling of anger stemming from the event.

"The words of a grieving relative need not be criticized," Elizabeth Miller of Bethlehem wrote in another letter to the editor. "The *Express-Times*' 'sick bastard' headline was not insensitive. It is intended to express to others that the raw emotion expressed by a grieving relative is real, not make-believe."

After Smith and Ballard finished discussing his guilty pleas, they moved on to a discussion about the sentencing portion of the trial. A jury would still have to be convened, but now instead of hearing arguments over whether Ballard committed the murders, they would be hearing testimony to determine whether he should get the death penalty. Michael Corriere then withdrew the motions he had previously filed seeking an out-of-county jury, meaning that the jurors would be selected from Northampton County after all.

While the jury was originally to be chosen from Wayne County, Corriere explained that upon reviewing the populations of both, they decided that a Northampton County jury would be in their client's best interests. As he told the *Morning Call,* the Northampton County population was more diversified than that in the heavily rural Wayne County, and Corriere believed Northampton jurors were less likely to opt for capital punishment.

But Sarah Cassi believed there was much more to it than that. Just a few weeks before, the defense had been arguing that a Northampton County jury couldn't possibly judge Ballard fairly, and now suddenly they reversed course? No, Cassi believed, this turn of events put the interview Ballard had given Riley Yates into a whole new perspective. The timing of Ballard's guilty plea only three days after Yates's story ran couldn't possibly be a coincidence. Now that the story had been printed, Ballard believed it was more likely that prospective Northampton County jurors would have read it, and might be more sympathetic to Ballard's side of the story.

He had to have some idea he would plead guilty or have a trial, and he wanted his story out there, Cassi thought. *He thinks in his mind that he is smart enough to get a jury to believe him.*

With the sentencing phase ready to proceed, Ballard

was led out of the courtroom, but not before one more emotional outburst from the crowd.

"You're a real pussy, Ballard!" a man shouted as Ballard was escorted by guards out of the courtroom. The chains from his shackles could be heard dragging on the floor for several minutes after he was out of the courtroom.

Outside, reporters scrambled to interview members of the victims' family for their reactions to Ballard's guilty pleas. Geraldine Dorwart told Cassi that the seven months since Ballard had pleaded not guilty—and the idea of a long trial ahead—had been the worst days of her life, and that the pleas had brought her a little bit of closure.

"It was a prayer that was answered," Geraldine said. When asked what, if anything, she would say to the jurors during the sentencing hearing, she replied, "I would tell them he killed me seven months ago."

Speaking to the *Morning Call,* Shelly Youwakim expressed her disbelief of Ballard's hopes to avoid the death penalty.

"He had no reason to go there purposefully to kill an eighty-something-year-old grandfather in a wheelchair who couldn't see and couldn't hear," Youwakim said. "It's ridiculous. And he doesn't want to die?"

The only person who spoke in Ballard's defense was Danielle Kaufman. She told the *Express-Times* she was pleased Ballard had pleaded guilty because she believed a long and drawn-out trial "would have been hard on everyone and it would have been for nothing." She also expressed her firm belief that Ballard didn't deserve to die.

"He did a horrible, horrible thing . . . [but] he's not a bad person. He's not," she told the newspaper. "I'll never say Michael's a bad person because he's not."

While many were shocked by Ballard's decision to plead guilty, John Morganelli knew exactly what Ballard was up to. The district attorney knew it was extremely rare for a defendant to plead to first-degree murder when capital punishment was still a possibility. But he also knew that Ballard was making his best possible play to spare himself from death.

Like everyone else, Morganelli had read Yates's story, with Ballard's claims that he didn't want to die. But he also knew that Ballard was a smart man who knew as well as anyone that hardly anybody ever gets executed in Pennsylvania. Based on the evidence he had reviewed, which included the correspondence and phone calls Ballard had made from prison, Morganelli knew that Ballard was trying to avoid the death penalty not because he feared death, but because he would have a much better quality of life serving a life sentence than he would on death row.

Life without parole meant more time outside, more time for visitors, more freedom and flexibility. And Ballard had spent the majority of his life in prison. Morganelli believed that serving life as opposed to death row would be the norm for a man like Ballard, and what kind of a punishment would that be for killing four people?

Morganelli was convinced that Ballard was just doing what he had always done. He was trying to manipulate the system, just as he had done with the parole board and with the media. And the worst part was, considering the state of capital punishment in Pennsylvania, and with jurors so reluctant to hand out death sentences, Morganelli knew there was a chance that Ballard just might get his way.

Jury selection for the death penalty phase of Ballard's case began on May 2, a Monday, and lasted throughout the rest of the week. Visitors already had to walk through a metal detector as they entered the courthouse but for added security, Judge Edward Smith arranged for a second security station to be set up directly outside his courtroom to make sure that nobody brought in weapons or cell phones. Sixty-seven prospective jurors were brought in and questioned by John Morganelli, Michael Corriere, and James Connell.

Geraldine Dorwart and Shelly Youwakim sat in the crowd for some of the selection, as did a gaggle of news reporters, sheriff's deputies, and courtroom staff. Ballard actively engaged his attorneys throughout the hearing, whispering into their ears and regularly giving advice on which jurors he felt would be the best choices. At times, he even laughed and appeared to be making jokes with his lawyers, upsetting some in the crowd.

"Smirking and laughing and having a good old time," Shelly said to the *Morning Call* of Ballard's demeanor. "He thinks he's on vacation . . . It's like a field trip."

But during the actual questioning of the potential jurors, Ballard remained somber and appeared relatively emotionless. Geraldine, on the other hand, struggled to rein in her emotions, hanging her head and fighting back tears as Connell explained to one prospective juror how horrible and graphic some of the evidence and testimony would be.

"There will be crying," Connell told one of them, according to the *Express-Times*. "There will be. We all expect that."

Each side had twenty strikes, or chances to eliminate potential jurors. Some courtroom observers were surprised by some of the people both sides allowed in. One man, when questioned, said he believed the death penalty should be the mandatory punishment for somebody who kills four people. *Express-Times* reporter Sarah Cassi overheard Geraldine lean over to Shelly and whisper, "He's going." But after the man assured the defense attorney he could set aside his beliefs and follow the judge's instructions, the defense allowed him to join the jury.

Another prospective juror, Bill Falsone, thought he was almost certainly not going to be chosen. His son,

Nick, was an assistant managing editor for the *Express-Times,* which had been covering the trial extensively. Not only that, but he had strong reservations about the death penalty: It was not so much that he opposed it, but he did not know whether he could personally impose it on someone else, no matter what they did.

"I'm very anxious about taking someone else's life," he said.

But Morganelli had a good feeling about Falsone, particularly after he assured the district attorney that, despite his personal feelings, he could do his duty and follow the letter of the law. Morganelli felt this was a man with a sense of civic responsibility and, even though he knew it was risky—it only took one juror to sink a death penalty verdict—he allowed Falsone to join the jury.

By the time the week was out, twelve jurors and four alternates were selected, and the trial was ready to begin the following Monday, May 9. Before the closing of proceedings on Friday, Ballard, over the objections of his attorney, asked for a brief delay. May 9, he explained, was Denise Merhi's birthday, a day that Ballard felt would be an overly emotional time for both himself and the victim's family.

It made Geraldine and the other family members sick to hear Ballard speaking about Denise at all, let alone feigning interest in their feelings on her birthday. Regardless, Judge Smith had no intention of delaying the trial.

"It's time for this case to begin," he said. "You're the most important person in this case. Your life is on the line."

On May 8, the day before the trial began, the *Morning Call* published a letter that reporter Riley Yates had received from Ballard in prison. Dated April 27, it was written shortly after Ballard had pleaded guilty. In the letter, Ballard appeared frustrated by the negative way he was continuing to be portrayed, despite his best efforts to humanize himself.

Ballard claimed in the letter that he wanted closure, and that he hoped his guilty plea would allow the "healing process" to begin. He also claimed that he deserved credit for having pleaded guilty, that he wasn't getting his due.

Ballard wrote, according to a portion of the letter printed in the *Morning Call:*

"You see, the reality of what that hearing represented and really meant is lost on those that want to call me a 'sick bastard,' 'a mad dog,' 'cold blooded,' and so on. Because if I was that 'cold-blooded monster,' I would have kept pursuing a trial. And so for weeks on end, hour in, hour out, day in, day out I could have had every single friend and family member on the stand facing a barrage of questions solely intended on impeaching, discrediting and destroying the character and images of those four individuals. And all the while that's going on, everyone in the gallery could sit there and look at poster-sized photos of their friends and family members at the crime scene, and of their autopsies. But I didn't choose to do that; from the get-go I've accepted my responsibility and have only wanted to explain."

The letter, and the notion that Ballard deserved credit for his actions, further infuriated members of the victims' families and the general public alike. Sharon Geosits, a Northampton resident, expressed her disgust in a letter to the editor later printed in the *Morning Call.*

"Families torn apart forever because of what Michael Ballard 'admitted' doing and he wants the jury to give him 'credit' while showing no remorse for his senseless act!" she wrote. "His arrogance is beyond belief. The only credit Michael Ballard deserves for his admission of guilt is death."

CHAPTER 24

As Ballard's death penalty trial began May 9, the court-room was packed with more than fifty family members and friends of the four victims. Many of them wore green, Denise Merhi's favorite color. Ballard, wearing a short-sleeved blue dress shirt and jeans, spoke quietly with his lawyers and did his best to avoid gazing at the crowd. There were few in the audience for him, with the exception of Danielle Kaufman, who sat in her usual spot in the second row behind him.

John Morganelli began the proceedings with his open-ing statement, where he emphasized the "methodical and businesslike" way that Ballard murdered Denise in retali-ation for spending time with other men, then killed three others just for being in the wrong place at the wrong time.

He tried to discourage the jury from showing any mercy toward Ballard because, the district attorney said, he had already failed when given a second and third chance: dur-ing both times he was released on parole. He also reminded them that Ballard had killed not only these four victims, but also Donald Richard back in 1991.

"Not one, not two, not three, not four, but five. This

case is about the deaths of five innocent people," Morgan-elli said. "Five people, all of whom loved life, all of whom had family and friends that they cared about and who cared about them. And all of whom died a violent and painful death at the hands of this defendant, Michael Bal-lard."

And, he pointed out, Denise's two young children could easily have been killed as well if they had been home that day.

"They could have been numbers six and seven," Mor-ganelli said.

During Michael Corriere's opening statement, he did his best to try to humanize Michael Ballard, just as Bal-lard had tried to do during his interview days earlier with the *Morning Call*. He said that Ballard loved Denise, truly loved her, and was so devastated upon learning that she was spending time with other men that he couldn't take it. He recalled how the two spoke of getting married and having children, that they even exchanged rings dur-ing a secret ceremony.

"This was probably his first real romantic relationship where it was anything other than physical," Corriere said. ". . . He was so devastated. To him, he couldn't take it. He couldn't think. He just had to react."

Geraldine rushed out of the courthouse as Corriere spoke, crying and appearing nauseous. When asked later by reporters, she explained that it was the talk of ex-changing rings that set her off. She had no idea they had done that.

Later that day, the jury also heard testimony from Northampton County Coroner Zachary Lysek, forensic pathologist Samuel Land, and Denise's cousin Debbie Hawkey. Debbie described having walked into the house during the middle of the killings, and seeing the shadow of someone she believed to be Michael Ballard just before fleeing the house. It had never been publicly revealed how close Debbie had been to becoming a fifth victim herself. Her testimony was a major part of the news stories that ran the next day.

Marilyn Rivera also testified, speaking about everything from becoming friends with Denise to the phone calls Marilyn received from Ballard the day before the murders. Testifying was extremely difficult for Marilyn, so much so that she had to sneak away to the bathroom to cry. It was made even harder by Geraldine's cold attitude toward her. The family still hadn't spoken with Marilyn since Denise's wake, and Geraldine would hardly even look at Marilyn the day of her testimony.

When Marilyn finished her testimony and stepped down from the witness stand, she glanced over at Ballard. Though she had avoided eye contact with him throughout her entire testimony, she couldn't help looking at him as she walked away. When their eyes met, Ballard smiled at her. It was a casual smile, a look of recognition as when two longtime friends see each other on the street. Marilyn was disgusted by it, and couldn't help but feel that the smile had a second meaning.

It's almost a little bit sarcastic, she thought. *Like he's saying, "I know what I did."*

Later, as Land and Lysek spoke, photographs from the crime scene were shown on a projector screen on the courtroom wall, opposite the jury box. The bloody images showed the final position of each of the victims after they were killed. Steve Zernhelt curled in a fetal position next to dried bloodstains on the carpet. Denise Merhi splayed out on the blood-drenched kitchen floor. Alvin Marsh sitting in his wheelchair, his throat slashed open. And Dennis Marsh lying dead in the basement, the words DENISE IS A WHORE written in blood on the wall above him.

The photographs were horrifying for the family and

friends sitting in the audience. Geraldine, having left after Corriere's opening statement, was spared the gruesome sights, but Janet Zernhelt was not so fortunate. She cried as the photo of her deceased husband appeared on the screen, grasping the hand of a family member sitting next to her.

Finally, the time had come for members of the victims' families to have their say in court. The second day of the trial would include testimony from Geraldine Dorwart, Janet Zernhelt, and others, all of whom prepared victim impact statements.

But as the families arrived at the courthouse that day, they learned that the defense attorneys had raised objections to portions of the statements, and certain sentences were going to be edited, reworded, or omitted altogether.

Judge Smith explained that, under the law, victim impact statements were limited to focusing on the victims themselves, the individual qualities they possessed in their lives, and the impact their loss had on the person testifying. The law strictly prohibits such statements from going beyond that, prohibiting speakers any mention of the crime itself, the outrage they feel as a result of that crime, and what punishment they believe should be imposed. And so Smith apologetically explained that some of the statements had to be modified.

The family members sat in the crowd and listened as Morganelli, Corriere, and Smith discussed the various objections raised by the defense. Morganelli explained that he had already reviewed all of the statements for appropriateness and he tried to defend against objections as they were raised. Nevertheless, changes were made. Some were a matter of a word or two, as when "senseless murder" was changed to "murder." One sentence that read that Steve Zernhelt was "a hero who came to the rescue with nothing other than his bare hands" had to be removed because it was too specific in describing the crime.

Corriere objected to one sentence from Jaime Zern-helt, Steve's daughter, who claimed he "became the whole neighborhood hero that day." The defense attorney said it was not fair for Jaime to speak for the entire community in declaring her father a neighborhood hero. Upon hearing this, one person from the courtroom audience shouted, "He was!" Nevertheless, Smith agreed and the sentence was struck.

Jaime closed her eyes and shook her head. The process pained Geraldine. After all this time waiting to have her say, having the statements edited was almost like being victimized all over again. On the other hand, Bill Fal-sone, sitting in the jury box, understood why it had to be done. The law had to be followed.

When the time for testimony came, Luther Marsh, Alvin Marsh's brother, spoke of growing up with Alvin, and said he has had many nightmares since the day of the murder about the grisly way his brother had been killed. Chris Stet-tler, Denise's first cousin, made a statement that was echoed by several others who testified: he hated the idea that eighty-seven-year-old Alvin Marsh, a veteran of the US Navy, survived World War II only to later die a death like this one.

"It feels like he died without the honor he deserved," Chris said.

Geraldine spoke about the pain of losing her child, and how terrible she felt that Denise would no longer be able to enjoy all of Trystan and Annikah's new experiences as they grew up.

"Denise deserved to make many more memories with her two beautiful children, family and friends," she said. "Denise won't be there to help her children along the path of life. She won't be able to take dozens of photos the way she always did when Trystan and Annikah go to proms, graduation, and weddings and put these treasures into the already-started scrapbooks."

The testimony was difficult for Janet Zernhelt, who tried her best to describe life without her husband of thirty-four years. Her home was no longer a place of comfort, she said, and she could no longer sleep without the assistance of pills.

As she neared the end of the statement, Janet broke into tears and banged on the wooden witness stand with both fists. *Express-Times* reporter Sarah Cassi honestly believed Janet was nearing the point of an emotional breakdown. To the reporter, Janet looked like a woman who had reached a point where words could not express the turmoil she was feeling inside, so she was trying to physically express it by hitting the witness stand.

"I look out the window and pray that Steve will pull up in his van," she said. "I cry every day driving to and from work. Everyone asks, 'Are you okay?' All I can think about is I'll never be okay. Never, ever be okay. I love my husband so much. He was my best friend."

But the most harrowing testimony came from Jaime Zernhelt. Although Jaime was able to maintain her composure much better than her mother had, her words were no less impactful. She said her father's murder had impacted her so much that her therapist suggested she receive the same kind of treatment that soldiers returning from war received for post-traumatic stress disorder.

Jaime said that to this day, she still would call her parents' answering machine just to hear her father's voice on the message. Working as a first-grade teacher, Jaime said there were days when she would start crying in the middle of her class, and her six-year-old students would comfort her by saying, "It's okay because your daddy loves you, and he's watching you from heaven."

"The weekend following this tragedy, my fiancé Lenny had planned on asking my father's permission to marry me," Jaime said. "He never got that chance. This September I'm getting married, something I've been looking forward to my whole life since I was a little girl. My daddy won't walk me down the aisle. He won't be there to see his little girl become a wife and some day a mother."

By the time Jaime was done, nearly half of the jury was in tears, despite explicit orders from Judge Smith earlier that they were to avoid expressing emotion wherever possible. But Bill Falsone couldn't help it. Listening to Jaime talk about Steve Zernhelt never getting the chance to meet his grandchildren struck a deep chord with Bill, who had grandchildren himself. Even years later, thinking back on Jaime's words would make him tear up.

"If you were human and you had a pulse, it just got to you," he said.

Even Michael Ballard himself, who had seemed emotionless and nonresponsive during most of the testimony, appeared to be moved by what Jaime Zernhelt had to say. Wearing a pink short-sleeved shirt and jeans, he hunched over the table as she spoke and wiped at his eyes. He clearly understood how damaging her testimony had been to his defense.

During a break in the trial, Morganelli arranged to meet with Wilfredo Riddick, the inmate who had claimed that Ballard confessed to several murders while they were serving time together in Frackville. Riddick had been brought from the state prison to Northampton County Prison to await Morganelli's decision about whether to call him or not.

Wearing a green prison jumpsuit, the shackled Riddick was escorted by sheriff's deputies into the district attorney's office, where he was brought into the law library to talk with Morganelli. Seated at a rectangular table in that room, Morganelli informed him that he planned to go over Riddick's previous statements to Trooper Raymond Judge.

"Well, what am I getting out of this thing?" Riddick asked.

"Nothing," Morganelli replied with only a moment's hesitation.

Riddick said he had several demands that had to be met before he would speak with Morganelli, namely that the district attorney's office arrange for early release and guarantee he be set free shortly after testifying against Ballard.

"Look, the only thing we do for people like you is we would send a letter stating you cooperated in the case," Morganelli said. "That's it. We don't negotiate time or deals or anything like that."

Riddick leaned back in his seat and frowned.

"Well, I've sort of got amnesia now," he said.

Morganelli had heard enough. He had neither the time nor the inclination to sit and play games with a convicted felon. Morganelli had already harbored suspicions that Ballard's statements to Riddick were nothing more than tough talk to make Ballard appear like a dangerous man to his fellow inmates. The district attorney also knew that Riddick wouldn't come across as the most reliable witness to a jury.

Furthermore, and perhaps more important, Morganelli didn't need Riddick. The only real value of his testimony was Ballard's claims that he killed Steve Zernhelt to eliminate witnesses, which was an aggravating factor for the death penalty. Morganelli would have to withdraw that aggravating factor, but the others would still stand.

"Okay, no problem," Morganelli said, standing up. "I'll probably write a letter now saying you didn't cooperate and make sure you serve your max."

Without another word to Riddick, Morganelli walked out of the room and instructed the sheriff's deputies to take the inmate back to prison.

CHAPTER 25

With Morganelli no longer planning to call Wilfredo Riddick to the stand, it was time for the defense to present their case. Corriere had made it clear that Ballard would not testify on his own behalf. Instead, the attorney intended to play an audio recording of a phone call a tearful Ballard made to his father from the prison July 6.

Morganelli had objected to the jury hearing the conversation, calling the move a thinly veiled effort to generate sympathy for Ballard without having him testify, thus giving Morganelli no chance to cross-examine him.

Judge Smith considered the objection, but after listening to the tape himself, he overruled it. The judge felt that there was no risk of the tape generating sympathy because there was nothing in the recording that was sympathetic. He showed no remorse for having killed Denise in the recording and, although he did become emotional while talking to his father, all of Ballard's sympathy was for himself, not her.

"I did everything I was supposed to do and she played me like a fiddle. Played with my fucking heart," Ballard's voice said in the audio recording. As it played, Denise's aunt Susan Stahler started to cry from the courtroom audience, her shoulders shaking as she tried to fight back her sobs.

Corriere also called Penny Lynn Sines, who had worked closely with Ballard when she was a correctional counselor at SCI–Laurel Highlands. She was ultimately one of the several people who made a recommendation for his 2006 parole.

Seeking to create sympathy for his client, Corriere questioned Sines about Ballard having volunteered to work at the prison's hospice unit for elderly prisoners. Sines explained that it was a particularly unpopular job at the prison because it involved such unpleasant work as interacting with sick inmates, answering their requests, and cleaning out their bedpans. Nevertheless, she said, Ballard willingly did it for two years.

But when it came time for his cross-examination, Morganelli had other subjects he wished to discuss. He questioned Sines about her role in Ballard's release. She explained that the decision was far from hers alone, that she was one of several staff members from the prison, the state parole board, and the Pennsylvania Department of Corrections who prepared Ballard's pre-parole case file by reviewing, among other things, his criminal history, the completion of institutional programs, and his history of prison misconducts.

It was the last part that Morganelli focused on. He questioned Sines about nearly a dozen infractions Ballard had committed in prison between 1993 and 2005, including his refusals to obey orders, possession of controlled substances, trying to punch a corrections officer, and becoming violent with a guard while he tried to inspect Ballard's cell. Morganelli took his time describing each infraction in great detail for the jury and questioning why Sines voted to release him despite those infractions.

Correire objected to the line of questioning, suggesting it was irrelevant. During a sidebar discussion with the two attorneys, outside the earshot of the jury and courtroom audience, Judge Smith warned Morganelli he did not want the witness to be placed on trial for the sins of the entire parole department. The district attorney agreed, but said he believed the questions were relevant because they spoke to Sines's credibility.

"I want to show that she overlooked a long history of discipline problems in the prison," Morganelli told the judge. ". . . Her judgment was bad. Her judgment was bad in putting Ballard out there. Her judgment was bad in overlooking discipline problems, and it goes to impeaching her ultimate testimony, which is that he was a good guy to put into the elderly home."

Smith overruled Corriere's objections and allowed Morganelli to continue. Sines acknowledged the long list of prison misconduct reports were accurate but said there were far fewer incidents during his later time in prison, that Ballard never had problems with the elderly patients he cared for, and that he received "average work reports." She had interviewed Ballard multiple times, she said, but even so she was only one of many people involved in his release.

Nevertheless, when his cross-examination was complete, Morganelli felt satisfied that he had damaged her credibility in the eyes of the jury.

Corriere next presented a number of witnesses from Ballard's past, from whom the defense attorney sought to present Ballard's childhood as one of great difficulty amid a broken home. In particular, he sought to portray Mickey Ballard as an uncaring father who had essentially thrown his son out on the street.

James Acker, an officer with Washington County Sheriff's Office in Arkansas, testified about arresting Mickey

Ballard in 1981. He described Mickey charging toward him with a fireplace poker and threatening to kill him before Acker hit him on the head with his flashlight, all while a young Michael Ballard watched.

"My first inclination was to shoot him, but I didn't want to do that, so I used the flashlight," said Acker, who added that he never knew Mickey to get into legal trouble again, that he attended the funeral of Mickey's mother five years later, and that Mickey was very cordial with him.

A number of other figures from Ballard's early years took the stand after Acker. Lavern Cook, Ballard's former caretaker, spoke about how Mickey Ballard all but abandoned his son during the boy's childhood. She described how a young Michael Ballard used to wait at the window for Mickey to visit him during holidays and birthdays, and how crushed Ballard was when Mickey never showed up.

Rhonda Maples, a friend from Ballard's childhood, described how Ballard would come to school with bruises, and said that when she asked about them, Michael claimed they had come from his father. She spoke of the time that she was waiting for Michael outside of his father's home, and overhead Mickey yelling at him, calling him "good for nothing" and a "no-good worthless bastard."

Justin Cook Letwich, Lavern's son, reaffirmed some of that testimony. He described the time that Mickey Ballard, in a drunken state, accidentally fired a gun inside Lavern's house, shooting out one of the windows. Justin also claimed he would often see Ballard appearing bruised and beaten up.

"He would always tell me that, 'Me and Dad got in a fight,'" Letwich testified.

Morganelli sought to cast doubt on the idea that Mickey Ballard was an abusive father somehow responsible for

Ballard's crimes. During cross-examination, Morganelli asked each witness if they ever actually saw Mickey hit his son, and each had to admit they had not. The district attorney pointed out that Ballard still maintained contact with his father and, when interviewed at the prison, had claimed he had a good relationship with his parents. In fact, Ballard specifically and adamantly denied that his parents had ever physically abused him during his childhood, Morgnanelli said.

Ballard showed little emotion during the testimony about his father, but a few rows behind him, Danielle Kaufman seemed visibly uneasy about it. She understood that Ballard's attorney was doing his job, and that presenting Mickey Ballard in such an unflattering light was a strategy they were using to help Michael. But based on her correspondence with Ballard, she did not believe his father had been abusive.

I don't like how he's throwing his dad under the bus, she thought.

Mickey Ballard himself had been subpoenaed in case they planned to call him to testify, but when they later informed him they would not be asking him to speak, he did not bother coming to the trial at all. Mickey later said he was not pleased with how he was portrayed by the defense attorneys.

"They didn't even give me the damn courtesy to speak at the trial, so I don't have much regard for how they treated me there," he later said. "I felt like I should have had a say."

By Friday, May 13, the fourth day of the trial, Corriere was ready to present testimony by the psychologists and mitigation specialists. Coupled with the previous testimony from family and friends, the defense attorney sought to use the defense experts to emphasize Ballard's difficult childhood, emotional problems, and brain damage, with the hope of persuading at least one juror that there were enough mitigating factors to spare him the death penalty. It was a difficult balancing act for Corriere, who had to make his case without sounding like he was making excuses for his client.

Louise Luck, Ballard's mitigation specialist, spoke about the extreme dysfunction Ballard had experienced throughout his childhood, from the abandonment by his mother, and the trust issues it created for Ballard with women, to his father throwing Ballard out of his home. Luck spoke of Ballard living in homes with no running water, going to the bathroom in a bucket, and having only a single pair of jeans while growing up.

"Life was pretty sparse," she said. ". . . His mother deserted him. It was anything but a loving environment. It was an angry environment."

Between the psychological trauma Ballard suffered at such a critical developmental stage, and the brain damage from his multiple head injuries, Luck said Ballard was more susceptible to alcohol, experienced increased aggression and decreased empathy, and had great difficulty in controlling his emotions.

It was difficult testimony for members of the victims' families to hear. The final straw for Geraldine Dorwart was when Luck testified that relatives might have sexually molested Ballard when he was five years old. Upon hearing that, she and other members of the family stormed out of the courtroom. Questioned outside by reporters, Geraldine described listening to the testimony as nothing more than an extension of her family's suffering.

"It's horrible," she told *Morning Call* reporter Riley Yates. "People thought the worst was over. It's not over . . . Now we have to hear his excuses."

Geraldine told the reporter that everybody has gone

through difficulties in their childhood and throughout
their lives.

"He is no different than anybody else," she said. "But
does that give him the right to take those four lives like
that?"

Back inside the courtroom, Morganelli was doing the
best that he could to discredit Luck's testimony on cross-
examination. He accused her of over-emphasizing all the
sympathetic elements of Ballard's past and ignoring everything else from her report.

To drive the point home, he spoke of the letter Ballard
had written to Luck describing a dream he had about killing people with a shotgun at Denise's house, all the while
laughing hysterically until he woke up.

The district attorney also cited other writings from Ballard in which he called Denise a "harlot" and rationalized
killing her as a way of absolving the sins of her infidelity.

"I judged her in righteousness and I prayed on it," Ballard had written in the letter. Just as he had written in
some of his religious ramblings to Danielle Kaufman,
Ballard claimed he decided to cleanse the home he shared
with Denise from her sins, and implied that by killing her
he had actually saved her.

"The rest of us live in sin, while my baby's free from
sin," he wrote. As Morganelli finished his questioning, he
was confident that when the jury later recalled Luck's
testimony, they would remember those statements from
Ballard, not the claims she made about his difficult past
or head injuries.

The forensic psychologist Gerald Cooke spoke next,
and Corriere also tried to use his testimony to portray
Ballard in a more sympathetic light. Cooke explained that
he, like others, had diagnosed Ballard as having anti-social
personality disorder and severe depression problems. The

brain injuries he suffered from fights and motorcycle accidents meant Ballard had significant trouble controlling his emotions, particularly in stressful situations.

Morganelli tried to cast doubt on Cooke's testimony by pointing out that Ballard could vividly remember details of the murder and other memories from his past, and he questioned how that could be if Ballard really suffered from a brain disorder. Cooke countered that such memories might not be affected by this type of disorder but admitted that Ballard's IQ nevertheless fell in the upper side of the average range.

Before testimony wrapped on Friday, Corriere presented one more witness: Walter Chruby, an inmate who had served time at SCI–Laurel Highlands at the same time Ballard was there. Chruby, who testified via videoconference, said he had major kidney problems and often ended up in the medical unit, where Ballard worked as a janitor and always showed Chruby a great amount of kindness.

"Mike was a great guy to all of us," Chruby said.

Corriere hoped that, as with Penny Lynn Sines, the testimony from Chruby would show that there was a kinder, gentler side of Ballard that thrived even in a prison atmosphere. But, just as he had with Sines, Morganelli sought to cut that idea off at the knees.

"What are you in for?" Morganelli started off with his cross-examination.

"I'm serving a life sentence for first-degree murder," Chruby replied. He had stabbed a seventy-three-year-old woman thirty-three times inside her home at State College, Pennsylvania, in 1995.

"No further questions," Morganelli said in response.

When the trial resumed the following Monday, May 16, Corriere announced something that took the entire courtroom by storm: The defense was about to rest.

The defense attorney still had a slate of defense experts—James Garbarino, Robert Sadoff, Frank Dattilio, and Susan Rushing—who had yet to testify, but Corriere made the tactical decision not to put them on the stand. Corriere believed—and he admitted it openly when questioned later by reporters—that allowing them to testify would only open the door for Morganelli to bring up extremely provocative and damaging details about Ballard's letters to Danielle Kaufman during his cross-examination.

It was a risky move, as it meant excluding much of the findings that could possibly have helped his client, but Corriere believed it was the right one. One only had to look at Morganelli's responses to the testimony of Luck and Cooke to see how he had taken every negative aspect of their reports and magnified it for the jury.

If the district attorney could segue from the other defense witnesses into Danielle's letters, it would allow him to bring up Ballard's detailed descriptions of the murders, or his claim that he "should have raped" Denise's daughter. There were the letters smeared with his own blood. The requests for Danielle to dig up dirt on other inmates for him. The threats he made against a Northampton County Prison guard.

Corriere believed the benefit of keeping that information away from the jurors far outweighed the loss of the more positive aspects of their testimony. And, if Morganelli's reaction was any indication, the district attorney felt the same way. He told reporters from the *Express-Times* and *Morning Call* that he still hoped to introduce some of Danielle's letters into the record, and he planned to do some legal research about whether he would be able to. Nothing ever came of it.

Corriere briefly recalled Trooper Raymond Judge to ask questions about the ninety-six text messages Ballard and Denise had exchanged with each other in the days prior to the murders. The attorney emphasized those early messages where Denise expressed excitement about having Ballard's baby, and Ballard's attempts to reassure her when Denise expressed concern that others might see her as a "whore." After that brief effort to remind the jury of that human side of Ballard, Corriere officially brought his defense to a rest.

CHAPTER 26

If eliminating parole is not the solution to stopping violent crime from repeat offenders like Michael Ballard, then what is? Perhaps it lies in addressing a crippling prison overpopulation problem in the United States, particularly due to a disproportionately high number of convictions for drug-related crimes. If such sentences were reduced, parole boards might be able to give proper attention to serious, violent offenders like Michael Ballard.

By the time Ballard appeared before the Pennsylvania Board of Probation and Parole, it had been experiencing a backlog that was consistent with an enormous growth in prison populations. This was true not only in Pennsylvania but throughout the nation. And it all seems to correlate with the start of the War on Drugs.

Although the term *War on Drugs* was first used by Richard Nixon in 1971, it is widely thought to have been "declared" by Ronald Reagan on November 14, 1982. Since that time, sentencing guidelines have become far stricter for drug offenses, most notably with the passage of the federal Anti–Drug Abuse Acts of 1986 and 1988. Many states have made parole much more difficult, and mandatory minimum sentences, recidivist statutes, and other new laws have been put in place to keep inmates incarcerated much longer for non-violent drug-related crimes.

In September 2006, when the Pennsylvania parole board considered Ballard's first request for parole, it was one of 1,713 parole and re-parole decisions made that month alone. When Ballard reappeared before them again in December 2009 following his second brief incarceration, his was one of 1,614 cases that month.

Those figures are enormous compared with those twenty years earlier, when the number of parole cases stemming from arrests from the War on Drugs was just starting to take hold. In 1989, the monthly average was 528 parole decisions, less than one-third the number of cases on the board's plate both times Ballard came before them.

Those figures are consistent with the growth in overall actions taken by the Pennsylvania Board of Probation and Parole over the years. In 1989, they considered 6,341 parole and re-parole decisions. That figure continued to climb over the years until it had swelled to 22,734 by 2011, according to the board. That's an increase of just over 358 percent in twenty-two years.

That growth in parole cases raises a question. If the board had fewer cases related to drugs and non-violent offenses before them, and more time for violent criminals, might decisions to release people like Michael Ballard have gone differently?

Pennsylvania is far from unique when it comes to such burgeoning numbers. According to the US Department of Justice, there were 478,368 inmates in prisons or jails as of 1980, before the War on Drugs was declared. At that time, it was a record high figure. By 1990, that number had jumped to 1,148,702, which was higher than the totals from 1980, 1970 (338,029), and 1960 (332,945) combined.

By 2000, the US prison population had grown to 1,391,261, according to the department, and by 2010 it jumped again to 1,612,395. There had been a growth of nearly 340 percent since 1980.

There are more people imprisoned in the United States than anywhere else in the world. According to the International Centre for Prison Studies, there were 2.29 million prisoners in the US in 2008. This figure was slightly higher than other studies because it included both pre-trail detainees and sentenced prisoners.

The closest country behind the United States was China with 1.57 million prisoners. But its population of 1.3 billion was more than four times that of the United States' 304 million in 2008. With just under 4.5 percent of the world's population that year, the US housed more than 23 percent of the world's prisoners.

The country's prisoner population rate of 756 per 100,000 was also higher than any other nation, a rate that had been significantly lower before the War on Drugs existed. From 1880 to 1970, that rate had always stayed between one hundred and two hundred per hundred thousand, according to the Center for Economic and Policy Research.

Prison overcrowding in Pennsylvania follows a pattern similar to that of the nation. The state's inmate population has doubled over a twenty-year span, jumping from 24,952 in 1992 to 51,638 in 2012, according to the Pennsylvania Department of Corrections. New prisons had to be built to keep pace, jumping from five state prisons in 1967 to twenty-seven by 2012. According to the Council of State Governments Justice Center, those prisons had a capacity of 45,280 that year, showing that the state was operating at 114 percent capacity.

It's not only an unsettling problem, but also an expensive one. At an annual cost of $32,986 per inmate, prison expenditures in Pennsylvania grew from $1.05 billion in 2001 to $1.86 billion in 2011, according to the council. At a national level, spending for federal, state, and local corrections ballooned from $18 billion in 1982 to $78 billion in 2008, according to the Center for Economic and Policy Research.

Despite the high number of incarcerations in the United States, only 20 percent of the country's inmates in 2007 had been incarcerated for violent crimes such as murder, rape, and aggravated assault, according to David Rudovsky, a senior fellow at the University of Pennsylvania Law School and one of the country's leading experts on civil rights and criminal defense. About 31 percent were in prison for drug violations alone at that time, according to Rudovsky, and 32 percent were in for burglaries and other non-violent crimes.

Between 1980 and 2007, the number of drug-related arrests in the United States more than tripled, according to the US Department of Justice, growing from 580,900 to 1,841,200. By 2007, 493,800 people had been incarcerated for drug offenses, an increase of 1,100 percent compared with the 41,100 offenders in 1980, according to the Sentencing Project advocacy group. In fact, the number of incarcerated drug offenders had now actually exceeded the entire 1980 prison population of 474,368.

But the whole point of the War on Drugs was to target major drug kingpins and traffickers—those who also tended to be violent criminals—and bring them to justice. That simply was not happening. Instead, most of the arrests tended to target mid- to low-level dealers or non-violent drug users.

According to the Sentencing Project, about 75 percent

of drug offenders in state prisons across the country in 2002 were there only for drug or non-violent offenses, and about 58 percent had no history of violence or high-level drug selling activity at all. In 2005, 81.7 percent of national drug arrests were for possession rather than for dealing, according to the project, and 42.6 percent of drug arrests were for marijuana offenses. In fact, 79 percent of the growth in drug arrests from the 1990s was related to marijuana possession rather than hard drugs.

In Pennsylvania, where Michael Ballard committed his murders, laws stemming from the War on Drugs intending to target violent offenders were so unsuccessful that one of the original authors of those laws began fighting to reform them.

Pennsylvania state senator Stewart Greenleaf, a former prosecutor from Montgomery County, came to the legislature in 1978 with a tough-on-crime approach and wrote many of the state's mandatory minimum sentence laws later signed by Governor Tom Ridge. Under those laws, for example, a first conviction for possession of more than ten grams of methamphetamine—which comes out to less than three teaspoons of sugar—required a maximum sentence of four years in prison regardless of any extenuating circumstances. Critics of the law, like the advocacy group Families Against Mandatory Minimums, pointed out that such a sentence was higher than the two-year minimum requirement for aggravated assault against a child under sixteen.

By 2011, Pennsylvania prisons were so overcrowded with non-violent offenders that Senator Greenleaf started making efforts to reform the laws he had helped create. He proposed bills that would allow courts in the state to waive mandatory minimums if there was, according to the bill, "a compelling reason to believe that a substantial injustice would occur by applying the mandatory sentence." His attempts at reform got stuck in committee and never went anywhere.

"The purpose of those bills was to address the violent criminals. But we also got in our net many little fish, meaning the nonviolent offenders," Greenleaf told the *Philadelphia Inquirer*. Discussing the costs of incarcerating those offenders, Greenleaf told the paper, "I'd spend all that money and more if I thought it was helping public safety. But it's not."

If Pennsylvania prisons had not been overcrowded with so many "little fish," and the Pennsylvania parole board had more time to focus on bigger fish such as violent offenders—if the board had more energy to spend on psychological examinations or other evaluations before Michael Ballard was up for parole—would he have been released in the first place? Or, even if he had been, would the system have been able to supervise him more efficiently after his release? Could his four murders have been prevented? And, with so many states facing prison overpopulation problems because of the War on Drugs, how many other Michael Ballards have been released across the country?

CHAPTER 27

After the defense rested, the twelve Ballard jurors were led by uniformed sheriff's deputies into the nondescript conference room where they were to hold their deliberations. They took their seats in office chairs around a long table, where a plate of brownies had been brought in by one of the jurors. After a brief discussion, it was decided that Bill Falsone, an outgoing and personable man, would serve as the jury foreman.

Falsone decided that the jury should start off with a discussion about the law to be sure they understood it. After fifteen or twenty minutes, it became clear that everybody was clear on the law. To arrive at a death penalty decision, the jury had to agree that the prosecution had established at least one of the two aggravating factors: that he had committed another murder in the past, or that his crime involved multiple victims. In Falsone's mind, the answer was obvious.

He's two for two, he thought.

"Okay, it seems like everybody understands the law correctly, so let's take a vote and see where we sit, and then we'll go from there," Falsone said.

The jury was required to vote on each of the four victims individually. They decided to start with Denise Merhi. When Falsone took a look at his fellow jurors, he had no idea from the appearance of their faces how any of them would vote.

I have a feeling we're in for some long deliberations, he thought.

"All right, all those in favor of the death penalty, raise your hands," Falsone said.

Twelve hands immediately rose in the air.

Falsone was stunned. He recalled the jury selection process, when he made clear that he harbored his own reservations about capital punishment. While he knew that he could follow the law, he was also sure that some of the other jurors would have held the same reservations as he did, and that at least one would hesitate to vote for death.

But once the vote was finished for Denise, they held another for Dennis Marsh, then for Alvin Marsh Jr., and then for Steve Zernhelt. For each, the vote was the same: twelve jurors in favor of the death penalty.

Wow, Falsone thought. *I don't think you could get twelve people to agree on what to order for lunch so quickly.*

Just two hours after they had been escorted out of the courtroom, the jury was ready to deliver its verdict. Those in the audience were shocked at how quickly it had gone, having been warned that such deliberations could last for days and days when somebody's life was on the line. What they didn't know was that the deliberations themselves took only about forty-five minutes; the remaining time was taken up simply by the logistics of moving the jury back and forth and informing the lawyers they had reached a decision.

Falsone stood and read to Judge Edward Smith the

verdict for all four first-degree murder convictions: death. The jury foreman never once looked at Ballard, unable to do it even after the jury was escorted away. But despite the mixed feelings he'd had about the death penalty coming in, Falsone knew he had made the right decision.

He wiped out three generations of a family, Falsone thought. *This is what he deserves.*

Despite specific instructions from Judge Smith to restrain from showing emotion in the courtroom, an outburst of celebration erupted after the decision was read. Many members of the packed courtroom leapt to their feet, letting out shouts of "Yes!" and throwing their fists into the air. Janet Zernhelt started to cry at her seat while her daughter Jaime sobbed on her fiancé's shoulder. Janet's two sons stared straight at Ballard, never taking their eyes off him.

After thanking the jury members for their service, Judge Smith brought a quick end to the hearing, officially concluding a trial that had lasted seven weekdays.

"I will not abuse you with words, as the sentence I impose is punishment enough," Smith said, according to the *Morning Call.*

Ballard himself expressed no surprise or despair as the decision was read. In fact, he showed no emotion whatsoever. In her years covering the courts, reporter Sarah Cassi had seen a wide range of defendant reactions to verdicts, and concluded that most who react emotionlessly appeared to be in a state of shock, struggling to maintain a stone-faced expression and keep control as the overwhelming realization of their verdict sinks in.

With Ballard, that was not the case at all. He glanced at the jury as they were being led away, shook hands with his attorneys, and exhibited a completely neutral facial expression, as if this were any other day in his life.

To him, it's just like, "Oh well, that's that," Cassi

thought as Ballard was escorted away for the final time. *Like, "Oh well, the decision is made."*

There was a rush of excitement in the air as the courtroom cleared out and everybody gathered in the hallway outside.

"Justice has come," Geraldine Dorwart said to the *Morning Call.* "I get to go home and tell the kids now."

Members of the victims' families waited for their chances to thank and give hugs to John Morganelli, Assistant District Attorney Kelly Lewis, and Trooper Raymond Judge. Among them was Morganelli's mother, who had come out to watch her son secure the first successful death penalty conviction of his career and, Northampton County's first since Josoph Henry in 1987.

"Your son is a brilliant man," one woman said to Morganelli's mother, according to the *Express-Times.* But Morganelli himself feigned modesty while speaking to the reporters gathered around him.

"There's no celebration on my end," he said. "I just believe Mr. Ballard deserved the verdict."

Michael Corriere and James Connell left the courthouse with little comment, other than a polite offering of congratulations to Morganelli for his victory. Others also declined to speak with the media, including Janet Zernhelt, although her daughter served as a spokeswoman of sorts for the family.

Jaime Zernhelt expressed an immense sense of relief with the verdict. Whether Ballard ever actually was executed or not, she said, the family took at least some comfort in the fact that the worst possible penalty had been imposed against him. Even if he had gotten life in prison, she didn't believe the family could truly feel comfortable that something couldn't happen that might allow him to become free one day.

"Ballard deserves it," Jaime Zernhelt told the *Express-Times*. "I couldn't be more thankful. Justice got served."

"I have no words for him," she said when asked what, if anything, she would say to Ballard. She later added to the *Morning Call,* "It's a relief I don't have to listen to his name anymore."

Shelly Youwakim, Denise's cousin who had made headlines earlier in the trial by calling Ballard a "sick bastard," was now so overcome with emotion that she found herself having trouble saying anything. But, while struggling to maintain her composure, she found she did have one thing to say about Ballard:

"The devil does not prevail."

EPILOGUE

To the surprise of some in the community at Northampton borough, both Geraldine Dorwart and Janet Zernhelt still live in the houses where they lost their loved ones. Both had given thought to moving out, to living somewhere else far away from where those tragedies took place. But as Geraldine told the newspapers: It is still her grandchildren's home, and she has no intention of taking them away from it.

Geraldine continues to maintain custody of her grandchildren Annikah and Trystan. In an interview with the *Morning Call* one year after Denise's death, she said she was haunted by nightmares of loved ones who had died years ago blaming her for the murder of Denise, demanding to know why she'd failed to prevent it. She told the newspaper that Ballard had "put me in hell." In court, she said it was extremely difficult for her to continue living, but her responsibility toward her grandchildren was what kept her going.

"It's difficult, day-to-day, every day is," Geraldine said. "Some days I don't want to get out of bed, but the kids are my responsibility . . . That's what keeps me going is my two grandchildren. And I know they have no one but me when they wake up."

Steven Zernhelt received numerous posthumous honors for the bravery he exhibited in running to help his neighbors, including the Carnegie Hero Fund Commission's Carnegie Medal and Kiwanis International's Robert P. Connelly Medal for Heroism. The Pennsylvania State Police bestowed a similar honor on Zernhelt during a June 2012 ceremony in Hershey, Pennsylvania, which Janet Zernhelt described as a special honor, although a bittersweet one that brought back memories of her husband's untimely death.

Jaime Zernhelt continues to work as a teacher. Janet's son Justin Zernhelt works as an associate technician for an electronics company, and Ryan Zernhelt is a third-party planning manager for a national cosmetics company. Justin moved back with his mother, at her request, to help her cope with the pain of living without Steve.

Michael Ballard continues to insist he's remorseful for having killed Steve Zernhelt, and has said he would be willing to speak with the family in person, but the Zernhelts have no intention of granting him such relief.

"Nothing he could say would be worthwhile," Janet said.

Trooper Raymond Judge remains with the Pennsylvania State Police, where he was named 2010 Trooper of the Year for his role in solving the Ballard case and three other homicides. Among them were the cold-case conviction of Lucinda Andrews; the arrest of rapist and killer Darius Maurer; and the conviction of Barry Soldridge Jr., who fatally shot his ex-girlfriend and her boyfriend with a rifle in Lehigh Township.

John Morganelli continues to work as Northampton County district attorney, having run unopposed for a sixth term in November 2011. Almost exactly one year after the Ballard trial, Morganelli personally prosecuted his second successful death penalty case: a man who shot a police officer. The defendant, George Hitcho Jr., fatally shot Freemansburg police officer Robert Lasso in the head with a shotgun as the officer responded to a disturbance call at Hitcho's home.

Danielle Kaufman continued exchanging occasional letters with Ballard after the trial, but his responses became even more accusatory toward her. He blames her for the fact that he now sits on death row, according to Danielle, and she found herself continually apologizing to him in all of her letters. Eventually, Ballard ended contact with her altogether. Danielle later said she believes Ballard belongs where he is, and that he blames her only because he cannot accept responsibility for his actions. Nevertheless, Danielle said she still loves Ballard, and would resume their relationship "in a second" if he was interested.

Mickey Ballard still lives in West Fork, Arkansas. He has declined to speak about his son's case because he does not want to jeopardize the ongoing appeal, but he said that he believes his son was treated unfairly by the criminal justice system.

"Our judicial system's a money system," Mickey said. "If you've got the money, you can buy the justice. That's my philosophy."

Michael Ballard is still in the middle of his appeals process. Ballard's attorneys are arguing that Judge Edward Smith erroneously allowed the jury to see crime scene photos and grisly autopsy images that offered no value except to inflame them. He also argued that the victim impact statements, which Smith carefully reviewed and redacted, were excessive and unfair to Ballard's defense.

Under state law, a death penalty verdict is automatically appealed to the Pennsylvania Supreme Court, the first step in a lengthy process that could take decades. In the case of many on death row in Pennsylvania, it lasts the entire natural life of the convict. Ballard believes there is still a chance a higher court could overturn his verdict.

"You don't know about this legal system," he said during a nine-hour jailhouse interview with the authors of this book. "Anything could happen."

Ballard is currently incarcerated at State Correctional Institution–Greene, a super-maximum-security prison near Waynesburg, Pennsylvania, one of two state institutions for the state's death row inmates. The 128-acre institution is home to 1,729 prisoners, including 160 inmates on death row who are segregated from the general prison population.

Ballard lives in an eight-by-ten-foot cell, is allowed only one visit per week, and can never have physical contact with any of his visitors. He may leave the cell for two hours of exercise five days per week, take three showers per week, and spend two hours in the law library if requested.

"I live as a goddamn pet," he said. "I am taken out for exercise. I am told when to eat. I live in a goddamn cage. I am a pet. This is not a goddamned life."

Ballard maintains that he feels remorse for the deaths of Steven Zernhelt and Alvin Marsh Jr., but not for Dennis Marsh, and most certainly not for Denise Merhi.

"If I could literally dig her the fuck up and do this to her again, I would," Ballard said. "That's the amount of rage I still have toward her."